NOT WIT

Not with Wisdom of Words

Nonrational Persuasion in the New Testament

Gary S. Selby

WILLIAM B. EERDMANS PUBLISHING COMPANY
GRAND RAPIDS, MICHIGAN / CAMBRIDGE, U.K.

Published 2016 by
Wm. B. Eerdmans Publishing Co.
2140 Oak Industrial Drive N.E., Grand Rapids, Michigan 49505 /
P.O. Box 163, Cambridge CB3 9PU U.K.

Printed in the United States of America

21 20 19 18 17 16   7 6 5 4 3 2 1

Library of Congress Cataloging-in-Publication Data

Names: Selby, Gary S.
Title: Not with wisdom of words: nonrational persuasion in the New Testament
    / Gary S. Selby.
Description: Grand Rapids, Michigan: Eerdmans Publishing Company, 2016. |
    Includes index.
Identifiers: LCCN 2015040171 | ISBN 9780802873002 (pbk.: alk. paper)
Subjects: LCSH: Bible. New Testament — Criticism, interpretation, etc. |
    Experience (Religion)
Classification: LCC BS2361.3 .S45 2016 | DDC 225.6 — dc23
    LC record available at http://lccn.loc.gov/2015040171

www.eerdmans.com

For Tammy,
My partner in the journey

Contents

Preface

Imagine attending a lecture about French food. You file into the auditorium and take your seat just as the speaker approaches the podium. She announces her topic and then begins to explain the particular practices that make French cuisine unique. She describes the different ingredients that combine to create the tastes that many find so exquisite. Most of all, she gives reasons why French food is superior to other kinds of cuisine, citing its popularity, its tradition, its health benefits, and so forth. How might such a presentation affect you? You would certainly know more about French cuisine than when you started. You might come away believing that French food would be good to eat. But you wouldn't actually know what French food *tastes* like, and you certainly wouldn't be a lover of French cooking. For that to happen, you would actually have to taste it.

That distinction between talking *about* something and actually experiencing it — and the role that each played in the New Testament authors' understanding of Christian faith — is the focus of this book. Of course, the writers of the New Testament sometimes explain or argue in order to help their listeners understand some concept or convince them that something is true or important. But I am particularly interested in the ways they also try to use language to bring their audiences into an imaginative, visceral experience of that truth, how they create opportunities for their audiences to "taste and see that the Lord is good" (Ps. 34:8).

One example that brought the difference home to me was comparing two speeches by Martin Luther King, Jr. Several years ago I came across one of King's early sermons, "The Death of Evil on the Seashore," which he gave in 1955 at the Dexter Avenue Baptist Church in Montgomery, Alabama. He briefly recounted the Exodus story and then offered a succession of examples and statistical evidence to "prove" that black experience followed the same basic story line as the biblical narrative. I was struck by how pedestrian the sermon seemed, how lacking in the soaring oratory that we came to expect of King. The sermon informed and explained rather than inspired. It placed the audience in a position of considering whether to agree with his argument or not. At most, hearers came away intellectually convinced that their situation was like the ancient one.

How different that was from his final speech, given the night before he was killed. At one point, King pauses and seems to look off into the distance, and then declares, "I've been to the mountaintop and I've seen the Promised Land." In that moment, his hearers are no longer standing at a distance evaluating the merits of an argument, considering whether their story is *like* Israel's. At that moment, they are "in" the story — they *are* the children of God, King *is* Moses, and they stand at the edge of the Jordan River. At that moment, explanation has been engulfed by imaginative experience. Future hope has become present reality.

In what follows, I draw upon what both ancient and contemporary communication theorists have called "transport," that is, the power of language to take you "out of the place where you are standing" (the root meaning of "ecstasy," or ἐκστάσις), in order to examine how New Testament writers sought to create "transportive" experiences for their audiences. My hope is to shed light on the character of early Christian persuasion and, more broadly, on how early Christians understood faith — that it was not just mental assent to rational arguments, but that it also involved a holistic experience of the divine presence. The ancient writers understood that if believers were to remain faithful in the face of the strong currents pushing against faith, they would not only need strong arguments and clear explanations, they would also need those imaginative, emotional experiences that made their beliefs "real." But my interest is not in the ancient church alone. What I have learned from researching this book has also profoundly shaped how I think about religious communication in the present, including what and how I personally communicate to the church. Thus, my hope is that this study will also speak to how we think about communication in the contemporary church.

I am deeply grateful to all who have encouraged me in this project, in ways both large and small. I especially want to thank Pepperdine University for the gift of a sabbatical to conduct research, and to the folks at Rochester College, Rochester, MI, and Emmanuel Seminary, Johnson City, TN, for welcoming me so graciously. I am grateful to the Fairhaven Ministries Retreat Center, Roan Mountain, TN, for a quiet and beautiful place to think and write. I thank my Pepperdine students who have read and explored early versions of this book with me, and especially, the editorial staff at Eerdmans, who have been wonderful to work with. Finally, to my sons and daughters-in-law, Joel and Ashley, and Tyler and Katie, and to my wife, Tammy, thank you for being in my court.

Introduction

But we do not want you to be uninformed, brothers and sisters, about those who have died, so that you may not grieve as others who have no hope.[1]

1 Thessalonians 4:13

Although the precise details of the rhetorical situation that prompted the apostle Paul to write these words are open to debate, this much is clear: several members of the Thessalonian community have died in the weeks or months following his sudden, unplanned departure from their city. These deaths have been a source of intense grief for the Thessalonian Christians, who are under the impression that their fellow believers who have died prior to the parousia will not partake in the joys of that event or, at least, will not enjoy them fully. In response to their confusion and heartache, Paul initially offers an rational argument that explains the order of events at Christ's coming. His claim features a chain of deductive logic beginning with a major premise to which he assumes his audience already gives their assent: "We believe that Jesus died and rose again" (v. 14a). Out of that premise he draws this conclusion: "Even so, through Jesus, God will bring with him those who have died" (v. 14b). With this logical proposition as the foundation for his argument, Paul "declares" to them this "word of the Lord, that we who are alive, who are left until the coming of the Lord, will by no means precede

---

1. Unless otherwise noted, biblical citations are from the New Revised Standard Version (NRSV). Where the New International Version (NIV) is used for clarity, this will be noted in the text.

those who have died" (v. 15). At this point, the Thessalonians have the essential information they need in order to understand the state of those who have died in Christ.

Paul apparently assumes, however, that rational explanation alone is not sufficient to assuage the Thessalonians' grief, for in the next breath (vv. 16-17), he offers a brief, yet also highly structured, imaginative vision of the parousia — a vision that adds virtually nothing by way of content to what he had already told them:

> For the Lord himself, with a cry of command, with the archangel's call and with the sound of God's trumpet, will descend from heaven, and the dead in Christ will rise first. Then we who are alive, who are left, will be caught up in the clouds together with them to meet the Lord in the air; and so we will be with the Lord forever.

Using poetic form and vivid, multi-sensory apocalyptic language and imagery, Paul does more than simply explain how the end will occur; rather, he invites the Thessalonians to imagine it. Only then does he conclude, "Therefore encourage each other with these words" (v. 18).

This passage is one of many texts in the New Testament that employ such poetic forms in the service of theological instruction and moral exhortation. Part of their power involves their potential for evoking strong emotion — something that the rhetorical tradition viewed as essential to persuasion. But what sets these texts apart from typical argumentation is the fact that they are imaginative. They appeal, in Ryken's words, "to our image-making and image-perceiving capacity"; they "incarnate ideas in the form of poetic images, stories of characters in action, and situations in which readers can imaginatively participate. We might say that . . . [they] appeal to our understanding through our imagination."[2] In other words, these passages do not merely explain ideas or supply evidence for rational processes of argumentation, but instead use language to transport their hearers into a phenomenological experience of their theological claims. Although they are clearly intended to be persuasive, affecting their audiences' behaviors and perceptions of the world, whatever persuasive effect they achieve does not result primarily from the kinds of intellectual processes outlined in the

---

2. Leland Ryken, *Words of Delight: A Literary Introduction to the Bible* (Grand Rapids: Baker Books, 1992), 14-15.

discipline to which most scholars have turned in their efforts to understand the NT's persuasive character, that of classical rhetoric.

Rhetoric and the New Testament

The last twenty-five years have witnessed an abundance of research exploring the NT from the perspective of rhetorical criticism, an approach given strong impetus by the publication in 1984 of George Kennedy's *New Testament Interpretation through Rhetorical Criticism*.[3] This turn to a rhetorical reading of Scripture represented a welcome shift from decades of NT research that focused on uncovering the layers of form and tradition that supposedly preceded the development of the NT documents into their present shape, an approach that might be viewed as an "archaeology of discourse" project aimed at discovering the original historical processes and events that gave rise to the Christian movement.[4] By contrast, rhetorical scholars aimed not so much at discovering a text's history or even its theological meaning, but rather at exploring how the texts might have functioned persuasively for the audiences to whom they were directed.[5] As Witherington wisely observed, even for those ultimately interested in the text's theological content, a rhetorical approach to Scripture interposed a crucial step into the enterprise of biblical interpretation by compelling the interpreter to ask what the text is *doing* before asking what the text *means*.[6] In this way, rhetorical criticism has become an indispensible tool for the study of biblical texts.

---

3. George A. Kennedy, *New Testament Interpretation through Rhetorical Criticism* (Chapel Hill: University of North Carolina Press, 1984). For an account of the history and development of the rhetorical turn in NT studies, see Thomas H. Olbricht, "George Kennedy's Scholarship in the Context of North American Rhetorical Studies," in *Words Well Spoken: George Kennedy's Rhetoric of the New Testament*, ed. C. Clifton Black and Duane F. Watson (Waco: Baylor University Press, 2008), 21-40; and Duane F. Watson, "The Influence of George Kennedy on Rhetorical Criticism of the New Testament," pp. 41-62 in the same volume.

4. Many mark the desire to shift away from form criticism to James Muilenburg's presidential address before the annual meeting of the Society of Biblical Literature in 1968, titled "After Form Criticism What?" The address was subsequently published as "Form Criticism and Beyond," *Journal of Biblical Literature* 88 (1969): 1-18.

5. An early but still helpful introduction to the rhetorical criticism of the NT is Burton L. Mack's *Rhetoric and the New Testament* (Minneapolis: Fortress, 1990).

6. Witherington's explanation of the difference that rhetoric makes to biblical interpretation offers an excellent discussion of how a rhetorical-critical perspective can help the interpreter, as he puts it, not "over- or under-interpret" a passage. See Ben Witherington III, *New*

While contributing much to our understanding of the New Testament, however, rhetorical studies of the NT have tended to approach biblical discourse with a strongly rationalistic bias, for reasons that will become clear in the next chapter. They have tended to see the biblical texts primarily as propositional and demonstrative — in Kennedy's words, "based on formally valid inference from accepted premises."[7] As Thiselton noted, such analyses have too often been confined to an "exclusively intellectualistic, didactic, cognitive realm," despite the obvious fact that "the function of much . . . of the biblical material is *transformative* (not simply informative)."[8] This assumption about the nature of NT discourse is evident in what has been among the strongest recent statements of the importance of classical rhetoric for understanding early Christian discourse, Witherington's comprehensive volume, *New Testament Rhetoric*. In the opening of that work, the author counseled the NT interpreter to begin by determining "the species of rhetoric in play" (e.g., deliberative, forensic, or epideictic), and then to "find the proposition and peroration of the discourse," as a prelude to discovering "where the argument is going."[9] While good advice as far as it goes, most of the analysis that follows, even of texts identified as "epideictic," seems to assume that the NT was largely a collection of speeches aimed primarily at seeking assent to theological propositions.[10]

Recognizing this rationalistic focus in NT rhetorical studies, Vernon Robbins's essay, "Rhetography: A New Way of Seeing the Familiar Text," published in the festschrift honoring Kennedy's contributions to NT studies, complained that the rhetorical turn in NT interpretation had "placed primary emphasis on speech (logos) in texts . . . at the expense of rhetography in literature," which he defined as the element of discourse that has to do

---

Testament Rhetoric: An Introductory Guide to the Art of Persuasion in and of the New Testament (Eugene: Cascade, 2009), 214-35.

7. Kennedy, *New Testament Interpretation*, 6. Kennedy himself notes that "sacred language" is often "imagistic and metaphorical, lending the reality of sensory appearances a new meaning," but his focus is clearly on the way that the biblical text offers evidence for claims in ways that appeal to "human rationality" (pp. 6-7).

8. Anthony C. Thiselton, *The First Epistle to the Corinthians: A Commentary on the Greek Text* (Grand Rapids: Eerdmans, 2000), 41 (italics his).

9. Witherington, *New Testament Rhetoric*, 21.

10. As Humphrey pointed out in her review of Witherington, this focus on argument leaves unexamined texts that, as she put it, "require analysis using more than Greco-Roman rhetoric." Edith M. Humphrey, review of *New Testament Rhetoric: An Introductory Guide to the Art of Persuasion in and of the New Testament*, by Ben Witherington III, *Interpretation* 65 (2011): 317.

with the "graphic images people create in their minds as a result of the visual texture of a text." The result, he argued, has been "the development of more and more abstract forms of rhetorical interpretation in the tradition of classical rhetoric that focus attention so completely on the 'rhetology' of the discourse [e.g., its argumentative character] that it ignores the substantive sequences of movements in the 'rhetography' of the discourse."[11]

Although numerous examples of this rationalistic orientation to early Christian discourse can be offered, perhaps the most instructive ones might be found in the analysis of the very type of visionary language with which this chapter opened, apocalyptic discourse. In his articulation of his concept of "rhetorolects," the term he used to explain the basic persuasive forms of early Christian rhetoric, Robbins analyzed the use of the "apocalyptic discourse" rhetorolect in 1 Thess. 4:3-6. He focused on the "*reasoning* of apocalyptic discourse" (emphasis added), comprised of a "thesis" concerning God's will that the Thessalonians engage in appropriate Christian behavior, supported by a "rationale" that "The Lord is the avenger in all these things."[12] Similarly, in her analysis of one of the NT's other major apocalyptic texts, Jesus' temple speech in Mark 13, Collins described the vision as merely a "rhetorically shaped esoteric instruction of a prophetic and apocalyptic nature," as if the speech's sole purpose were to convey secret information. She went on to introduce her analysis in terms of the "structure and logic of the argument," reducing the speech's function to two explanatory purposes, prediction and instruction.[13] When he advocated for the rhetorical analysis of the NT's apocalyptic passages, Carey urged the interpreter to identify apocalyptic motifs that functioned "as argumentative resources," revealing the ways that early Christians "applied the resources of apocalyptic argumentation."[14] While it is certainly the case that the NT's apocalyptic language does serve argumentative or explanatory functions, the result of such approach to critical analysis is a tendency to reduce a potent, imaginative vision to mere propositional argument in a way that marginalizes or

11. Vernon Robbins, "Rhetography: A New Way of Seeing the Familiar Text," in *Words Well Spoken*, ed. Black and Watson, 81-83.

12. Vernon Robbins, "The Dialectical Nature of Early Christian Discourse," *Scriptura* 59 (1996):353-62. (Citations are from the author's revision of 9 December 2001, available online, http://www.religion.emory.edu/faculty/robbins/dialect/dialect353.html).

13. Adela Yarbro Collins, "The Apocalyptic Rhetoric of Mark 13 in Historical Context," *Biblical Research* 41 (1996): 13.

14. Greg Carey, "How to Do Things with (Apocalyptic) Words: Rhetorical Dimensions of Apocalyptic Discourse," *Lexington Theological Quarterly* 33 (1998): 95.

even dismisses the central feature of the discourse, that is, its experiential, visionary character.

When scholars have recognized that the NT writer was doing something besides simply offering a logical argument in support of a factual claim, their reliance on a rhetorical frame has at times become a straightjacket limiting their ability to explain how that alternative form of discourse might have functioned. Thus, at the end of an otherwise outstanding analysis of Paul's encomium of love in 1 Cor. 13, Smit reached this conclusion: "This passage is a rhetorical feat in which Paul tries giving pleasure to his public by artistic means. He gives a small demonstration of his oratorical ability in order to reap the public's admiration."[15] In short, when the discourse moves away from logical argumentation and didactic explanation, rhetorical scholars have not been sure what to make of it.

Such an approach to the NT, I shall argue, simply cannot do justice to the breadth of discourse that we find there, especially to such forms as poetry, hymn, vision, dramatic performance, and the like. But this approach also betrays a far too narrow understanding of the kind of religious faith that such texts were intended to engender. Traditional rhetorical analyses of the NT seem to assume that faith, even in early Christianity, was an intellectual response to argumentation and abstract reasoning, explainable by means of the mechanisms of persuasion envisioned in classical rhetoric. Consequently, a rhetorical approach to the NT, as it has often been practiced, not only tends to overlook the poetic character of these forms of religious discourse but also to misunderstand the role that such texts were expected to play in the formation of Christian faith — for example, how Paul's dramatic vision of the end might have been expected to nurture fervent hope in the face of crushing loss.

Discourse and the Problem of Faith

Although argument and explanation clearly played a role in the process of religious conversion and faith, these poetic texts suggest that the NT writers, especially Paul, also assumed that something more was needed than

15. J. Smit, "The Genre of 1 Corinthians 13 in the Light of Classical Rhetoric," *Novum Testamentum* 33 (1991): 213. Smit did note that "this captivating game . . . is not disinterested. Values are at stake. With the help of 'great' love, Paul demonstrates how small the value of the charismata is so that the fascination with which the Corinthians cherish the extraordinary gifts is diminished."

arguments which supported theological claims. Indeed, if the conversion stories in Acts are any indication, the NT assumes that some kind of extra-rational experience was a central element in the process of coming to faith, alongside the rational explication of the Christian gospel. The account of Pentecost in Acts 2 is paradigmatic in its recounting of the outpouring of the Holy Spirit, which causes the apostles, all Galilean men, to speak in tongues. The result is that visitors from the Jewish diaspora gathered in Jerusalem for Pentecost — "Parthians, Medes, Elamites, and residents of Mesopotamia, Judea and Cappadocia, Pontus and Asia, Phrygia and Pamphylia, Egypt and the parts of Libya belonging to Cyrene, and visitors from Rome, both Jews and proselytes, Cretans and Arabs" — are all able to hear them "speaking about God's deeds of power" in their native languages (Acts 2:8-11). The bystanders who witness this display are "amazed" (ἐξίστημι, vv. 7 and 12) and perplexed and ask, "What does this mean?" (v. 12). Their question then leads into Peter's proclamation of the gospel, which places what they have just witnessed within a narrative that gives it meaning as a climactic sign of the fulfillment of Hebrew messianic prophecy, the centerpiece of which is the death and resurrection of Jesus Christ and the outpouring of the Holy Spirit on "all flesh" (v. 17). In response to his sermon, the account states, 3000 are baptized.

In the following chapter, Peter and John heal a man disabled from birth who used to beg for alms at the temple gate. Later, when the crowd recognizes the man, now healed, "walking and leaping and praising God" (3:8), they are "filled with wonder [θάμβος] and amazement [ἔκστασις] at what had happened to him" (3:10). As with chap. 2, this demonstration of the power of God creates the opportunity for Peter to proclaim the gospel, again in a way that provides meaning to the experience the crowd has just undergone.

Numerous other examples might be offered to show this pattern: Cornelius, the first recorded Gentile convert, who is given instructions to send for Peter by an angel who appears to him one day when he is praying — and who experiences an outpouring of the Holy Spirit similar to the one that occurred at Pentecost just as Peter is in the midst of preaching to him and his household (Acts 10:1-48); Lydia, of whom it was said that "the Lord opened her heart to listen eagerly to what was said by Paul" (Acts 16:14); the Philippian jailor, who witnesses an earthquake that opens the doors to the jail where Paul and his companions had been chained, affording Paul the opportunity to proclaim the gospel to the jailor and his household (Acts 16:25-34); even Paul, to whom Jesus appears as he travels the road to Damascus (Acts

9:1-8). Paul will later recount his dramatic conversion experience in Gal. 1, emphasizing that he received his message by revelation from God, and not from any human being:

> You have heard, no doubt, of my earlier life in Judaism. I was violently persecuting the church of God and was trying to destroy it. I advanced in Judaism beyond many among my people of the same age, for I was far more zealous for the traditions of my ancestors. But when God, who had set me apart before I was born and called me through his grace, was pleased to reveal his Son to me, so that I might proclaim him among the Gentiles, I did not confer with any human being (Gal. 1:13-16).

In each case, Christian faith was not simply the result of a logical presentation of arguments to which listeners gave intellectual assent — although a conceptual explanation of the gospel was certainly part of the process. In other words, religious conversion was rarely conceived in early Christianity as arising out of the kinds of persuasive processes that lay at the heart of the classical rhetorical tradition. As Kennedy himself put it, "Christian preaching is . . . not persuasion, but proclamation, and is based on authority and grace, not on proof." Citing Augustine's *De Doctrina Christiana* (4.21), he explained,

> A good listener warms to it not so much by diligently analyzing it as by pronouncing it energetically. Its truth must be apprehended by the listening, not proved by the speaker. The reaction of a person in the audience to the *kerygma* is like his reaction to a miracle, the direct evidence of authority: he believes or he does not.[16]

In short, the faith process involved not simply a rational response to logical proofs but rather an often dramatic, extrarational and life-altering encounter with God, accompanied by the experience of amazement, literally, ecstasy (ἔκστασις).

---

16. George A. Kennedy, *Classical Rhetoric and Its Christian and Secular Tradition from Ancient to Modern Times* (Chapel Hill: University of North Carolina Press, 1980), 127. Kennedy distinguished between the proclamation and reception of the Christian gospel and the tradition of rhetoric in this way: "In its purest and most fundamental form . . . the basic modes of proof of Judeo-Christian rhetoric are grace, authority, and logos, the divine message, which can be understood by man. These correspond in a very incomplete way to the pathos, ethos, and rational logos of Aristotelian rhetoric" (p. 123).

Many contemporary scholars see faith in a similar, holistic way — in theologian Paul Tillich's words, as an "act of the total personality." Tillich particularly emphasized what he called the "ecstatic" character of faith, which included yet also transcended rational processes. As he put it,

> Faith as the embracing and centered act of the personality is "ecstatic." It transcends the drives of the nonrational unconscious and the structures of the rational conscious. It transcends them, but does not destroy them. The ecstatic character of faith does not exclude its rational character although it is not identical with it, and it includes nonrational strivings without being identical with them.

Tillich also noted that although faith included will, faith was "not a creation of the will. In the ecstasy of faith the will to accept and to surrender is an element, but not the cause."[17] The will, he believed, seemed to play more a role of making sense of and ultimately embracing the transformative reorientation of life that grew out of some kind of transcendent experience, rather than being at the root of conversion. Scholars who research the psychology of religion likewise emphasize the role of these all-encompassing, transcendent experiences in the formation of faith. Such "ultimacy experiences . . . point to ultimate concerns and elicit our most intense cognitive-emotional-spiritual engagement/commitment."[18] Spilka, Hood, Hunsberger, and Gorsuch point out that social scientists who study the psychology of conversion emphasize the pervasive impact of religious experience on dimensions of personality. Their findings underscore the way that such experiences foster profound change in what are called "mid-level functions" of personality (attitudes, feelings, and behaviors), as well as "self-defining personality functions," which have to do with one's "purpose in life, meaning, identity."[19]

In particular, contemporary writings on faith distinguish between faith as a holistic reorientation of one's personality and identity, and mere "belief," which they understand as mental assent or the "holding of certain ideas."[20] As Tillich put it, "The most ordinary misinterpretation of faith" is to view

---

17. Paul Tillich, *Dynamics of Faith* (New York: Harper and Row, 1957), 4, 6-7.

18. Patrick McNamara, *The Neuroscience of Religious Experience* (Cambridge: Cambridge University Press, 2009), 148.

19. Bernard Spilka, Ralph W. Hood, Jr., Bruce Hunsberger, and Richard Gorsuch, *The Psychology of Religion: An Empirical Approach*, 3rd ed. (New York: Guilford, 2003).

20. James W. Fowler, *Stages of Faith: The Psychology of Development and the Quest for Meaning* (New York: HarperCollins, 1981), 11.

faith simply a kind of knowledge based on "a low degree of evidence."[21] By contrast, Wilfred Smith argued,

> Faith is deeper, richer, more personal. It is engendered by a religious tradition, in some cases, and to some degree by its doctrines; but it is a quality of the person and not the system. It is an orientation of the personality, to oneself, to one's neighbor, to the universe; a total response; a way of seeing whatever one sees and of handling whatever one handles; a capacity to live at more than a mundane level; to see, to feel, to act in terms of, a transcendent dimension.[22]

Contemporary philosopher James K. A. Smith poignantly captured this sense of faith as a fundamental, holistic orientation to the world, as well as the role that experience plays in shaping that orientation, when he described humans as "liturgical animals" rather than "thinking machines." In his formulation of the character of faith, Smith drew on philosopher Charles Taylor's notion of the "social imaginary," which Taylor defined in this way:

> By social imaginary I mean something much broader and deeper than the intellectual schemes people may entertain when they think about social reality in a disengaged mode. I am thinking, rather, of the ways people imagine their social existence, how they fit together with others, how things go on between them and their fellows, the expectations that are normally met, and the deeper normative notions and images that underlie these expectations.

In contrast to an abstract or theoretical understanding of the world, he continued, the social imaginary is "that largely unstructured and inarticulate understanding of our whole situation, within which the particular features of our world show up for us in the sense that they have. It can never be adequately expressed in the form of explicit doctrines because of its unlimited and indefinite nature."[23]

On this basis, Smith rejected the anthropology that ignores the status of humans as "embodied creatures," which assumes that ideas precede actions

---

21. Tillich, *Dynamics of Faith*, 31.

22. Wilfred C. Smith, *Faith and Belief* (Princeton: Princeton University Press, 1979), 12.

23. Charles Taylor, *Modern Social Imaginaries* (Durham, NC: Duke University Press, 2004), 23, 25.

and that most human behavior results from explicit cognitive processes. Against that view, Smith argued that humans are oriented to the world through practice and experience. As he put it,

> We don't go around all day *thinking* about how to get to the classroom or *thinking* about how to brush our teeth or *perceiving* our friends. Most of the time, we are simply involved in the world. We navigate our way and orient ourselves for the most part without thinking about it — like driving home from work by a route so familiar that we can do it without even being "conscious," and thus sometimes find ourselves in the driveway unable to remember driving home.[24]

Much of the human response to the world, in other words, is visceral, a "gut reaction," arising not from conscious intellectual processes but from what Scripture calls the *kardia*, the heart. And as he noted, this part of the human self is shaped by repeated experiences, by liturgies practiced not only with the mind but also with voice and body. To quote Smith once more:

> Before we articulate a "worldview," we worship. Before we put into words the lineaments of an ontology or an epistemology, we pray for God's healing and illumination. Before we theorize the nature of God, we sing [God's] praises. Before we codify the doctrine of Christ's two natures, we receive the body of Christ in the Eucharist. Before we think, we pray. That's the kind of animals we are, first and foremost: loving, desiring, affective, liturgical animals who, for the most part, don't inhabit the world as thinkers or cognitive machines.[25]

---

24. James K. A. Smith, *Desiring the Kingdom: Worship, Worldview, and Cultural Formation* (Grand Rapids: Baker Academic, 2009), 50.

25. James K. A. Smith, "Beyond Integration: Re-narrating Christian Scholarship in Postmodernity," in *Beyond Integration: Inter/Disciplinary Possibilities for the Future of Christian Higher Education*, ed. Todd C. Ream, Jerry A. Pattengale, and David L. Riggs (Abilene: Abilene Christian University Press, 2012), 23. Smith is particularly critical of contemporary preaching for the way it often reflects this same intellectualistic bias that rhetorical scholars have sometimes imposed on the NT. As he put it, "While the mall, Victoria's Secret, and Jerry Bruckheimer are grabbing hold of our gut by means of our body and its senses — in stories and images, sights and sounds, and commercial versions of 'smells and bells' — the church's response is oddly rationalist. It plunks us down in a 'worship' service, the culmination of which is a forty-five minute didactic sermon, a sort of holy lecture, trying to *convince* us of the dangers by implanting doctrines and beliefs. . . . The church still tends to see us as Cartesian

What all of these scholars underscore and, indeed, what seems inherent in the NT's accounts of religious conversion, is an understanding that faith is a holistic, all-encompassing reorientation of one's personality and worldview, and that this reorientation typically involves some kind of transcendent, ecstatic state of consciousness in the experience of the believer. This understanding of faith and, especially, the role that the experience of ecstasy plays in its creation, holds a clue for how we might understand the persuasive character of the NT's texts that resist easy categorization within the tradition of classical rhetoric.

An Alternative Perspective

Among the numerous scholars who have explored the NT's rhetorical character, a small handful have recognized and sought to address forms of early Christian discourse that did not necessarily lend themselves to traditional rhetorical analysis. For example, although he remained clearly in the conceptual world of argumentative persuasion, Pernot urged scholars to examine such pervasive forms of religious discourse as hymn and prayer on their own merits, arguing that such research would lead to an identification of the unique rhetorical mechanisms specific to such forms. The key, he argued, was to view them not as "a mere transposition of judicial, deliberative, and epideictic categories," but rather as forms of discourse "*sui generis,* characterized by structures, arguments, stylistic forms, and an *actio*" of their own.[26] Others scholars have been especially drawn to the visual component of Christian rhetoric. Humphrey's *And I Turned to See the Voice*, for example, complained that rhetorical criticism had not found a way to account for the NT texts that claimed to report visionary experiences. Focusing on the way that "*word* and *image* work together" in these texts (emphasis in original), she highlighted the integral contribution that both made to the process of argumentation:

> Some visions bring speech to an apt and powerful conclusion; others direct the polemic of a narrative through recapitulation or strategic placement; still others, embryonic in form, subtly shape the message of the

---

minds. While secular liturgies are after our hearts . . . the church thinks it only has to get into our heads" (*Desiring the Kingdom*, 126-27).

26. Laurent Pernot, "The Rhetoric of Religion," *Rhetorica* 24 (2006): 241-42.

passage in which they are embedded; and extensive visions allow the readers' imaginations freer reign even while they are guided by propositions included within the vision sequence.[27]

Although her study still focused primarily on the argumentative dimensions of visions, she nevertheless challenged scholars to broaden the focus of their analysis beyond that of traditional rhetorical-critical studies.

Similarly, Robbins himself called interpreters to include the "visual texture" of texts, which he described in this way: "A speaker or writer composes, intentionally or unintentionally, a context of communication through statements or signs that conjure visual images in the mind which, in turn, evoke 'familiar' contexts that provide meaning for a hearer or reader." In other words, every discourse contains cues that assume or presuppose an imaginative setting in which the discourse is taking place. Indeed, he pointed out, even classical rhetoric's traditional genres included this visual dimension, as the "speaker/writer or interpreter is asked to envision attributes of the speakers and characteristics of the audience where a speech occurs," whether the political assembly, the courtroom, or the public celebration. The speech's contextual cues, in turn, invite the audience to picture that setting, in a way that lends support to the argument conveyed by the discourse itself. As an example, in his analysis of Paul's use of judicial rhetoric to defend himself, which runs through 1 Cor. 1–5, Robbins noted how the text employs apocalyptic discourse to move the imaginative setting of the speech "beyond a courtroom in a city-state to the imperial divine courtroom of apocalyptic rhetoric."[28]

Robbins's call to expand the focus beyond the analysis of the argument is a welcome invitation to examine the inescapable visual dimension of even texts that were more clearly envisioned as being rhetorical in the sense of being aimed at intellectual conviction. Yet even here, the focus is still on how those elements serve the interests of rational argument.

Among these scholars who have sought to expand the boundaries of what constitutes persuasion in early Christianity, however, at least three have highlighted the *nonrational* or *extrarational* dimensions of some early Christian discourse, focusing especially on the way that such discourse created imaginative experiences rather than offering rational arguments.

27. Edith M. Humphrey, *And I Turned to See the Voice: The Rhetoric of Vision in the New Testament* (Grand Rapids: Baker Academic, 2007), 26, 28.

28. Robbins, "Rhetography," 81, 83, 92.

Their studies, moreover, have sought to explore the role that such imaginative discourse might have played in the development and sustaining of religious faith. First was Kirkwood's work on parables,[29] which, he emphasized, had the power, together with other forms of storytelling, to provoke self-confrontation in their audience, arousing "both sympathetic and hostile listeners to recognize and overcome those thoughts, feelings, attitudes, and actions which impede their spiritual growth." At the heart of this power was the unique potential for a tale to "arrest for a few minutes the listener's otherwise incessant intellectualizing"[30] — what Stark aptly called the "hermeneutics of suspicion"[31] — by evoking "in listeners a brief experience of nonrational awareness." In other words, rather than giving instruction *about* some emotion or state of awareness, stories have the power to place listeners in an imaginative state in which they possess that awareness or mood in their actual consciousness, providing them, in Kirkwood's words, with "an experiential introduction to a new state of mind."[32]

Second was Sullivan's important study, "*Kairos* and the Rhetoric of Belief,"[33] which argued that the NT reflects an understanding of rhetoric that reaches back beyond Aristotle's formulation of rhetoric as *techne* to a stream of tradition associated with Gorgias, who emphasized the "magical and seductive marvels of *logos*." This stream viewed the *kairos* as a moment when "inspiration produces *logos*" and "when the power, *dunamis*, of *logos* breaks through the stasis of doxatic rhetoric, making decision and action possible." What is striking about Sullivan's argument is the way that it highlights the essential character of at least some early Christian proclamation as a "nonrational or supra-rational rhetoric" that produces "what might be called a kairotic experience, which presents a single alternative, filling the entire consciousness of the auditor." Drawing on Rudolf Otto's notion of the "holy," such rhetoric makes certain realities "present" for an audience:

---

29. William G. Kirkwood, "Storytelling and Self-confrontation: Parables as Communication Strategies," *Quarterly Journal of Speech* 69 (1983): 58-74.

30. Kirkwood, "Storytelling and Self-confrontation," 58, 64. See also his "Parables as Metaphors and Examples," *Quarterly Journal of Speech* 71 (1985): 422-40.

31. Ryan J. Stark, "Some Aspects of Christian Mystical Rhetoric, Philosophy, and Poetry," *Philosophy and Rhetoric* 41 (2008): 260.

32. Kirkwood, "Storytelling and Self-confrontation," 64-65.

33. Dale L. Sullivan, "*Kairos* and the Rhetoric of Belief," *Quarterly Journal of Speech* 78 (1992): 317-32.

One could say that the speaker can simply awaken the audience to the presence of something far greater than themselves. . . . If we associate kairotic rhetoric with Otto's numinous experience, we can conclude . . . that an orator cannot argue a person into acknowledging the presence of God; the orator can, at best, create a *kairos* which unleashes the glory of God.

The result of such an experience is that the audience encounters "a sense of the numinous," an experience that "can be associated with the power of imagination creating a vision that fills the consciousness." In the face of such discourse, the listener "confronts a force that does more than address his or her intellect."[34]

Both of these studies underscored the fact that the experiential character of early Christian discourse was integrally connected to the fundamental nature of religious faith. As Kirkwood observed, in most religious traditions "certain moods and states of mind (e.g., equanimity, quietude, awe, devotion) are not just the means, but the ends of spiritual discipline." Rather than being subordinate to other cognitive processes, in other words, these feelings and states of awareness are "significant in their own right." Thus, "a parable which arouses one of these moods is not necessarily serving some further argumentative end."[35] Similarly, as Sullivan pointed out, it should not surprise us that early Christian rhetoric offers a numinous experience rather than just rational argument, since "its end is not judgment (*krisis*) but belief (*pistis*); it is aimed not at the mind but the heart."[36] Such discourse uniquely fits the needs inherent in the creation and nurturing of religious faith.

Finally, although he did not deal primarily with early Christian discourse, Stark's essay, "Some Aspects of Christian Mystical Rhetoric, Philosophy, and Poetry,"[37] likewise emphasized the need to distinguish between what he termed "mystical rhetoric" and "secular rhetoric," arguing that because of their failure to distinguish between the two, scholars have "attempted to transmogrify Spirit into secular concepts, which distorts spirited language and leads to mischaracterizations of religious experience." Like Kirkwood, he noted that believers who wish to enter fully into mystical rhetoric must suspend their "overly critical stance," because such a stance actually diminishes the believers' openness to new insight. He offered an account of what

---

34. Sullivan, "*Kairos* and the Rhetoric of Belief," 317, 320, 326-27.
35. Kirkwood, "Storytelling and Self-Confrontation," 59, 66.
36. Sullivan, "*Kairos* and the Rhetoric of Belief," 327.
37. Stark, "Some Aspects of Christian Mystical Rhetoric, Philosophy, and Poetry," 260-77.

he called "mystical enthymemes," where numinous experiences created by the breaking in of the Holy Spirit supply the ground for the explication of an "argument" to view and respond to the world in a particular way. As he put it,

> The truth that the Spirit supplies is not cold knowledge alone, the frosty epistemology of Enlightenment rationalism, for example, or the ambivalent epistemology of contemporary pragmatism. Rather, the Spirit supplies an "upheaval of thought" . . . a rhetorical-logical-ethical-mystical apprehension of love and purpose — an epiphany — where pathos functions as the core epistemological medium.

Thus, he concluded, "Writing inspired by the Spirit has a participatory quality, which affords continuous chances of communion and illumination through supernatural transfers of energy."[38]

The thesis of this book is that the poetic texts of the NT represent the attempts of early Christian writers to create these numinous experiences for their audiences. They possessed a richer understanding of religious faith than could be sustained by the kind of "rational persuasion" envisioned in the dominant tradition of classical rhetoric, and so they offered more than simply reasonable arguments and explanations. Instead, they sought to use language to create vivid, transcendent, "extrarational" experiences that would provide for their hearers a momentary, phenomenological apprehension of theological reality. In doing so, I shall argue, the NT writers fundamentally altered the three central relationships in the rhetorical exchange, the relationship of the rhetor to the audience, the relationship of the audience members to one another, and most importantly, the relationship of the audience to the content itself. These poetic texts transformed the relationship of rhetor to audience by moving the rhetor out of a stance of explicitly attempting to change the audience's beliefs and behaviors. They transformed the relationship of audience members to each other, positioning them not as isolated critics of argument but as co-sharers in a powerful, numinous experience. Most importantly, these poetic texts shifted the relationship of the audience to the content itself, from a position of contemplating theological ideas as abstract conceptions or of considering the merits of the rhetor's arguments, to one where they encountered the content as a subjective experience. In short, these texts were aimed not at convincing but, rather, at inducing "ekstasis," literally, transport, carrying their listeners into an alternative realm

38. Stark, "Some Aspects of Christian Mystical Rhetoric, Philosophy, and Poetry," 260-65.

of reality, an experience that would fundamentally change their orientation in the physical and social worlds in which they lived.

In order to situate these texts within the landscape of ancient discourse, then, we turn not to the mainstream of classical rhetoric represented by Aristotle and those who followed him, but to an alternative conception of what Stephen Halliwell called "rhetorico-poetic" persuasion.[39] This tradition, represented in such thinkers as Gorgias and Longinus, incorporated into its understanding of persuasion key elements from the tradition of poetics, particularly those of *mimesis*, or representation, and *phantasia*, or visualization. Although they clearly understood the importance of argument and evidence, they also emphasized the power of language to transport hearers into an alternative state of consciousness. The conception embodied in this tradition, I shall argue, provided early Christianity with a crucial resource for sustaining believers' sense of the presence of God, and for providing them with a subjective experience of the theological realities that lay at the heart of their faith, allowing believers to "see" what they longed for but had not yet come to pass.

Chapter Outline

In chapter one, I offer an overview of the distinctions made within the classical tradition between rhetoric and poetic, noting the roots of that distinction within the political and social culture of the ancient world. I emphasize the role of what Aristotle and others called "mimesis," or representation, in the poetic tradition to create psychological experiences for the audience. In this chapter, I explore the conception of persuasion contained in Gorgias's *Encomium of Helen*, and particularly the treatise traditionally titled *On the Sublime*, attributed to a figure known as "Longinus." In both cases, I highlight the way that these authors understand the power of mimetic discourse to activate what the classical writers call *phantasia*, that is, the human capacity for visualization, in order to "bring before the eyes" ideas, experiences, and attitudes that were not directly or literally in the experience of the audience.

In chapters 2–5, I closely examine four such poetic texts that are embedded in the NT's most argumentative or "rhetorical" genre, the epistle. While these texts certainly do not exhaust the range of possibilities for examining

39. Stephen Halliwell, *Between Ecstasy and Truth: Interpretations of Greek Poetics from Homer to Longinus* (Oxford: Oxford University Press, 2011), 277.

the NT's poetic texts, they represent what might be viewed as a collection of paradigmatic poetic forms in the NT: an apocalyptic vision (1 Thessalonians 4:13-18), a "dramatic performance" (that is, a "speech-in-character," Romans 7:14-25), a "poem proper" (Paul's encomium of love, 1 Corinthians 13), and a liturgy (Ephesians 1:3-14). Although three come from the hand of Paul, the fourth, the liturgy of Eph. 1, is of uncertain authorship, a fact that may suggest a broader practice of language usage beyond that of Paul himself.

In chapters 6–7, I explore the implications of the use of poetic form for three central relationships in the rhetorical encounter, described above. Finally, the book's conclusion explores the larger implications of this study for our broader understanding of early Christian persuasion.

A Word on Methodology

Although strong inferential evidence suggests that Paul and other NT rhetors may have actually had rhetorical training, we have no direct evidence that they ever studied rhetoric formally or consulted a rhetorical handbook in order to write. However, it is axiomatic among most NT interpreters that a rhetorical consciousness pervaded the culture in which the NT texts were written, so that it would have been unavoidable for the writers not to have been shaped by that consciousness. Thus, when I consult classical treatises, it is not to assume that there was any kind of direct dependence; rather, those treatises, I am assuming, represented a common understanding of persuasion.

At times in this study, I will also draw upon contemporary theoretical understandings of persuasion. Obviously, this does not reflect the anachronistic assumption that these writers would have had access to conceptualizations of these theories. Rather, it simply reflects the understanding that practice precedes theory (even as theory, in turn, shapes practice), and that contemporary theorists thus offer explanations for how humans — who may have never read a shred of contemporary theory — attempt to influence each other. In this way, contemporary theories can sometimes uncover and illuminate ancient practice, even if the original writers were not completely aware of what they were doing.

CHAPTER ONE

Rhetoric, Poetics, and the Ecstasy of Faith

When Paul, in 1 Thess. 4:16-17, describes the parousia of Christ by enumerating the audible and visual portents that would accompany that event, the "cry of command," the "archangel's call" and the "sound of God's trumpet," he certainly intends to persuade his hearers to believe and to act in certain ways. This passage, like all of the NT's poetic texts, clearly supports the NT's theological claims. It does so, however, out of a dramatically different understanding of persuasion than that of merely supplying evidence for rational processes of argumentation. Instead, it uses language to embody or represent those claims in a way that provides hearers with something of a visceral, extrarational consciousness of the theological message. In short, it creates an imaginative experience that reflects the understanding of persuasion not so much of Aristotle's *Rhetoric,* but of his other classic treatment of the communicative arts, the *Poetics.*[1] Although the line between the two was never completely definitive, Aristotle clearly believed that the two arts employed markedly different modes of expression. As Baldwin put it, "Finding these to be distinct essentially, as . . . processes of conceiving, ordering and uttering, Aristotle treated them separately as two distinct technics, rhetoric and poetic."[2]

---

1. Unless otherwise noted, citations from Aristotle's *Rhetoric* and *Poetics* are from *The Rhetoric and the Poetics of Aristotle,* trans. W. Rhys Roberts and Ingram Bywater (New York: McGraw-Hill, 1984). Where, for purposes of preserving a more literal reading of the original language, I have quoted from the Loeb edition (*The "Art" of Rhetoric,* trans. John Henry Freese [Cambridge, MA: Harvard University Press, 1959]), the translator's name will be included in the citation.

2. Charles Sears Baldwin, *Ancient Rhetoric and Poetic* (Gloucester, MA: Peter Smith, 1959), 3.

This chapter explores the classical theory of poetics as it was outlined in Aristotle's *Poetics* as a vantage point for viewing the NT's poetic texts, focusing particularly on Aristotle's explanation of how mimesis, or artistic representation, functioned to influence the poet's audience. From there, the chapter explores what Halliwell calls the "rhetorico-poetic" tradition, a tradition of public communication that explicitly embraced mimetic processes alongside rational arguments in its understanding of persuasion. It is in this tradition, represented especially by such writers as Gorgias and Longinus, that early Christian persuasion finds its natural "home," because of the emphasis that such writers placed on using language to create the kind of "ecstatic" experiences that the NT understood as being foundational to religious faith. As a backdrop for considering the distinct understanding of persuasion that these writers brought to public discourse, we begin with a brief discussion of classical rhetoric's character as a rationalistic mode of persuasion.

Rhetoric as Rational Judgment

The tradition of rhetoric, as it was codified in the treatises that comprised what Kennedy called the "philosophical tradition," provided theoretical knowledge and practical strategies for engaging in civic persuasion in the primary avenues that were available for public speaking throughout most of Greco-Roman history, namely the courtroom and the legislative assembly.[3] Although he did envision a place for ceremonial rhetoric, Aristotle's focus on judicial and legislative locations for the practice of rhetoric as he envisioned it is clear in his complaint that the handbooks had neglected deliberative rhetoric — to his mind, the one "nobler and more worthy of a statesman" (*Rhet.*, 1.1) — in favor of judicial rhetoric. This also explains Aristotle's anemic treatment of epideictic, which Kennedy attributes to the

---

3. As Kennedy described it, the tradition of "philosophical rhetoric" was a reaction to the sophists that tended to "deemphasize the speaker and to stress the validity of his message and the nature of his effect on the audience," and that had "close ties with dialectic or logic, and sometimes with psychology" (*Classical Rhetoric and Its Christian and Secular Tradition from Ancient to Modern Times* [Chapel Hill: University of North Carolina Press, 1980], 17). Robbins likewise recognized classical rhetoric's roots in the courtroom and the legislative assembly, but also includes the civic ceremony; see his "Rhetography: A New Way of Seeing the Familiar Text," in *Words Well Spoken: George Kennedy's Rhetoric of the New Testament*, ed. C. Clifton Black and Duane F. Watson (Waco: Baylor University Press, 2008), 82.

relative paucity of opportunities for public speaking outside those two primary settings.[4] This focus continues throughout the Hellenistic and Roman traditions, and Cicero would endorse it by citing with approval his Greek forebears who "separated from other uses of speech that portion of oratory which is concerned with public discussions of the law-courts and of debate, and left that branch only to the orator" (*De or.*, 1.6.22).[5]

The fact that the conceptualization of rhetoric as an art grew out of the exigencies of the courtroom and the legislative assembly profoundly shaped its epistemology and what it envisioned as its *telos*. Aristotle declared, "The object of Rhetoric is judgment [κρίσεως] — for judgments are pronounced in deliberative rhetoric and judicial proceedings are a judgment" (*Rhet.*, 2.1, Freese). Although he would later admit the need to arouse emotion, he nevertheless opened his treatise by claiming that in the courtroom, exercising judgment was akin to using a ruler to measure the length of an object: arousing "anger, jealousy, or compassion" in the jury would be tantamount to "warp[ing] a carpenter's rule before using it" (*Rhet.*, 1.1). Commenting on these passages, Black asserted that Aristotelian rhetoric was aimed at a decision, "a kind of conclusion, drawn on the merits of competing claims."[6] In a similar way, even Isocrates, traditionally categorized as a sophist, argued that rhetoric, the ability to "speak before a crowd," was the external counterpart to inner deliberation, the ability of wise persons to "skillfully debate their problems in their own minds" (*Antid.*, 256-57).[7] Much later, the youthful Cicero would introduce his treatise *De Inventione* by mentioning the breadth of what might be covered in a rhetorical handbook but then focusing his readers' attention to "the most important of all the divisions," which was invention, the discovery of the cause or claim that would be offered for the audience's assent. The *Rhetorica ad Herennium* reflects the same focus.

---

4. Although in later antiquity a "large number of epideictic forms were practiced," he said, opportunities for public speaking that was not deliberative or judicial were limited to "ceremonial oratory and public festivals and funerals. In such speeches, praise of a god, a man, or a city was the dominant theme" (George A. Kennedy, *New History of Classical Rhetoric* [Princeton: Princeton University Press, 2009], 61).

5. See also Kennedy, *New History*, 62, 65.

6. Edwin Black, *Rhetorical Criticism: A Study in Method* (New York: Macmillan, 1965), 109.

7. Kennedy offered this characterization: "Modern scholars often distinguish an Isocratean tradition in classical rhetoric, contrasted with an Aristotelian tradition. So understood, the Isocratean tradition emphasizes written rather than spoken discourse, epideictic rather than deliberative or judicial speech, style rather than argument, amplification and smoothness rather than forcefulness" (*New History*, 49).

It offers a copious treatment of style and, as Reid pointed out, it actually includes "embellishment" — the use of "similes, examples, previous judgments, and other means which serve to expand and enrich the argument" — as an integral dimension of the "complete argument."[8] Nevertheless, it clearly subordinates these persuasive elements to the ultimate goal of helping the audience grasp the import of the facts of the case, on the assumption that doing so will enhance their ability to pass judgment on the claims being presented for their evaluation.

A number of scholars have pointed out that this understanding of rhetoric's *telos* as judgment gave Greco-Roman rhetoric its fundamentally rationalistic character, reflected in Aristotle's assertion that "enthymemes . . . are the substance of persuasion," and that matters such as "the rousing of prejudice, pity, anger, and similar emotions" are "non-essentials" (*Rhet.*, 1.1); thus, the central goal of rhetorical training was to become "skilled in the enthymeme" (*Rhet.*, 1.1). What attention he did give to delivery and style was a concession to the "defects of our hearers," since "we ought in fairness to fight our case with no help beyond the bare facts: nothing, therefore, should matter except the proof of those facts" (*Rhet.*, 3.1). These examples support Enos's claim that Aristotle clearly took a "restrictive view of rhetoric as essentially an explicit, rational process."[9] Sullivan argued, moreover, that this rationalistic character was rooted in Aristotle's conceptualization of rhetoric not as a skill (ἐμπειρία), but as an art (τέχνη), the "faculty of discovering in any given case the available means of persuasion" (*Rhet.*, 1.1):

8. Reid concluded, "Other writers tended to treat embellishment as an aspect of style, but here it functions as part of the reasoning process that proves persuasive for listeners" (Robert S. Reid, "*Ad Herennium* Argument Strategies in 1 Corinthians," *Journal of Greco-Roman Christianity and Judaism*, 3 [2006]: 198). Reid's essay argues that this form of argument, including the "embellishment," lay behind the composition of 1 Corinthians. See especially the treatment in the *Ad Herennium* of "vivid description," a figure of thought "which contains a clear, lucid, and impressive exposition of the consequences of an act" (*ad Her.*, 4.39), as well as its discussion of embellishment as part of the "complete argument" (2.28, 2.46.29).

9. Richard Lee Enos, "Aristotle, Empedocles, and the Notion of Rhetoric," in *In Search of Justice: The Indiana Tradition in Speech Communication,* ed. Richard J. Jensen and John C. Hammerback (Amsterdam: Rodopi, 1987), 7. Enos asserted that "when Aristotle refused to acknowledge the nonrational aspects of rhetoric, he dismissed a long-established mode of expressing thoughts and sentiments and tainted the sophistic movement for centuries afterwards. In short, Aristotle's *Rhetoric* portrays its discipline more as a revolution than an evolution in thought, a department from irrationality rather than an evolutionary step in the historical development of consciousness about discourse."

Unlike someone who uses an *empeiria*, which is a skill without knowledge of principles, one who practices a *techne* can explain what he or she is doing because the principles are explicit. . . . Thus, we might think of *empeiria* as a skill with much tacit knowledge, while *techne* is a science that has surfaced the tacit dimensions of the craft.[10]

This shift from skill to art, he concluded, inherently gave rhetoric a rationalistic character. But as he further explained, Aristotle also privileged the rational over the nonrational by making judgment, the logical appraisal of competing claims, rather than the belief or conviction that something was true or real, the *telos* of rhetoric. Thus, "unlike a rhetoric that has belief or conviction as the goal, Aristotle's rhetoric produces a systematic procedure, for judgment is primarily a rational process." Aristotle's *Rhetoric* thus represented a "divorce of rhetoric from the magical and seductive marvels of *logos* as defined by Gorgias,"[11] for such marvels clouded the audience's ability to weigh critically the claims offered for their assent. As Kennedy tersely concluded, "The irrational powers of language have no attraction for him."[12]

Poetics and Imaginative Transformation

For most writers in the classical tradition, poetry represented a marked departure from the rationalistic character of rhetoric. Cicero reflected that understanding when, in *De or.*, he has Callus say,

The truth is that the poet is a very near kinsman of the orator, rather more heavily fettered as regards rhythm, but with ampler freedom in his choice of words, while in the use of many sorts of ornament he is his ally

10. Dale L. Sullivan, "*Kairos* and the Rhetoric of Belief," *Quarterly Journal of Speech* 78 (1992): 323.

11. Sullivan, "*Kairos* and the Rhetoric of Belief," 323-24, 320. As Sullivan further observed, Aristotle's focus on judgment rather than belief led him to give "certain key words (*pistis, dunamis*) special meanings." In the case of *pistis*, or "proof," he emphasized an instrumental rather than teleological understanding; in the case of *dunamis*, which in the sophistic tradition denoted a "power that breaks out," he defined it as "everything necessary to bring something into existence. And since Aristotle believed that the art of rhetoric was sufficient, a person who exercises *dunamis* simply exercises the *techne* of rhetoric by putting its rules and principles into action" (324).

12. Kennedy, *Classical Rhetoric*, 78.

and almost his counterpart; in one respect at all events something like identity exists, since he sets no boundaries or limits to his claim, such as would prevent him from ranging whither he will with the same freedom and license as the other (1.16.70-71).

Of course, as the above passage also indicates, the two traditions were never completely separate, especially when it came to discussions of style. Aristotle recognized, for example, that poetic discourse could be used within rhetorical texts, just as a speech might appear on the lips of a character in a drama.[13] Halliwell also noted in his introduction to the *Poetics* that Aristotle's discussion of "diction" in chaps. 20-22 is closely related to book 3 of the *Rhetoric*.[14] We find a similar integration, typical of Roman rhetoric, in the *ad Her.*, which mines poetry and oratory as equally fruitful sites for discovering illustrations of various schemes and tropes (e.g., 4.1.2, 4.5.8, 4.32.43). Nevertheless, the art of poetry reflected a fundamentally different understanding of how discourse influences its hearers from that of rhetoric. That understanding, I shall argue, was far better suited than that of rhetoric to religious communication, which took place not in the courtroom or the legislative assembly, but in the church, and which had as its end not judgment, but faith.

The qualities that set poetic apart from rhetoric emerge clearly in Aristotle's own account of that alternative art. In contrast to rhetoric, centered in proofs and, especially, the enthymeme, Aristotle stated that the defining characteristic of all poetic arts, from epic, tragedy, and comedy to "flute-playing and lyre-playing," is that they are "modes of imitation" (*Poet.*, 1). For example, he notes the representational nature of dance: "Rhythm alone, without harmony, is the means of the dancer's imitations; for even he, by the rhythms of his attitudes, may represent men's characters, as well as what they do and suffer" (*Poet.*, 1). Unlike the rhetor, who needed to employ the proofs of ethos to enhance his or her personal standing before the audience, Aristotle urged the poet to "say very little *in propria persona,* as he is no imitator when he is doing that" (*Poet.*, 24). His warning captures the distinction between explanation and representation that lay at the heart of rhetoric's division from poetic. Howell describes that distinction in this way:

13. See, e.g., Aristotle, *Poetics*, 6. For an extensive treatment of the connections between rhetoric and poetic in the classical tradition, see Ruth Webb, "Poetry and Rhetoric," in *Handbook of Classical Rhetoric in the Hellenistic Period, 330 B.C.–A.D. 400*, ed. Stanley E. Porter (Leiden: Brill, 1997), 339-69.

14. Stephen Halliwell, "Introduction" in Aristotle, *Poetics*, translated and ed. Stephen Halliwell (Cambridge, MA: Harvard University Press, 1995), 5.

The difference between poetical and rhetorical literature would appear in Aristotle's eyes to be a difference between two separate approaches to the realities of human life. Faced with the problem of doing something about a crisis in their society, the poet and the orator respond in different ways. The poet deals with the problem by telling a story or by presenting a dramatic action.[15]

Rather than describing or explaining something, the poet imitates or represents it in some way.

Aristotle went on to note the power of this representational performance to engage an audience, an awareness reflected in his famous definition of the particular genre that occupied most of the *Poetics*, tragedy:

> A tragedy . . . is the imitation of an action that is serious and also, as having magnitude, complete in itself; in language with pleasurable accessories, each kind brought in separately in the parts of the work; in a dramatic, not in a narrative form; with incidents arousing pity and fear, wherewith to accomplish its catharsis of such emotions (*Poet.*, 6).

As his definition suggests, at the heart of tragedy lies a psychological process that involves evoking pity in the audience toward characters in the play who have suffered tragic consequences, as well as fear at the possibility of facing a similar fate. Although scholars have disagreed over what, exactly, Aristotle intended in his use of the medical term "catharsis," whether "purification" or "purgation," most agree that the spectators underwent some kind of change as a result of being caught up in the drama. As Lear explained it, catharsis had to do with the way that tragedy evokes intense emotion within the "safe" confines of the theater. The tragic poet confronts us with dimensions of the human condition that we would rather ignore, in particular, the reality that disastrous consequences sometimes result from choices made out of the best of intentions. The problem, he observed, is how best or most appropriately to experience those tragic emotions:

> On the one hand, the possibility of tragedy in ordinary life is too remote to justify real fear, on the other hand, it is too important and too close to ignore. Tragic poetry provides an arena in which one can imaginatively

15. Wilbur Samuel Howell, *Poetics, Rhetoric, and Logic: Studies in the Basic Disciplines of Criticism* (Ithaca: Cornell University Press, 1975), 56-57.

experience the tragic emotions: the performance of a play "captures our souls." However, it is crucial to the pleasure we derive from tragedy, that we never lose sight of the fact that we are an audience, enjoying a work of art. Otherwise, the pleasurable katharsis of pity and fear would collapse into the merely painful experience of those emotions.[16]

In this way, the relief we feel in the theater arises from our experience of strong emotion within a setting that is safely imaginative.

As a number of scholars have pointed out, Aristotle believed that this psychological experience was far more than mere entertainment; it was transformative. Taylor, for example, argued that tragedy served the dual function of displacing inappropriate emotions and reinforcing positive ones in a way that instilled them in the character of the audience:

> When Aristotle says that tragedy through pity and fear effects a purification from such-like passions, his meaning is, that it purified from those perturbations, which happen in the fable, and which for the most part are the cause of the peripeteia, and of the unhappy event of the fable. Thus for instance, Sophocles, through pity and terror excited by the character of Ajax, intends a purification from anger and impiety towards the gods, because through this anger and impiety those misfortunes happened to Ajax.[17]

As evidence for this contention, Taylor cited Aristotle's observation, made in the *Ethics*, that by being repeatedly exposed to particular emotions or qualities of character, such as timidity or anger, a person tends to take on those qualities or emotions as habitual.

Offering a slightly different perspective on this transformative function, Nussbaum argued that tragedy introduced the crucial dimension of the fragility of human well-being to the classical ethic of the good by highlighting the essential inability of humans to hold absolute control over their own fates.[18] Kosman similarly suggested that tragedy directs our gaze to the vulnerability of human well-being and invites us to acknowledge our fears about that vulnerability:

16. Jonathan Lear, "Katharsis," in *Essays on Aristotle's Poetics*, ed. Amélie Oksenberg Rorty (Princeton: Princeton University Press, 1992), 334.

17. Thomas Taylor, "Note on Catharsis," in *Aristotle's Poetics and English Literature*, ed. Elder Olson (Chicago: University of Chicago Press, 1965), 79.

18. Martha Nussbaum, *The Fragility of Goodness: Luck and Ethics in Greek Tragedy and Philosophy* (Cambridge: Cambridge University Press, 1986).

These are the realistic fears that politically nurtured virtue may not always be sufficient for the well-being at which it aims, and that our happiness is subject to the stern and seemingly irrational control of a destiny which may at any moment sunder the tenuous connection between virtue and well-being, a destiny which is the result neither of some inner flaw of character nor of some external *daimōn* of ill-fortune, but of the very actions that we have thoughtfully and courageously chosen. The *Poetics* offers us the hope that we may be able, by acknowledging these fears, to cleanse our affective lives of their pollution, and be restored to the fellowship of parlous human agency.[19]

While differing somewhat in their emphasis, these accounts share in common the conviction that through its engagement in dramatic performance, an audience may be awakened to realities of human existence hitherto unacknowledged, to certain kinds of self-knowledge, and to new ways of seeing the world.

Central to this transformative process is what Aristotle called "mimesis." As Woodruff described it, mimesis is a "functional deception" that places an audience in a position where they imaginatively experience states of consciousness that normally would only be experienced by other, natural means. For example, "the usual way to feel or to become heroic has nothing to do with music; but music can be contrived in such a way that it has this effect.... Mimesis breaks the natural order of design and effect. That is why it is wonderful and exciting, and that is why it gives us a safe way to learn facts about lions — through pictures — and a pleasant way to develop habits of mind — through music and dance."[20] In the same way, even though the events portrayed in a tragedy are not literally taking place, their dramatic depiction evokes the kinds of emotions that the audience would feel if they were actually happening. As Woodruff put it, "The script has the same effect on you that the actions would have had, if you had believed they were taking place. In this way the poet's mimesis is aimed at producing a result that is normally achieved by other means."[21]

Although much of the above discussion focuses on tragedy, it provides important insight into the nature of poetic discourse more generally, and into the way most writers in classical rhetoric distinguished poetic from

19. Aryeh Kosman, "Acting: *Drama* as the *Mimēsis* of *Praxis*," in *Essays on Aristotle's Poetics*, ed. Rorty, 68-69.

20. Paul Woodruff, "Aristotle on *Mimēsis*," in *Essays on Aristotle's Poetics*, ed. Rorty, 91-92.

21. Woodruff, "Aristotle on *Mimēsis*," 93.

rhetoric.[22] Rhetoric advances claims for an audience's assent; it seeks to demonstrate their truthfulness using evidence that supports them through a process of formal reasoning. Of course, the rhetorical tradition recognizes the importance of emotion to that process. As Aristotle puts it, the orator needs to put his hearers "into a certain frame of mind," for "if a man desires anything and has good hopes of getting it, if what is to come is pleasant, he thinks that it is sure to come to pass and will be good; but if a man is unemotional or not hopeful it is quite the reverse" (*Rhet.*, 2.1.4).[23] The *ad Herennium* similarly recognizes the importance of emotion, for example, in its observation that the function of the speech's introduction was to put the hearers in such a state of mind that they will be "attentive, receptive, and well-disposed," as well as in its connection of certain modes of delivery or style to particular emotional states (1.4.6).[24] In the Ciceronian tradition, arousing emotion comes to play a key role in the *officia oratoris* of teaching, pleasing, and moving the audience (*Or. Brut.*, 69; cf. *De or.*, 2.115). In rhetoric, however, pathos is not the goal, but merely the servant, of logos. As Howell put it, the "rhetor must state the facts and prove them acceptable to the reason, the emotions, and the moral sense of his hearers."[25]

Poetic discourse, by contrast, achieves its end not by marshaling evidence in support of a thesis, but by using language to create a mimetic performance in which hearers are transported into an imaginative consciousness of the discourse's content. Baldwin explained that whereas rhetoric was "primarily intellectual, a progress from idea to idea determined logically," poetic is "primarily imaginative, a progress from image to image determined emotionally."[26] Nussbaum highlighted the role of emotion in that process when she noted that the ethical content of a poetic text

22. Howell, for example, extends Aristotle's discussion to comedy, which "might be expected to produce the effect of laughter, and might seek this effect by painting a picture of the ridiculous or the deformed in such a way as not to cause pain or harm to others" (*Poetics, Rhetoric, and Logic*, 54).

23. Aristotle provides a sophisticated account of how the rhetor may stir the emotions, defining fear, for example, as a "pain or disturbance due to a mental picture of some destructive or painful evil in the future," and then describing how to make that future evil seem both imminent and likely — for "we do not fear things that are a long way off" — while also holding out "some faint expectation of escape" (*Rhet.*, 2.5).

24. The author claims, for example, that the "pathetic" tone, by "amplifying misfortunes, wins the hearer over to pity," and that the judicious use of the stylistic figure *aposiopesis* — deliberately leaving a statement unfinished — arouses feelings of suspicion (*ad Her.*, 3.13.24; 4.30.41).

25. Howell, *Poetics, Rhetoric, and Logic*, 56.

26. Baldwin, *Ancient Rhetoric and Poetic*, 3.

centrally involves emotional response. We discover what we think about these events partly by noticing how we feel; our investigation of our emotional geography is a major part of our search for self-knowledge. . . . Even this puts matters too intellectualistically: for . . . the emotional response can sometimes be not just a *means* to a practical knowledge, but a constituent part of the best sort of recognition or knowledge of one's practical situation.[27]

Nussbaum's suggestion that her explanation might be overly rationalistic is instructive since, Freeland pointed out, "the pleasure of catharsis is not in and of itself the pleasure of learning or thinking something, but rather of seeing and feeling something."[28] In other words, whereas in rhetoric emotion served the needs of logic, in poetics an emotional experience was a central outcome of the communicative performance. Poetic discourse afforded its hearers an opportunity, in a moment of imaginative transcendence, actually to experience the conviction, perspective, aspiration, or event that it represented.

The "Rhetorico-Poetic" Alternative

Although, as noted above, much of what was preserved in the rhetorical tradition clearly distinguished rhetoric from poetic, several scholars have recognized an alternative tradition that Halliwell called "rhetorico-poetic persuasiveness,"[29] which explicitly drew on mimetic processes in order to position auditors not as judges of logical argument but as participants in an extrarational experience. Among the earliest articulations of this understanding of persuasion was Gorgias's *Encomium of Helen,* in which Gorgias famously proclaimed, "All poetry can be called speech with meter" (9).[30] Throughout the treatise, Gorgias evinces an understanding of "logos" that

---

27. Nussbaum, *The Fragility of Goodness*, 15-16.

28. Cynthia A. Freeland, "Plot Imitates Action: Aesthetic Evaluation and Moral Realism in Aristotle's *Poetics,*" in *Essays on Aristotle's Poetics,* ed. Rorty, 124.

29. Stephen Halliwell, *Between Ecstasy and Truth: Interpretations of Greek Poetics from Homer to Longinus* (Oxford: Oxford University Press, 2011), 277.

30. Translation of Gorgias is from Rosamond Kent Sprague, ed., *The Older Sophists: a complete translation by several hands of the fragments in Die Fragmente der Vorsokratiker, edited by Diels-Kranz. With a new edition of Antiphon and Euthydemus* (Columbia: University of South Carolina Press, 1972).

integrates a poetic understanding of what Longinus would later describe as the transportive power of language. At several points he connects pleasure (τέρψις), a motif "strongly associated with the experience of poetry," with belief (πίστις), in a way that links poetry to conviction. Gorgias's discussion of the power of logos highlights what Halliwell called the "psychological absorption" that accompanies the experience of poetic discourse: "Its hearers shudder with terror, shed tears of pity, and yearn with sad longing" (9). He compares the ability of language to "drug and bewitch the soul" to a drug-induced hallucination, causing "what is incredible and invisible to appear before the eyes of the mind" (13-14). He thus deems "persuasion by speech" the equivalent to "abduction by force" (12). While clearly recognizing the dangers inherent in such power, Gorgias nevertheless also emphasizes the positive value of logos, particularly for the way that it enables a hearer's soul to feel "as its own an emotion aroused by the good and ill fortunes of other peoples' actions and lives" (9). As Halliwell noted, this description of poetry

> throws into relief the power of words not (simply) to mislead treacher-ously but to activate highly charged passions (pity, fear, grief) in response to the play of good and bad fortune, happiness and unhappiness, in the lives of others (ἐπ' ἀλλοτρίων τε πραγμάτων καὶ σωμάτων).[31]

While the "deceptions" and "fictions" (11) created by logos could lead to disaster and tragedy, as in the case of Helen and Paris, they could also perform "most divine works." What marked both was, Halliwell said, "the intensity of the soul-changing experience induced by words."[32]

Of particular importance for the present study is Gorgias's emphasis on the way that language creates vicarious experience for the audience. In the passage noted above, which describes the audience's intense emotional experience — shuddering with terror, shedding tears of pity, etc. — he emphasizes how the audience "feels *as its own*" emotions attendant to the "good and ill fortunes of *other people's* actions and lives" (9, emphasis added).

31. Halliwell identified this description of poetry (from section 9) as "one of the passages which made an impression on Plato" (*Between Ecstasy and Truth*, 273).

32. Halliwell, *Between Ecstasy and Truth*, 271-73. In this connection, Halliwell cites a frag-ment of Gorgias preserved in Plutarch, which describes tragedy as a genre that " 'through its stories and sufferings/passions' provides its audiences with 'a deception in which the one who succeeds in deceiving, rather than the one who fails to deceive, has right on his side, and in which the deceived is wiser than the undeceived.' "

This seems to suggest that the audience is responding to a depiction of such events as if they were real in their own experience. Similarly, in his description of "persuasions by means of fictions," Gorgias appears to attribute to speech the ability to create a vision of the past or future, in the absence of the audience's own ability to recollect accurately the past or future in their own minds. Underscoring this sense of language creating experience is the linkage he makes between this almost magical power of language to imprint the mind and the defense he offers for Helen at the end of the treatise, that she was swept up and influenced by the sight of Paris himself, a defense that turns on the way that both poetic language and visual arts such as sculpture and painting have the power to create intense longing. Halliwell summarized that connection in this way:

> Gorgias' argument invites us to recognize a parallelism between the two artforms (a parallelism anticipated by the trope "the eyes of belief," τοῖς τῆς δόξης ὄμμασιν, at 13), taking poetry to stand in the same relation to logos in general as visual art stands to vision in general.

Poetry offers the rhetor the possibility of creating "gratifying, moving figments of consciousness, as in the works of painters."[33]

As the rhetorical and poetic traditions both made clear, the primary strategy for creating this experience involved activating the human capacity known as *phantasia*, a word variously translated as imagination or perception, activated by a variety of language uses centered on "bringing before the eyes" images or experiences not literally before the audience. Although clearly suspicious of its power, Aristotle offers a remarkably cogent account of *phantasia*, which he closely associates with sense perception. In an oft-cited passage from the *Rhetoric* he calls *phantasia* a kind of "weak sensation" and connects that capacity to the experience of strong emotion: "If pleasure consists in the sensation of a certain emotion, and imagination is a weakened sensation, then both the man who remembers and the man who hopes will be attended by an imagination of what he remembers or hopes" (*Rhet.*, 1.11). As a number of scholars have noted, Aristotle did not restrict *phantasia* exclusively to visual images, but rather likened it to the "full range of cognitive and perceptive activities of humans," operating "both in the presence of sensible objects, interpreting them to the mind, and in their absence, bringing absent objects to the mind in what we would call variously

33. Halliwell, *Between Ecstasy and Truth*, 208, 282.

memory, contemplation, and imagination."[34] Nevertheless, for Aristotle and those who followed him, *phantasia* was particularly concerned with the capacity for visualizing and emotionally responding to objects, people, and events not literally in the field of vision, an understanding that informs the summary that Quintilian will give some four centuries later in his *Institutes of Oratory* (6.2.29, 32):

> There are certain experiences which the Greeks call *phantasiai,* and the Romans *visions* [*visiones*], whereby things absent are presented to our imaginations with such extreme vividness that they seem actually to be before our very eyes. . . . From such impressions arises that *enargeia* which Cicero calls *illumination* [*illustration*] and *actuality* [*evidential*], which makes us seem not so much to narrate [*dicere*] as to exhibit [*ostendere*] the actual scene.[35]

Thus, as O'Gorman noted, "Words can be made to move so as to activate the phantasmatic capacities of audience members. What is absent before the eyes physically is made present to the mind through *lexis* in the same way that an individual may 'put' images before her mind while imagining."[36]

Not surprisingly, this capacity to activate *phantasia* represented an important area of overlap between poetic and rhetoric in Aristotle's writings. In the *Poetics*, he counsels the dramatist, when "constructing plots," to "put the actual scenes as far as possible before his eyes," for only by "seeing everything with the vividness of an eye-witness" will the dramatist be able to write plays that satisfy their audiences (*Poet.*, 17). Indeed, he encouraged the poet to "act his story with the very gestures of his personages," since "he who feels the emotions to be described will be most convincing; distress and anger, for instance, are portrayed most truthfully by one who is feeling them at the moment" (*Poet.*, 17). In other words, by acting out the role in the process of

34. Ned O'Gorman, "Aristotle's *Phantasia* in the *Rhetoric*: *Lexis*, Appearance, and the Epideictic Function of Discourse," *Philosophy and Rhetoric* 38 (2005): 16-40, here 20. As Newman observed, this broader understanding can be seen in his discussion of the "sources from which metaphors should be taken: from the beautiful either in sound or in effect or in visualization or in some other form of sense perception." Sara Newman, "Aristotle's Notion of 'Bringing-Before-the-Eyes': Its Contributions to Aristotelian and Contemporary Conceptualizations of Metaphor, Style, and Audience," *Rhetorica* 20 (2002): 8.

35. This is the translation of O'Gorman ("Aristotle's *Phantasia*," 17), quoted here because of the way that it reflects a literal rendering of the original Latin.

36. O'Gorman, "Aristotle's *Phantasia*," 24.

writing, one could better construct a plot that truly brings the action before the eyes of the audience.

When it came to the place of *phantasia* in rhetoric, Aristotle predictably restricted it to discussions of emotion and style, necessary evils that were distinct from and subordinate to rhetoric's definitive source of proof, supplied by logical argument. Despite that ambivalence, however, his account still offers rich insight into how thinkers in the classical tradition understood the power of imagination. Regarding emotion, for example, he noted that the pleasure related to honor and reputation derives from the fact that "they make a man see himself in the character of a fine fellow" (*Rhet.*, 1.11), that anger involves the pleasure of imagining retaliation (*Rhet.*, 2.2), that fear grows out of the "mental picture of some destructive or painful evil in the future" (*Rhet.*, 2.5), and that confidence derives from the "mental picture of the nearness of what keeps us safe" (*Rhet.*, 2.5). Regarding this final emotion, Burke's distinction between the idea and the experience is instructive:

> There is a difference between an abstract term naming the "idea" of, say, security, and a concrete image designed to stand for this idea, and to "place it before our very eyes." For one thing, if the image employs the full resources of the imagination, it will not represent merely one idea, *but will contain a whole bundle of principles,* even ones that would be mutually contradictory if reduced to their purely ideational equivalents.[37]

So potent is the experience of imagination that it can overcome seemingly logical inconsistencies.

Aristotle's discussion of style likewise highlighted the use of image to activate the process of visualization. He explains, for example, that elegance in language is achieved when the rhetor "set[s] the scene before our eyes [πρὸ ὀμμάτων ποιεῖ]; for events ought to be seen in progress rather than in prospect" (*Rhet.*, 3.10). In particular, Aristotle's discussion of metaphor emphasizes comparisons that evoke not just a mental image, but a mental image suggesting movement and action, which imbue the language with the quality of actuality or vigor (ἐνεργείας). An example of such "liveliness" was Homer's ability to give "metaphorical life to lifeless things," as when the poet composed that the "arrow flew" and "the point of the spear in its fury drove full through his breastbone" (*Rhet.*, 3.11). Hawhee summarized the effect in

---

37. Kenneth Burke, *A Rhetoric of Motives* (Berkeley: University of California Press, 1969), 86-87.

this way: "With such vivid descriptions, the zipping and quivering arrows can't help but be visualized as such." Thus, she concluded,

> Movement and life, *kinēsis* and *zōē*, are what confer rhetorical presence; such a lively style therefore pours words as lively images into the eyes, creating "presence" and giving the impression that the description is now. That impression of course resides with phantasia. The lifeblood of lexis, bringing-before-the-eyes, and *energeia*, therefore stand . . . as the leading stylistic strategies for tapping *phantasia* and stirring the *pathē*.[38]

Although Aristotle "expresses skepticism about its reliability as a mental operation that issues in reliable knowledge,"[39] he clearly recognized the persuasive power of *phantasia*.

Perhaps no work better represents the "rhetorico-poetic" tradition than the first-century treatise *On the Sublime*. In the opening paragraphs, Longinus — whose reference to Genesis 1:1 as "a worthy conception of divine power" (*Subl.*, 9.9) indicates familiarity with the Old Testament[40] — sets off a marked contrast between discourse that results in a kind of "mere" intellectual conviction versus one which creates for the audience a vivid, imaginative experience:

> The effect of genius is not to persuade the audience but rather to transport them out of themselves. Invariably what inspires wonder, with its power of amazing us, always prevails over what is merely convincing and pleasing. For our persuasions are usually under our control, while these things exercise an irresistible power and mastery, and get the better of every listener. Again, experience in invention and the due disposal and marshaling of facts do not show themselves in one or two touches but emerge gradually from the whole tissue of the composition, while, on the other hand, a well-timed flash of sublimity shatters everything like a bolt of lightning and reveals the full power of the speaker at a single stroke (*Subl.*, 1.4).

---

38. Debra Hawhee, "Looking into Aristotle's Eyes: Toward a Theory of Rhetorical Vision," *Advances in the History of Rhetoric* 14 (2011): 154.

39. O'Gorman, "Aristotle's *Phantasia*," 19.

40. On the historicity and implications of this reference, see Casper C. de Jonge, "Dionysius and Longinus on the Sublime: Rhetoric and Religious Language," *American Journal of Philology* 133 (2012): 271-300.

This remarkable passage challenges the core understanding of rhetoric in the classical tradition, which viewed rational judgment as the goal of the art and which generally assigned to nonrational elements of discourse the task of "pleasing" the audience in order to make them more amenable to the arguments themselves. For Longinus an extrarational experience, *ekstasis*, was the goal, to which was subordinated the "merely convincing." O'Gorman captured this dramatic divergence from the classical tradition when he wrote,

> Rhetoric as the Aristotelian art-of-the-available-means-of-persuasion, . . . as the broad Isocratean philosophico-literary art for earthy political life, . . . or as the Ciceronian *artis* for the *res publica* . . . are not the Longinian conceptions of rhetoric. Longinus's treatise might as well have been entitled *Beyond Persuasion*, for its stated subject is not the available means of persuasion or the well-being of the public per se, but the road (*methodos*) to ecstasy (*ekstasis*) via 'height' or *hypsos* (*Subl.*, 1.4).[41]

In his discussion of the sublime, Longinus went on to explain the particular uses of language that created experiences of the sublime, uses centered in the sense-producing potential of *mimesis* and *phantasia*. Citing Homer's account of the gods in the *Iliad* as a marvelous "imaginative picture" (θεομαχίας φαντάσματα), he described the passage's effect in terms of visual experience:

> You see [ἐπιβλέπεις], friend, how the earth is split to its foundations, hell itself laid bare, the whole universe sundered and turned upside down; and meanwhile everything, heaven and hell, mortal and immortal alike, shares in the conflict and danger of that battle (*Subl.*, 9.6).

Similarly, he extolled Sappho's ability to evoke in her readers the "emotions incident to the passion of love," noting how she summons "at the same time, soul, body, hearing, tongue, sight, skin" (*Subl.*, 10.2-3). His account suggests that poetic language actually has the potential to produce a gestalt of emotion and physical sensation like that accompanying the flush of romantic attraction. Later in the treatise, he explained that certain figures could mimic emotional states because of their mimetic qualities. As one example,

41. Ned O'Gorman, "Longinus's Sublime Rhetoric, or How Rhetoric Came into Its Own," *Rhetoric Society Quarterly* 34 (2004): 71-89, here 73.

he explained that the figure *hyperbaton*, which "consists in arranging words and thoughts out of the natural order," was the "truest mark of vehement emotion," because it mimics how people, when they are actually angry, frightened, or indignant, "often put forward one point and then spring off to another with various illogical interpolations, and then wheel around again to their original position, while, under the stress of their excitement, like a ship before a veering wind, they lay their words and thoughts first on one tack then another" (*Subl.*, 22.1). Thus, in the "best prose writers, the use of *hyperbata* allows imitation (μίμεσις) to approach the effects of nature" and, as a speech by Dionysius the Phocaean recorded in Herodotus found, in a way that not only gives "great effect of vehemence" but also "drags his audience with him to share the perils of these long *hyperbata*" (*Subl.*, 22.3).

As these examples show, Longinus clearly understood what the shift from logical argumentation to a poetic form represented for the experience of the audience. The former meant encountering claims and evidence as abstract ideas to be considered; the latter meant undergoing an imaginative transport in which auditors felt the emotions and physical sensations almost as if they were literally happening, in his words, as "a vivid actuality" (*Subl.*, 25.1). At the same time, Longinus also recognized that the two might be profitably joined together, with imaginative discourse supporting the aims of logical argumentation: "Visualization [φαντασία] when combined with factual arguments . . . not only convinces the audience, it positively masters them" (literally "makes them slaves/servants," δουλοῦται) (*Subl.*, 15.9). As evidence, he offered several examples from the famed orator Demosthenes, concluding with this observation:

> Besides developing his factual argument the orator has visualized the event and consequently his conception far exceeds the limits of mere persuasion. In all such cases, the stronger element seems naturally to catch our ears, so that our attention is drawn from the reasoning to the enthralling effect of the imagination (*Subl.*, 15.10-11).

As will become clear, this integration of mimesis and abstract explanation uniquely fit the needs of Christian faith, because it provided the potential to create for its hearers the kind of ecstatic religious experience in which their faith was rooted.

Ecstasy and Faith

As we noted in the introduction to this volume, the conversion stories in the NT seem to assume that although conceptual explanations of the gospel are certainly part of the process of coming to faith, that faith was never simply the result of a logical presentation of arguments that brought listeners to intellectual conviction. Instead, they encountered the mighty works of God and were overcome with amazement at what they saw and heard. The conceptual explanation — the preaching of the Gospel — more often provided an explanation for what the witnesses had just experienced. Rather than being a rational response to logical proofs, then, faith was viewed in early Christianity as a vivid, extrarational and life-altering encounter with God, accompanied by the experience of amazement, literally, ecstasy (ἔκστασις).

When viewed from this perspective, Longinus's choice of the term "transport" (ἔκστασις) as the mark of rhetorical genius is extraordinary. O'Gorman observed that this term was "commonly used in ancient Greek to describe mental states beyond reason."[42] Whereas an audience might ignore or dismiss logical arguments ("persuasions are usually under our control"), Longinus believed that the experience of "transport" or "ecstasy" became deeply imprinted on an audience's mind, shaping their perceptions of the world: "It is difficult, nay impossible, to resist its effect; and the memory of it is stubborn and indelible" (*Subl.*, 7.3-4). O'Gorman offers further examples of what we noted in the introduction of this book, that this term is often used in the NT to "describe that wonder, awe, or astonishment that comes to those who witness the supernatural works of the Lord." It describes the reaction of the disciples who, seeing Jesus raise the daughter of Jairus, the synagogue ruler, from the dead, are "overcome with amazement" (Mark 5:42). Similarly, when Jesus heals the paralytic who is lowered through the roof of the house where he is teaching, the witnesses crowded into the house undergo this reaction: "Amazement seized all of them" (Luke 5:26). When the three women, intent on embalming the body of Jesus, arrive at the tomb and encounter an angel who announces the resurrection, they flee from the tomb, "for terror and amazement had seized them" (Mark 16:8). And of course, in the examples noted earlier, in Acts 2 and 3, the crowds' reaction to their experience of God's power is "amazement," or, as Longinus puts it, "transport." What is striking about Longinus is that he believed that language could be used to affect an audience in the same way. As he puts it, whereas

42. O'Gorman, "Longinus's Sublime Rhetoric," 74.

the "marshaling of facts" might result in some change in the audience's beliefs over the course of a composition, "a well-timed flash of sublimity shat-
ters everything like a bolt of lightning" (*Subl.*, 1.4).

Given the crucial role that these extrarational encounters seemed to play
in the stories of conversion as they are presented in the NT, it would indeed
be odd if the NT writers had *not* sought some discursive means of capturing
or representing these experiences for their hearers. Kennedy highlighted the
challenge that these early church leaders faced in their attempts to bolster
the faith of their listeners when he noted that it is

> frequently the case that the Judeo-Christian orator is addressing an audi-
> ence on whom the Spirit has worked in the past and for whom the pre-
> requisite grace has been provided earlier, but whose experience of conver-
> sion is no longer valid. There is a possibility of reminding such an audience
> of the religious experience it has already known, recalling individuals to
> the truth through rational and emotional means.

To be sure, as Kennedy suggested, the NT writers did "remind" their audiences of the "religious experience[s]" they had "already known." But as we
shall see, they did more than remind audiences of the ecstasies of the past.
Instead, they used poetic form and language to create and recreate those experiences in the present. Along the lines envisioned in the "rhetorico-poetic"
tradition represented by Gorgias and Longinus, they exploited the mimetic
qualities of particular stylistic forms and language in a way that was intended
to activate their audience's capacity for *phantasia*. The result, Longinus said,
was that "you seem to see what you describe and bring it vividly before
the eyes of your audience" (*Subl.*, 15.1-2). In the presence of such language,
the NT writers hoped, their hearers would do more than recall an ecstatic
occurrence from the past; rather, it would be as if they were subjectively
encountering that reality in their present experience.

Conclusion

The purpose of this chapter has been to lay out the theoretical framework
that will guide the analysis of the NT's use of poetic discourse, which is the
focus of this study. It began by observing that the tradition of classical rhetorical theory, as it was represented by Aristotle and even Isocrates, as well as
by Roman theorists like Cicero and the author of the *ad Herennium*, viewed

rhetorical persuasion as fundamentally a rationalistic process in which arguments led to conclusions through a chain of logical reasoning. By contrast, Aristotle explained that poetic achieved its influence not by argumentation, but by mimesis, that is, by using language to create an extrarational apprehension of whatever idea or experience it presented. Rather than considering the merits of the discourse's claims, poetic discourse sought to place auditors "in" the subjective experience it related by activating the audience's capacity for *phantasia*, or imagination. The chapter went on to describe an alternative tradition of public communication from that of philosophical rhetoric, represented by Gorgias and Longinus, which embraced the power of mimesis and *phantasia* as key elements of persuasion.

The chapter argued, finally, that this latter understanding of persuasive discourse would have meshed naturally into early Christianity's understanding of faith. The stories of conversion presented in the NT suggest that Christian faith was never simply the outcome of logical reasoning. Instead, those stories accentuate some kind of visceral experience of God's presence and power as a crucial accompaniment to being instructed in the content of the gospel. Indeed, as noted in the introduction, the experience of certain emotions was not envisioned in early Christianity as merely preparing for or supporting the acceptance of abstract theological ideas. Rather, in some cases, those sustained states of emotion were themselves the goal of Christian spirituality.

The tradition of poetics offered early Christianity an important resource for sustaining believers' sense of the presence of God and for providing them with a subjective experience of the theological realities that lay at the heart of their faith. In his discussion of catharsis in tragedy, Lear argued that the dramatic form offered the audience an opportunity to contemplate events and to experience emotions as if they were true, but all within the relative emotional safety of the theater.[43] The audience could thus confront elements of human experience that, were they to occur in "real life," would be overwhelmingly painful and disturbing. The NT's poetic texts employ similarly imaginative uses of language, but with a very different function. Rather than providing a "safe" forum for experiencing the tragic, these texts allowed their audiences to apprehend realities that they believed and hoped for intellectually, but that had not yet become real in their day-to-day experience, allowing believers to hear and "see" what they longed for but which had not yet occurred.

43. Lear, "Katharsis," 333-35.

CHAPTER TWO

Visions of the End (1 Thessalonians 4:13-18)

In his eighth homily on 1 Thessalonians, fourth-century preacher and church father John Chrysostom attempted to capture the conceptual background of Paul's vision of the end in 1 Thess. 4:16-17:

> When a king drives into a city, those who are in honor go out to meet him; but the condemned await the judge within. And upon the coming of an affectionate father, his children indeed, and those who are worthy to be his children, are taken out in a chariot, that they may see and kiss him; but those of the domestics who have offended remain within. We are carried upon the chariot of our Father. Seest thou how great is the honor? and as He descends, we go forth to meet Him, and, what is more blessed than all, so we shall be with Him.[1]

His description brings before the imagination of his audience a scene of celebration for those who go out to welcome the king, as a way of evoking the emotions he expected would have been called forth when Paul spoke of Christ's return "with a cry of command, with the archangel's call and with the sound of God's trumpet." Especially he sought to depict the delight with which believers who had died before the parousia would be raised to welcome their triumphant king. His depiction suggests that he recognized the evocative character of Paul's vision — that it was intended to do more than simply explain the order of events at the eschaton, but rather, to provide a momentary, transcendent experience of that joyful event for a congregation

---

1. Available online, http://www.ccel.org/ccel/schaff/npnf113.iv.v.viii.html (accessed April 9, 2013).

of believers who were facing persecution, who felt abandoned by Paul, their "father in the faith," and who had been thrown into grief and confusion by the deaths of some of their fellow Christians.

The purpose of this chapter is to examine that vision, alluded to at several points thus far in this book, as an instance of the NT's use of mimesis in its efforts to inculcate a Christian worldview. Most scholars who have examined the epistle from a rhetorical perspective agree that Paul employs the epideictic genre while composing this vision. We should, therefore, not be surprised to find emotive language in Paul's discourse, since such an evocative style was most often associated with ceremonial rhetoric. At the same time, in the way that Longinus suggested, I shall argue that Paul's vision went far beyond stirring emotions in order to make an audience more amenable to considering a logical proposition, although it clearly does support adherence to theological ideas. Rather, it is an example of a text for which experiencing the vision *was* the goal. In other words, it was aimed not merely at seeking assent to a factual claim, but at promoting a sustained experience of emotion, in this case, the emotion of hopefulness. In what follows, I explore the background and rhetorical situation to the letter and then discuss the content and overall persuasive strategy of the epistle as a whole, highlighting the epistle's pervasive eschatological tone. Finally, I examine Paul's treatment of the "righteous dead" in 4:13-18 and, particularly, his dramatic vision of the parousia in vv. 16-17.

Hope in the Face of Oppression and Grief

Unlike Paul's other epistles, 1 Thess. does not appear to address a congregation entertaining obvious doctrinal heresy or engaged in ethical misconduct, nor one in obvious revolt against his authority as the community's founder. Paul's tone throughout seems positive and encouraging and, at most, he exhorts his readers to continue their present behavior, only to "do so more and more" (4:1-10). In the absence of a clear issue or problem, determining the precise rhetorical situation is a difficult task, complicated further by questions about the historicity of Luke's account of the establishment of the Thessalonian church (Acts 17), and by discrepancies between that account and the information about the church's origin provided in the epistle itself. Luke records that Paul's mission in Thessalonica lasted only three weeks, a period viewed by many as far too short a time in which to establish a viable congregation. Further, in 1 Thess. Paul describes intense opposition to the church as coming from the Gentiles ("your own compatriots," 2:14), whereas in Acts the opposition is Jewish. Also, Acts 17:14 has Paul leaving Timothy behind in Berea (the city he went to after leaving Thessalonica), whereas Paul himself implies that Timothy accompanied him to Athens, and from there, he sent Timothy back to Thessalonica (1 Thess. 3:1-2).[2] Despite these difficulties, however, there is a sufficient correlation between the two texts to offer an account of the establishment of the Thessalonian church in at least a broad outline and, from that account, to determine the situation to which Paul is responding in his epistle.[3]

Paul's ministry among the Thessalonians, both accounts make clear, occurred midway through his second missionary journey, probably around 49 C.E. He arrived in Thessalonica from Philippi accompanied by a group of co-workers that included Silas and Timothy. For at least "three Sabbath days" he debated with the Jews in the local synagogue, arguing "from the scriptures, explaining and proving that it was necessary for the Messiah to suffer and to rise from the dead" (Acts 17:3). According to Luke, some Jews were persuaded, as were "a great many of the devout Greeks and not a few of the leading women" (Acts 17:4). Other Jews, however, seeing this response, instigated a riotous mob against Paul and his companions so that, in Luke's words, they "set the city in an uproar" (Acts 17:5). Because of the volatility of the situation, the believers sent Paul and Silas (and presumably Timothy) away from the city under cover of darkness, and they arrived shortly after in the city of Berea. Whether or not Paul's sojourn in Thessalonica lasted only three weeks as Luke implies,[4] both accounts make clear that the period of time was much shorter than either he or the Thessalonians expected. Further, his mission to Thessalonica ended abruptly and under violent circumstances, so that in 1 Thess. 2:17 Paul can speak of his being "made orphans by being separated from you" (ἀπορφανισθέντες ἀφ' ὑμῶν). As both accounts also make clear, the Thessalonians welcomed the gospel "in spite of great opposition" (1 Thess. 2:2).

After facing similar opposition to his preaching in Berea, Paul made his

2. For a full discussion of these issues, see Chris Manus, "Luke's Account of Paul in Thessalonica (Acts 17–19)," in *The Thessalonian Correspondence*, ed. Raymond F. Collins (Leuven: Leuven University Press, 1990), 27-38.

3. For a reconstruction of Paul's mission to the Thessalonians, see Gene L. Green, *The Letters to the Thessalonians* (Grand Rapids: Eerdmans, 2002), 47-52; and Ben Witherington III, *1 and 2 Thessalonians: A Socio-Rhetorical Commentary* (Grand Rapids: Eerdmans, 2006), 36-44.

4. As Brown observed, Luke's account represents a "compressed and highly stylized picture" that does not necessarily limit his stay to only three weeks (Raymond E. Brown, *An Introduction to the New Testament* [New York: Doubleday, 1997], 458).

way to Athens[5] where, feeling such concern for the fledgling Thessalonian church, he decided to "be left alone" and to send Timothy back to Thessalonica, "to strengthen and encourage you for the sake of your faith" (1 Thess. 3:2). Meanwhile, Paul continued on to Corinth, where he remained for eighteen months, establishing another community of believers there. While Paul was in Corinth, Timothy returned with news of the Thessalonians' welfare, which Paul describes in 1 Thess. 3:6: "But Timothy has just now come to us from you, and has brought us the good news of your faith and love." He thus implies that Timothy's return is the specific event that has prompted him to write what we now have in the epistle of 1 Thessalonians.

The report that Timothy brought back to Paul appears to have had at least three important elements which, taken together, comprise the epistle's rhetorical situation. First, Timothy reported that the Thessalonians continued to suffer persecution, a problem to which Paul will explicitly refer several times in his letter, even going so far as to tell them that persecution "is what we are destined for" (3:3-4). Second, the epistle contains strong evidence that among Timothy's news was the report that in their discouragement, the Thessalonians feel abandoned by Paul, their "father in the faith." This is indicated by Paul's preoccupation in chaps. 1–3 with reassuring the Thessalonians of his concern for them and his emphasis on the closeness of their relationship.[6] He praises God for the way they received him (1:6-10), and he

---

5. Site of his famous address before the Areopagus, recorded in Acts 17:22-34.

6. A number of scholars have viewed this section as an apology intended to answer charges against Paul raised by opponents in Thessalonica. See James Everett Frame, *A Critical and Exegetical Commentary on the Epistles of St. Paul to the Thessalonians* (New York: Scribners, 1912), 4, 9; E. J. Bicknell, *The First and Second Epistles to the Thessalonians* (London: Methuen, 1932), xvii-xviii; William Hendriksen, *Exposition of I and II Thessalonians* (Grand Rapids: Baker, 1955), 12; Leon Morris, *First and Second Epistles to the Thessalonians* (Grand Rapids: Eerdmans, 1959), 22; Hendrikus Boers, "The Form Critical Study of Paul's Letters: I Thessalonians as a Case Study," *New Testament Studies* 22 (1975-76): 153; and Robert Jewett, *The Thessalonian Correspondence: Pauline Rhetoric and Millenarian Piety* (Philadelphia: Fortress, 1986), 102-4. However, there is no evidence in 1 Thess. that Paul is responding to specific charges brought against him by opponents there. Further, these verses lack the tone and argument found in Paul's other, clearly apologetic writings (see, especially, 1 Cor. 1:18–4:21; 2 Cor. 10:1–12:21; and Gal. 1:6–2:21; 4:12-20). To the contrary, in the opening chapters of 1 Thessalonians Paul repeatedly attempts to convince the Thessalonians of his deep love and concern for them, which suggests that he is reassuring his audience in the face of their feelings of despondency and abandonment, rather than defending himself against their accusations. For further discussion, see Frank W. Hughes, "The Rhetoric of 1 Thessalonians," in *The Thessalonian Correspondence*, ed. Collins, 95; and Abraham J. Malherbe, " 'Gentle as a Nurse': The Cynic Background to I Thess. ii," *Novum Testamentum* 12 (1970): 202.

points to his determination to preach the gospel in spite of severe opposition as evidence that his appeal "does not spring from deceit or impure motives or trickery," (2:3). He reminds them of his presence among them: "gentle . . . like a nurse tenderly caring for her own children" (2:8).[7] "So deeply do we care for you," he continues, "that we are determined to share with you not only the gospel of God but our own selves, because you have become very dear to us" (2:8). He gives as his reason for sending Timothy to them his anxious desire to know their welfare, to the point that he "could bear it no longer" (3:1). They were "infants" in the faith and Paul, their "nurse" and "father," has suddenly left them to face intense persecution alone.[8]

To many scholars, however, the most important factor in Paul's rhetorical situation was Timothy's news that several in the Thessalonian congregation had died during the intervening time between Paul's departure and Timothy's visit, raising serious questions in the believers' minds and perhaps even threatening the faith of some.[9] Although we cannot be certain, Witherington has raised the possibility that these deaths may even been linked to the ongoing persecution, since it has come not only from Jews but also at the hands of "your own compatriots" (2:14), which could refer to Gentile authorities or perhaps, as Mitchell suggested, even "sporadic . . . mob action."[10] As to why, exactly, these deaths so disturbed the Thessalo-

---

7. For a study of the background of this image in Hellenistic philosophy, see Malherbe, "Gentle as a Nurse," 201-17. On the question of whether Paul uses ἤπιοι (nurse) or νήπιοι (infant) in v. 7, however, see Stephen Fowl, "A Metaphor in Distress: A Reading of NHΠIOI in 1 Thessalonians 2:7," *New Testament Studies* 36 (1990): 469-73. See also Jeffrey A. D. Weima, "But We Became Infants Among You": The Case for NHΠIOI in 1 Thess 2.7," *New Testament Studies* 46 (2000): 547-64, who argues in favor of the alternative reading, "infants," based on external evidence as well as what he views as its internal argumentative function, which contrasts the innocence suggested by the metaphor of infants with Paul's denial of ulterior motives for his mission to Thessalonica (2:5-7).

8. In describing himself as an orphan (2:17), Paul may well be playing on the Thessalonians' own feelings of abandonment, even using the same language that they have used to describe themselves in relation to Paul.

9. Johanson reflected that assumption in this assertion: "It was the deaths of fellow Christians before the parousia that constitutes the primary exigency to which the various persuasive strategies of the letter as a whole are directed" (Bruce C. Johanson, *To All the Brethren: A Text-Linguistic and Rhetorical Approach to 1 Thessalonians* [Stockholm: Almqvist & Wiksell, 1987], 58). See also Helmut Koester, "1 Thessalonians: Experiment in Christian Writing," in *Continuity and Discontinuity in Church History*, ed. F. F. Church and T. George (Leiden: Brill, 1979), 33-44.

10. Witherington, *1 and 2 Thessalonians*, 139; Margaret M. Mitchell, "1 and 2 Thessalonians," in *Cambridge Companion to St. Paul*, ed. James D. G. Dunn (Cambridge: Cambridge University Press, 2003), 55.

nians, scholars take several different positions, although most agree that it revolves around their understanding regarding the resurrection of the dead and its relation to the parousia. Frame argued quite early that the grief was caused "not because they did not believe in the resurrection of the saints, but because they imagined, some of them at least, that their beloved dead would not enjoy the same advantage as the survivors at the coming of the Lord."[11] Green, on the other hand, viewed the problem not so much as one of mistaken understanding but simply as a reflection of the threat that death posed to their faith:

> At the moment of confronting the reality of death, the Thessalonians did not allow their confession to inform their reaction to this human tragedy. Alternately, they may simply not have understood the full reality of the resurrection from the dead, especially in light of the general Gentile consensus that such things simply did not happen.[12]

Most, however, believe that the Thessalonians' grief stemmed from a mistaken or at least an incomplete understanding of the resurrection, leading to the possible impression that one had to be alive to participate in the bliss of the parousia. Nicholl reconstructed the situation in this way:

> In the light of Paul's imminentist expectation, it seems perfectly possible that, even though he almost certainly believed in the future resurrection of the dead saints, at the mission Paul could have preached on the resurrection of Christ and taught on the parousia and judgment, and yet still omitted to mention the future resurrection of physically dead Christians, presumably because of his premature, forced departure from Thessalonica.[13]

---

11. James E. Frame, *St. Paul's Epistles to the Thessalonians* (London: Longman, 1880), 61. Klijn noted that the tension between the relative positions of the living and the dead at the end-time was a familiar problem in apocalyptic literature, that the two groups are often discussed and compared, and that usually "the conclusion is that the survivors are in a much better position than those who die before the end" (A. F. J. Klijn, "1 Thessalonians 4:13-18 and Its Backround in Apocalyptic Literature," in *Paul and Paulinism*, ed. Morna D. Hooker and S. G. Wilson [London: SPCK, 1982], 68-72).

12. Gene L. Green, *The Letters to the Thessalonians* (Grand Rapids: Eerdmans, 2002), 47-52.

13. Colin R. Nicholl, *From Hope to Despair in Thessalonica: Situating 1 and 2 Thessalonians* (Cambridge: Cambridge University Press, 2004), 36-37. Morris similarly offers this account:

Although he was less convinced that Paul neglected to preach about the resurrection during his brief time with the Thessalonians, Witherington concurred that Paul's untimely exit "probably prevented adequate teaching, and some Thessalonians had apparently died unexpectedly after Paul left, raising questions about the afterlife."[14] In any case, the deaths had apparently created a "theological and pastoral crisis." As Mitchell pointed out, "These deaths were taken by some to invalidate Paul's kerygma, consequently sowing doubts about the legitimacy of his claim to speak, not just his own humanly fallible words, but God's own truth."[15] Paul thus needed to reassure them so that they would not "grieve as others [οἱ λοιποί, i.e., the 'pagans'] do who have no hope" (4:13).

This situation, one of a church grieving and confused over the deaths of fellow believers, facing persecution, and feeling forsaken by their founder, called for a response that was neither argumentative nor heavily weighted with doctrinal instruction. In fact, most scholars who have approached the epistle from a rhetorical perspective have concluded that it represents the genre of epideictic oratory, which was "primarily about testimony and appreciation, not . . . argumentation and proofs. But the audience is not just to appreciate. They are being reminded of what is true — what they . . . already know. They are being urged to embrace these truths or virtues."[16] Most have noted as well the overwhelmingly consolatory nature of the epistle, that it was intended to reassure his audience of his love and concern, to strengthen

---

"Christ would come and take them all to himself. But some of them had died, and that raised a problem. Did it mean that the deceased would miss their share of the events of that day? Did it perhaps throw discredit on the whole idea of the Parousia?" (*First and Second Epistles to the Thessalonians*, 22). Similarly, Plevnik, working from the idea of the epistle's apocalyptic background, argued that the problem concerned the expectation that at the parousia, believers would undergo an "assumption," that is, that they would be caught up in the heavens and transformed or "translated" into a new manner of existence — which, in that tradition, required one to be alive at the end. "They would naturally think that the dead could not participate in the assumption — one had to be *alive* to be assumed" (Joseph Plevnik, "The Taking Up of the Faithful and the Resurrection of the Dead in 1 Thessalonians 4:13-18," *Catholic Biblical Quarterly* 46 [1984]: 281). For a cogent refutation of this general understanding of the background to 1 Thess., see Bruce N. Kaye, "Eschatology and Ethics in 1 and 2 Thessalonians," *Novum Testamentum* 17 (1975): 47-57.

14. Witherington, *1 and 2 Thessalonians*, 130.

15. Mitchell, "1 and 2 Thessalonians," 55.

16. Witherington, *1 and 2 Thessalonians*, 22. For his overall argument regarding the epistle's rhetorical genre, see pp. 20-22. For an extended discussion of attempts to classify the letter that reaches a similar conclusion, see Steve Walton, "What Has Aristotle to Do with Paul? Rhetorical Criticism and 1 Thessalonians," *Tyndale Bulletin* 46 (1995): 229-50.

them in the face of persecution, and to address their troubling questions about the fate of those who have died, aims which Olbricht emphasized in his summary of the letter's purpose:

> It might be said that Paul's purpose was to do precisely what he said he did when he was there, "encouraging [παρακαλέω], comforting [παραμυθέομαι] and urging [μαρτύρομαι] you to lead lives worthy of God" (1 Thess. 2:12), which was likewise the reason he sent Timothy, "to strengthen [στηρίζω] and encourage [παρακαλέω] you" (3:2), and the reason behind the charge to the Thessalonians: "Therefore encourage [παρακαλέω] one another and build each other up [οἰκοδομέω], just as in fact you are doing" (5:11).[17]

At the same time, however, the fact remains that Paul is writing to an infant congregation comprised primarily of Gentiles who have embraced the movement with no prior acquaintance with Christian teaching (see 1:9). As Paul's account of their conversation puts it, they "turned to God" from lifestyles that included the worship of idols (1:9), sexual promiscuity (4:3-8), and drunkenness (5:7-8). Thus, even as he consoles and reassures them, he must also exhort them in the strongest terms possible to continue their commitment to the gospel and to pursue lifestyles that reflect the moral demands of their Christian faith.

In short, Paul faces the dilemma of how to encourage and reassure his audience, while also challenging them to seek lifestyles that reflect their Christian faith. They need to feel confident in God's ultimate triumph over those who now oppress them and even over death itself, but they must also take seriously God's unequivocal call to holiness (4:7). His response is to draw upon a body of apocalyptic language and imagery current in the early

---

17. Thomas H. Olbricht, "An Aristotelian Rhetorical Analysis of 1 Thessalonians," in *Greeks, Romans and Christians: Essays in Honor of Abraham J. Malherbe*, ed. David L. Balch, Everett Ferguson, and Wayne E. Meeks (Minneapolis: Fortress, 1990), 227. A number of scholars have emphasized the consolatory nature of the epistle, with particular focus on its relationship to the "letter of consolation" in the Hellenistic epistolary tradition. See, especially, Abraham J. Malherbe, "Exhortation in First Thessalonians," *Novum Testamentum* 25 (1983): 238-56; and Karl P. Donfried, "The Theology of 1 Thessalonians as a Reflection of Its Purpose," in *To Touch the Text: Biblical and Related Studies in Honor of Joseph A. Fitzmyer, S.J.*, ed. M. P. Horgan and P. J. Kobelski (New York: Crossroad, 1989), 243-60. But see Witherington, *1 and 2 Thessalonians*, 20-22, who argues convincingly that, as much as the letter is concerned with consolation, in terms of genre it falls more clearly in the category of epideictic rhetoric.

Christian church and that had been central to his own kerygma, which he employs to structure the letter and to imbue it with a sense of eschatological expectation as a basis for faithfulness and ethical living.[18] Central to that response is a brief but vivid mimetic representation of that central event, the second coming of Christ.

The Epistle's Eschatological Framework

The epistle contains six brief eschatological passages (1:10; 2:12; 2:16; 2:19; 3:13; and 5:23), as well as two longer passages that describe the eschaton in vivid detail, prompting Best to observe that "there is an eschatological atmosphere in the whole letter."[19] The first brief reference concludes the epistle's thanksgiving section (1:2-10), the next three conclude three segments of a long narration that rehearses the history of Paul's mission to Thessalonica (2:1-12; 2:13-16; 2:17-20), while the fifth forms part of that narrative's overall conclusion (3:11-13). The final brief eschatological citation furnishes a climactic statement to the epistle's concluding benediction. The placement of these citations thus appears deliberate, with each functioning as a thematic discourse marker within the epistle's overall structure.

Beyond merely punctuating the discourse, however, these passages also evoke a number of themes regarding the end of time with which the audience is assumed to be familiar. Phrases such as "wait for his Son from heaven" and "the wrath that is coming" (1:10), as well as Paul's frequent references to Jesus' "coming" (παρουσία, 2:19; 3:13; 5:23), appear to function as a code for a larger body of eschatological information that the audience already knows, information that includes many salient themes from early Christian eschatology. They anticipate Christ's imminent return. Thus Paul reminds them that their conversion led to an eager expectation for the return of Christ "from heaven." His discourse assumes the final judgment, reflected in Paul's prayer that God will strengthen the Thessalonians "in holiness," so that they will be "blameless before our God and Father at the coming of our Lord Jesus with all his saints" (3:13; see also 5:23). These eschatological passages assume the separation between the righteous and the wicked at the

18. Kieffer highlights the connection between the eschatological theme of the letter and its ethical imperatives; see René Kieffer, "L'Eschatologie en 1 Thessaloniciens dans une perspective rhétorique," in *The Thessalonian Correspondence*, ed. Collins, 206-9.

19. Ernst Best, *A Commentary on the First and Second Epistles to the Thessalonians* (New York: Harper and Row, 1974), 14.

judgment, as well as the punishments and rewards that each was expected to receive from God. The Thessalonians, Paul reminds them, have been rescued "from the wrath that is coming" (1:10). They were taught to "lead a life worthy of God, who calls you into his own kingdom and glory" (2:12), shielded from the outpouring of God's wrath on those who have rejected or hindered the preaching of the gospel (2:16). In this way, Paul does not appear to use this language in order to convey new theological information to his audience, but rather to draw on ideas and images regarding the end with which his audience is already familiar, weaving a continuous thread of eschatological discourse throughout the epistle.

In addition to these brief eschatological citations, the epistle contains two longer passages, the vision of the end (4:13-18), which will be dealt with at greater length below, as well as a longer discussion of the time of Christ's arrival, in 5:1-11, which ostensibly answers questions raised by that vision. As with the brief eschatological citations, Paul sets out to answer their "questions" with reference to what he assumes they already know: "Now concerning the times and the seasons [Περὶ δὲ τῶν χρόνων καὶ τῶν καιρῶν], you do not need to have anything written to you. For you yourselves know very well [an emphatic construction, αὐτοὶ γὰρ ἀκριβῶς οἴδατε] that the day of the Lord will come like a thief in the night" (v. 2). The parousia, though imminent, will nevertheless come suddenly and unexpectedly. In v. 3, he elaborates on this fearful picture: "When they say, 'There is peace and security,' then sudden destruction will come upon them, as labor pains come upon a pregnant woman, and there will be no escape!" Having raised the specter of Jesus' sudden, cataclysmic return, Paul then "reassures" the Thessalonians that they have nothing to fear: "But you, beloved, are not in darkness, for that day to surprise you like a thief; for you are all children of the light and children of the day; we are not of the night or of the darkness" (vv. 4-5). Of course, Paul's "reassurance" has the performative force of an exhortation: They have nothing to fear *as long as* they remain "children of light." This leads into what comes closest to a direct exhortation to sobriety in the entire passage, in the form of the two second-person plural subjunctive verbs (καθεύδωμεν, γρηγορῶμεν), a grammatical form that conveys less a sense of direct command than that of a gently expressed hope or wish. Indeed, the only direct instruction comes at the end of the passage, where he urges them, "Therefore encourage one another and build each other up [διὸ παρακαλεῖτε ἀλλήλους καὶ οἰκοδομεῖτε εἰς τὸν ἕνα], as indeed you are doing."

What we find when we look across the epistle, then, is a consistent apocalyptic thread running through it that eventually leads to an exhortation to holy living. When viewed in light of the epistle's exhortations combined with the author's rhetorical situation, it becomes clear that this pervasive eschatological theme provides the logical and emotional context for Paul's appeals to faithfulness, brotherly love, and especially moral and ethical purity, in a way that deftly responds to his perception of that situation. In short, the eschatological references provide Paul with a way to reassure a church facing persecution, unsure of his own support and care, and grieving over fellow Christians who have died, while also insisting that they hold unswervingly to the gospel and to the ethical, moral, and communal requirements of their faith. In response, Paul employs visionary language at strategic moments in the discourse, which is itself primarily consolatory and reassuring. Each major section and subsection culminates in an eschatological pronouncement so that a strongly eschatological tone pervades the entire epistle. By using visionary language in this way, Paul evokes a perspective from which the Thessalonians are invited to see themselves and their circumstances. They are living near the end of time and awaiting the imminent return of Christ, the judgment before God, and the final reward and punishment that will be meted out at the last judgment. Viewed in this context, of course, their present circumstances take on a new perspective altogether. Persecution becomes a temporary experience made all the more bearable by the believers' anticipation of God's vengeance being poured out on those who now trouble them. Much more, this eschatological context heightens their need for faithfulness to God and holy living. For despite all of Paul's reassurance, his language makes clear that the Thessalonians' status as "blameless before God" at the judgment is not assured. Rather, it is something that he and they fervently hope for. But only through holy living will they avoid "the wrath to come" from which Jesus has rescued them.

Remarkably, however, Paul's discourse implies the ethical and behavioral implications rather than stating them explicitly, which likely reflects Paul's sensitivity to the rhetorical situation. He must deal with his audience with utmost gentleness, as befits his claimed position among them of "nurse" and "father," while at the same time exhorting them to faithfulness and moral purity. Paul's strategy for doing this is to evoke an eschatological worldview and present it simply as "what is." That discursively constructed eschatological reality, then, carries the weight of the exhortation, so that Paul does not have to threaten or appeal to his personal authority in order to gain their compliance — neither of which, given his circumstances, would have been a judicious strategy. Rather, when they accept his challenge to live soberly and righteously, they are simply responding to the natural implications of their situation, which Paul has merely reminded them of, rather than to his direct, persuasive appeals. In other words, if his audience indeed comes to view their lives from this eschatological perspective, they will, Paul hopes, come to accept the imperatives of faithfulness and moral purity. Paul is thus able to retain his position as the "gentle nurse," while at the same time providing a powerful incentive for the Thessalonians to live as they ought.

As noted above, Paul presents all of this as a reminder of what they already know. By contrast, the one element of this eschatological framework that is presented as information the Thessalonians *do not yet have* is the vision of the end in 4:13-18. Yet the entire worldview that he wishes them to adopt depends on a proper understanding of what is presented in that vision and the attendant emotional state of hopefulness that the vision seeks to instill, which at this point they do not possess. Thus, the foundation of Paul's persuasive strategy, the one piece on which the entire eschatological worldview hinges, is that dramatic vision of the parousia.

Paul's Vision of the End (1 Thess. 4:13-18)

Paul begins by raising the issue with a disclosure formula, "But we do not want you to be uninformed," which, as Johanson noted, "not only serves to signal a transition to a different topic, but also the introduction of new information, as indicated by θέλομεν together with the noetic verb."[20] His topic, of course, concerns "those who have died" (περὶ τῶν κοιμωνένων), literally, "those who sleep," lest they "grieve as others do who have no hope" (v. 13). His use of κοιμάω ("sleep") here and in vv. 14-15, in contrast to the usual and more direct term, οἱ νεκροί ("the dead," v. 16), appears intentional, suggesting the temporary nature of what has now so grieved the Thessalonians and offering, as Nicholl put it, a "first attempt to change the Thessalonian community's paradigm concerning Christian death."[21]

---

20. Johanson, *To All the Brethren*, 120. Nicholl likewise emphasizes the contrast between this introduction and the introductions of 4:9 and 5:1, which "strongly suggests that Paul is distinguishing between what his readers already know in 4:9 and 5:1 and what they do not yet know in 4:13" (*From Hope to Despair in Thessalonica*, 21).

21. Nicholl, *From Hope to Despair in Thessalonica*, 23. See also Witherington, *1 and 2 Thessalonians,* 131: "What we find beginning in Dan. 12.2 and continuing in *Testament of Judah* 25.4 and *Testament of Issachar* 7.9; 2 Macc. 12.44-45; and *1 Enoch* 91.10 and 92.3 however is a connection between sleeping and being awakened by the resurrection, an idea Paul further develops here and in 1 Cor. 15.20-21."

Certainly, the metaphor of sleep prepares for the vision in vv. 16-17, which prominently features three booming sounds that announce the parousia, presumably intended to "wake the dead." Paul then states the core "information" that answers their grief in v. 14 in the form of a conditional sentence (εἰ γὰρ . . . οὕτως καί . . .): "For we believe that Jesus died and rose again, and so we believe that God will bring with Jesus those who have fallen asleep in him." The protasis, cast in the first-person plural, cites what may actually be a pre-Pauline confession and, at the very least, posits a conviction that Paul and his audience are already assumed to share.[22] Then, using deductive reasoning, the apodosis presents the logical implication of that shared belief, that God will bring with Jesus those who have fallen asleep. Paul omits restating the "we believe" (πιστεύομεν) in the "then" clause of his statement, an ellipsis that draws in the audience by way of inviting them to supply the missing content. The statement of faith, finally, suggests that of all the members of the Thessalonian Christian community, living *and* dead, those who have died and await resurrection, have more closely followed the path of the Lord who died and rose again.

Then, in v. 15, Paul appears to shift from arguing logically regarding the resurrection, to simply declaring to them "the word of the Lord." Earlier in 2:13 he had praised them for the way that they had initially accepted his gospel, not as "a human word" (λόγον ἀνθρώπων), but "as what it really is, God's word" (λόγον θεοῦ). In the exhortation just preceding this passage, he summarizes his call to holiness by reminding them that "whoever rejects this rejects not human authority but God" (4:8). At the end of the epistle, he will urge them not to "despise the words of prophets" (προφητείας μὴ ἐξουθενεῖτε, 5:20). Now, he seems to take on the persona of the prophet in order to declare to them, ἐν λόγῳ κυρίου ("by a word of the Lord"), "that we who are alive, who are left until the coming of the Lord, will by no means precede those who have died" (lit. "those sleeping," τοὺς κοιμηθέντας). Of course, Paul's introductory formula, ἐν λόγῳ κυρίου, underscores his authority to disclose what will happen at the end and thus to address the misunderstanding that has caused the Thessalonians' grief. But by taking on the prophetic persona, he may also have sought to prepare his audience not for more logical argumentation, but instead for the apocalyptic vision that follows. As to the "word of the Lord" that he proclaims, it is striking that he presents the information somewhat awkwardly, not as a positive statement,

---

22. On the evidence that this is a "primitive Christian confession," see Witherington, *1 and 2 Thessalonians*, 132; see also Nicholl, *From Hope to Despair in Thessalonica*, 26.

but as a statement of what will *not* happen, using the emphatic negative (οὐ μή).[23] The living who now grieve the loss of their fellow Christians will "by no means" be at any advantage over the dead in Christ whom they now mourn.

At this point, then, Paul has given the Thessalonians the essential information they need in order to understand rationally the event that has caused them to "grieve as others do who have no hope" (v. 13). As a logical corollary to their shared belief in the resurrection of Christ, they can expect that their departed loved ones who now "sleep" will be raised and that, at the coming of the Lord, they will not be at any disadvantage vis-à-vis those who remain alive. Further, the text reflects a high degree of careful rhetorical intentionality, suggesting that Paul has taken pains to present his argument in as persuasive a manner as possible — as illustrated by his use of the metaphor of sleep to describe those who have died, his apparent citation of an early creedal statement as the basis for constructing a deductive argument based on their shared belief in the resurrection of Christ, and his shift to a prophetic voice in order to declare to them the "word of the Lord."

Yet for all that, Paul is not finished. He seems to assume that to quell the Thessalonians' anxiety and assuage their grief, more is needed than a cogent argument, delivered in flat prose, explaining the fate of the righteous dead at the parousia. As Plevnik argued, beyond simply stating "that the presence of the deceased faithful is guaranteed by the Christ-event of the past," Paul also "had to show them graphically how this would be made possible."[24] What is needed, rather, is a mimetic experience that allows them a brief glimpse of that event, which he offers in vv. 16-17:

> [16]For the Lord himself, with a cry of command, with the archangel's call and with the sound of God's trumpet, will descend from heaven, and the dead in Christ will rise first. [17]Then we who are alive, who are left, will be caught up in the clouds together with them to meet the Lord in the air; and so we will be with the Lord forever.

Several features of this passage evince its connection to the previous verses. The introductory conjunction, ὅτι ("for," "because," "since"), signals that what follows is an elaboration of what has just been said. Of course, the

---

23. Witherington calls the second half of the verse "grammatically awkward" (*1 and 2 Thessalonians*, 132-33).

24. Plevnik, "Taking Up of the Faithful," 281.

vision thematically reflects the material from the previous verses, especially in the way that the audible signals announcing the parousia build on the notion that the dead in Christ are merely "asleep." But vv. 16-17 also build on the previous verses in an even more subtle way. As noted above, Paul in v. 15 explains the order of events somewhat awkwardly, in negative terms, stating that "we who are alive, who are left until the coming of the Lord, will by no means precede those who have died." The vision, by contrast, presents the same information in positive terms, so that the two accounts are broadly related in a form of reverse parallelism, in roughly the same way that a photographic negative is related to the image itself. What is striking, however, is that for all of the ways that the vision relates to the prose information provided in vv. 14-15, it really adds little new information to what they have just been given, that there will be a resurrection and that those who have died will in no way be in an inferior position relative to those who are alive when Christ returns. The vision of vv. 16-17 simply takes up that same essential information and re-presents it in a poetic form.

Numerous features highlight the text's poetic character. Most obvious is the parallelism between the three participial phrases describing the signals that announce the parousia has begun: "with a cry of command, with the archangel's call, and with the sound of God's trumpet" (ἐν κελεύσματι, ἐν φωνῇ ἀρχαγγέλου καὶ ἐν σάλπιγγι θεοῦ). The overall vision also seems to follow something of a temporal and spatial progression, which provides a basic plot to the event: Christ descends, the dead rise, and then the living are "caught up in the clouds" to meet the Lord in the air. The audience is thus drawn into a narrative structure that begins with a cataclysmic disruption announced by loud shouts and trumpets and that resolves in a serene ending, "and so we will be with the Lord forever." That spatial language also adds an important sensory dimension to the vision — one expects to look to the skies to see what is being announced so dramatically — as does Paul's dramatic description of the living being, literally, seized or snatched up (ἁρπάζω, v. 17) to join the living. Of course, this multisensory character is especially reinforced by the auditory portents that herald the Lord's coming, the "cry of command, . . . the archangel's call and . . . the sound of God's trumpet."

A number of scholars have observed, however, that these terms did more than simply give the vision its multisensory character; they also likely conveyed a powerful set of associated visual and emotional meanings. Scholars have differed as to the precise source from which Paul drew these images, with some arguing that the background lies in the Jewish and Christian apocalyptic tradition.[25] Witherington suggested that Paul was probably "drawing on the *yom Yahweh* traditions, which referred to a trumpet blast announcing the event (cf. Isa. 27.13; Joel 2.1; Zech. 9.14; 2 Esd. 6.23; *Sibylline Oracles* 4.174; 2 Cor. 15.52)."[26] The trumpet blast and clouds in particular are standard elements of theophany in the Jewish tradition.[27] But there is also strong evidence that some of Paul's language may also have called to mind for a Gentile audience the events surrounding the royal visit of a powerful king, particularly the term ἀπάντησις ("meeting"). As Witherington noted, the term referred "to the actions of a greeting committee as it goes forth from the city to escort the royal person or dignitary into the city for his official visit."[28] Cicero, for example, refers to Julius Caesar's victory tour through Italy in 49 B.C.E. in these words: "You can imagine the town deputations [ἀπαντήσεις] and official compliments" (*Att.* 8.16.2); he likewise said of Augustus, "The boy is remarkably popular in the towns," noting that he was greeted with "amazing receptions [ἀπάντησις] and demonstrations of encouragement" (16.11.6).[29] Thus Nicholl concluded, "In the case of 1 Thess. 4:16-17a, ἀπάντησις would conjure up a picture of the dead and the living leaving their *polis*, the earth, to form a reception party to welcome their Lord."[30] Indeed, Donfried argued that the key terms

---

25. Weatherly summarized this position: "The language that Paul uses here would have been familiar to anyone who knew the traditions of Jewish apocalyptic literature. Its roots are in the Old Testament prophets, especially Dan. 7:13-14, where a vision of a series of political empires comes to an end with the coming of 'one like a Son of Man' on the clouds of heaven" (Jon A. Weatherly, *1 & 2 Thessalonians*, The College Press NIV Commentary [Joplin, MO: College Press, 1996], 157).

26. Witherington, *1 and 2 Thessalonians*, 16. See also Candida R. Moss and Joel S. Baden, "1 Thessalonians 4.13-18 in Rabbinic Perspective," *New Testament Studies* 58 (2012): 199-212, which explores the background of these images in the Jewish rabbinic tradition, which held that "at the advent of the eschaton the righteous will fly up to the new eschatological Jerusalem, either in the seventh heaven or floating on the clouds" (208). The problem with an exclusively Jewish background, however, is that while it may explain the source of the language for Paul, it would not necessarily be compelling to a primarily Gentile audience.

27. On the role of the clouds in Jewish eschatology, see Joseph Plevnik, "The Destination of the Apostle and of the Faithful: Second Corinthians 4:13b-14 and First Thessalonians 4:14," *Catholic Biblical Quarterly* 62 (2000): 83-95.

28. Witherington, *1 and 2 Thessalonians*, 138.

29. In both cases, Cicero inserts the Greek term in his Latin text, indicating that the word may have had something of a technical connotation.

30. Nicholl, *From Hope to Despair in Thessalonica*, 43. See also Bruce, who wrote, "These analogies (especially in association with the term παρουσία) suggest the possibility that the Lord is pictured here as escorted on the remainder of the journey to earth by his people — both

in the vision, παρουσία (coming), ἀπάντησις (meeting), and κύριος (lord), were all politically charged:

> When used as court language, *parousia* refers to the arrival of Caesar, a king or an official. *Apantēsis* refers to the citizens meeting a dignitary who is about to visit the city. . . . The term *kyrios*, especially when used in the same context as the two preceding terms, also has a definite political sense. . . . All of this, coupled with the use of *euangelion* and its possible association with the eastern ruler cult suggests that Paul and his associates could easily be understood as violating "the decrees of Caesar" in the most blatant manner.[31]

By thus "co-opting . . . imperial rhetoric to apply it to Jesus," Witherington concluded, Paul's language would have carried particular weight if the "dead in Christ in Thessalonike were victims of the persecutions elsewhere alluded to in this letter, which is certainly possible."[32]

In the face of the theological questions and, more importantly, the grief and anxiety caused by the unexpected deaths of their fellow believers, Paul needs to reassure his audience about the fate of those who have died "in the Lord," in a way that overcomes their own empirical experience of that loss, as well as the kinds of cultural understandings about death that they may well have brought to their faith. At the same time, he needs to reinforce the broader apocalyptic expectation of the parousia which, in connection to the brief eschatological references, as well as the longer passage about the "times and seasons" of that event, provide the ultimate foundation for his call to lead a holy life. Paul responds by offering a rational explanation based on what they already know — that Jesus died and rose again. In a carefully crafted argument, Paul deduces the logical implication of that belief for their expectation for the righteous dead, which he follows with a declaration "in the word of the Lord" regarding the precise order of events at the coming of Christ. Then, rather than adding further explanation, Paul recasts that information in the form of a powerful, image-filled vision of the end. As Bridges put it, Paul's vision is not so much aimed at "correcting false beliefs or even teaching new ones," but rather

those newly raised from the dead and those remaining alive" (F. F. Bruce, *1 & 2 Thessalonians* [Waco: Word, 1982], 103).

31. Karl P. Donfried, "The Imperial Cults and Political Conflict in 1 Thessalonians," in *Paul and Empire*, ed. R. A. Horsley (Harrisburg: Trinity, 1997), 215-23, here 217.

32. Witherington, *1 and 2 Thessalonians*, 140.

at "creating space for healing from disappointment."[33] Only after having provided them a transcendent, extrarational glimpse of that event can Paul give them his concluding exhortation in v. 18: "Therefore, encourage one another with these words."

Conclusion

Paul writes 1 Thessalonians to a community of believers who feel that he has abandoned them to face intense persecution and the deaths of their fellow believers, events that may even be related, on their own. His letter, written in an epideictic form, praises them for their faith and endurance and offers them consolation in the face of their loss. But it also underscores the urgent need to pursue lives of ethical and moral purity. Paul's overarching rhetorical strategy is to structure the entire letter around a series of eschatological references. These references infuse the letter with a strong sense of expectation for the second coming, the judgment, and the ultimate fate of the righteous and the unrighteous, a theme that allows Paul to offer consolation while also highlighting the need for righteous living. As I have argued in this chapter, undergirding that overall strategy is the vision of the end that Paul offers within his treatment of the righteous dead in 1 Thess. 4:13-18.

Essentially, Paul wants the Thessalonians to live out of a worldview that is dramatically different from that of their dominant culture and that flies in the face of their own empirical experience, a worldview centered in the conviction that holds, in the face of the power of Rome, ongoing persecution, and even death itself, that God is firmly in control, that Christ is returning, and that all will be made right. That worldview, he believes, will inspire the Christians in Thessalonica to the hopefulness and motivation they need to live faithfully in the midst of difficult circumstances. But in order for that conviction to become truly rooted in the social imaginary of the Thessalonians, they need to do more than learn "about" it — they need to see it. Paul offers them that glimpse of what he expects to be an earth-shattering event by using poetic form and vivid, provocative language. In doing so he captures some sense of the event's cataclysmic character, imbuing the vision with the sense of grandeur that Longinus understood was at the heart of creating an experience of "ecstasy." By bringing that event before their eyes,

---

33. Linda McKinnish Bridges, *1 & 2 Thessalonians* (Macon: Smyth and Helwys, 2008), 125.

Paul's words "shape a reality and consciousness that will not be shaken by external realities."[34]

Although it is certainly brief — only two verses — Paul's vision offers an important first clue about the nature of early Christian persuasion. Rather than simply arousing emotion in support of argument, Paul's treatment of the righteous dead is structured in the opposite way, where the vision and its attendant emotions are the culmination of the discursive process, where logical reasoning gives way to mimetic representation. That vision takes the audience out of their present difficult circumstances, collapsing temporal boundaries, and for a moment, dissolves the frontier between their world and the world to come. The fact that the vision takes up and recasts information that has already been provided them, rather than presenting new information, indicates Paul's own sense of the limitations of argument. For Christians to live out of this alternative worldview, they need to be able to see it and hear it. In Paul's vision, that reality, at least for a moment, becomes tangible in their experience.

---

34. Bridges, *1 & 2 Thessalonians*, 127.

CHAPTER THREE

Performing Despair (Romans 7:14-25)

For Longinus, the paragon of oratorical brilliance was none other than the Greek orator Demosthenes. What made him "far [exceed] . . . the limits of mere persuasion," was his ability to exploit the "enthralling effect of the imagination" in support of factual arguments. Such artful blending of imagination and logical reasoning, Longinus believed, "not only convinces the audience, it positively masters them" (*Subl.*, 15.9-11). Of the four poetic texts examined in this book, none comes closer to fulfilling Longinus's vision than Paul's "speech-in-character" in Romans 7:14-25. The passage comes at the end of a highly dialectical train of discourse that begins with a logical deduction concerning the Christians' freedom from the law of Moses, and moves from there to a painstaking explanation, framed as a response to a series of rhetorical questions, all raising questions about the role that the law played in salvation history. Reading it, one can almost imagine Paul and his audience engaged in a spirited back-and-forth debate, as he seeks to convince them of his position. But then, in vv. 14-25, Paul takes up that same theological claim made in the previous 13 verses and recasts it as a mimetic performance in which he actually plays the part of the anguished sinner, first engulfed in self-condemnation and then miraculously freed from the law's curse by the grace of God. The result, potentially at least, is the kind of imaginative absorption in the discourse that Longinus predicted.

This chapter examines Paul's dramatic portrayal of the law-keeper's guilt and self-condemnation as a crucial element in his effort to advance a radical claim about the role of the Mosaic law to which many in his audience would likely have strongly objected. But much more significantly, I argue, his representation played a crucial role in his broader attempt to bring about the unity of Jews and Gentiles in the Christian Church. He accomplished this by taking both groups through a common, vicarious experience of guilt, self-condemnation, and despair, to an experience of welcome release brought on by the sudden awareness of God's grace. In short, he hoped to give his hearers a consciousness of the stages of religious conversion as he understood it, as a way of creating in them the kind of disposition they would need to respond to God with gratitude and to each other with humility and forbearance. The chapter begins with a discussion of the rhetorical situation to which Paul addresses the letter as a whole, followed by an analysis of the overall argument of chapter 7. This prepares for the close analysis of the "speech-in-character" itself in vv. 14-25, followed by a discussion of the role that this dramatic performance played in the overall "argument" of Romans.

A Movement in Peril

The epistle to the Romans contains a number of clues that, when combined with details from other NT texts, allow for a fairly certain reconstruction of the background of Paul's letter to the church in Rome — a church he did not establish and over which, consequently, he had no clear authority.[1] In the opening of the letter, after giving thanks to the Roman Christians because their "faith is proclaimed throughout the world" and assuring them that "without ceasing I remember you always in my prayers," he tells them of his plans to visit them: "For I am longing to see you so that I may share with you some spiritual gift to strengthen you — or rather so that we may be mutually encouraged by each other's faith" (1:8-12). His hope, he says, is to "reap some

---

1. For discussions of the origins of Christianity in Rome, see F. F. Bruce, "Romans Debate — Continued," in *The Romans Debate*, ed. K. P. Donfried (Peabody, MA: Hendrickson, 1991), 334-59, esp. 337-38; Wolfgang Wiefel, "The Jewish Community in Ancient Rome and the Origins of Roman Christianity," in *The Romans Debate*, ed. Donfried, 85-101; Donald Guthrie, *New Testament Introduction* (Downers Grove: InterVarsity, 1970), 393-411; Werner Georg Kümmel, *Introduction to the New Testament*, trans. Howard Clark Kee (Nashville: Abingdon, 1996), 307-9; Douglas J. Moo, *The Epistle to the Romans* (Grand Rapids: Eerdmans, 1996), 3-5; Thomas H. Tobin, *Paul's Rhetoric and Its Contexts* (Peabody, MA: Hendrickson, 2004), 44-46; Ben Witherington III, with Darlene Hyatt, *Paul's Letter to the Romans: A Socio-Rhetorical Commentary* (Grand Rapids: Eerdmans, 2004), 8-9. Based on chap. 16, Witherington identified at least five different house churches that make up the broader Christian community in Rome. "Perhaps one reason there was no central organization to the church in Rome was that it had no apostolic foundation, nor was it simply an offshoot of the synagogue communities in Rome. It seems likely that the first Christians in Rome were ordinary Jews and God-fearers who had heard the gospel in Jerusalem and had brought the message home with them (see Acts 2.10-11)."

harvest among you as I have among the rest of the Gentiles" (1:13).[2] Toward the end of the epistle, he explains his plan to undertake a pioneering mission to Spain, becoming the first to carry the message of Christianity to that part of the empire (15:18-29), and he informs them of his desire that the church in Rome serve as his base of operation for this planned mission.[3] Before he can begin that mission, however, he must first deliver a contribution for the poor among the Jewish Christians in Jerusalem who suffer as a result of a famine in Palestine, which he has gathered from the churches established through his mission to the Gentiles in Asia Minor.[4] As he puts it, the Gentiles "owe it to them, for if they have come to share in their spiritual blessings, they ought to be of service to them in material things" (15:27).

Most scholars recognize that behind these details loomed a much larger crisis having to do with the relationship of Gentiles and Jews in the church and the related question about whether the Mosaic law had any ongoing authority for Christians. The controversy had been present from the moment that Gentiles were admitted to the faith without first undergoing the rite of circumcision (Acts 10–11). It had led to a major gathering of church leaders, the so-called "Jerusalem Council," which opened with the demand of a faction of believers identified with the sect of Pharisees insisting that "it is necessary for [the Gentiles] . . . to be circumcised and ordered to keep the law of Moses" (Acts 15:5). The question occupies most of Paul's epistle

2. Based on this explicit designation of his audience, most assume that the epistle is directed to a primarily Gentile audience, although there were probably at least some Jewish Christians included as well, as evidenced by the fact that he seems to address Jews directly in chap. 2 and greets a number of Jewish Christians by name in chap. 16. As Witherington put it, "Paul as the apostle to the Gentiles is primarily addressing Gentile Christians in Rome, although he is happy for Jewish Christians to overhear this conversation" (*Paul's Letter to the Romans*, 8). See also Moo, *Epistle to the Romans*, 9-13.

3. Specifically, he tells the Roman Christians that he wishes "to be sent on by you" (ὑφ' ὑμῶν προπεμφθῆναι, 15:24), describing their proposed relationship using an idiom that denotes financial as well as moral support. See Walter Bauer, *A Greek-English Lexicon of the New Testament and Other Early Christian Literature*, edited and trans. W. F. Arndt and F. W. Gingrich, 2nd ed. revised by F. W. Gingrich and F. W. Danker (Chicago: University of Chicago Press, 1979), 709. Robert Jewett argued on this basis that the letter is an adaptation of the subtype of epideictic rhetoric known as the "ambassador's speech," described in Theodore C. Burgess's definitive study, "Epideictic Literature," *Studies in Classical Philology* 3 (1900): 89-261. He pointed, as well, to the handbook of Pseudo-Libanius, which describes and offers a sample of the "diplomatic letter." Jewett also finds other examples of this ancient epistolary form in Euripides's play, "The Heracleidae," and Philo's *On the Embassy to Gaius*; see Robert Jewett, "Romans as an Ambassadorial Letter," *Interpretation* 36 (1982): 9-20.

4. See also Acts 24:17 and 2 Corinthians 8–9 for other references to this collection.

to the Galatians and, indeed, Tobin argued that Paul's response there had engendered at least some of the ongoing controversy that he must now address in Romans. As Tobin put it, Paul had become

> embroiled . . . in controversy with the churches of Jerusalem, Antioch, and eventually with the Galatian community he himself had founded. The intensity of his controversy with the Galatians led Paul to so sharpen the contrast between righteousness through faith and observance of the law that it became difficult to see how the law or its observances could ever have been commanded by God. These same stark contrasts seemed even to exclude the Jewish people from ultimately receiving the inheritance promised to them by God in the Scriptures.[5]

At the very least, Paul felt the need to quell rumors he feared had reached the Roman church, which represented his position as rank antinomianism: "Some people slander us by saying that we say, 'Let us do evil so that good may come'" (Rom. 3:8). As Moo stated, "Paul's battle against Judaizers . . . had gained for him a reputation of being 'anti-law' and perhaps even 'anti-Jewish.'"[6]

When Paul wrote Romans, then, he faced the dire possibility that the Jewish and Gentile strains of the Christian movement might part ways over questions concerning the role of the law and the place of the Jews in salvation history. That risk of schism threatened Paul's fundamental sense of calling and mission. As the epistle to the Romans itself makes clear, Paul saw himself as a crucial player in the plan which God had been unfolding since the beginning of time, a self-understanding which informed his entire mission. He was the "apostle to the Gentiles," whose role in God's grand scheme was to bring them into unity with the Jews in a single church, a mission to which, as noted above, he refers several times in the Roman epistle (e.g., 1:5, 13). Later, in something of an apology for the liberty he has taken in boldly writing to them, he says that he wished to remind them

> of the grace given to me by God to be a minister of Christ Jesus to the Gentiles in the priestly service of the gospel of God, so that the offering of the Gentiles may be acceptable, sanctified by the Holy Spirit. In Christ Jesus, then, I have reason to boast of my work for God. For I will not ven-

---

5. Tobin, *Paul's Rhetoric*, 77.
6. Moo, *Epistle to the Romans*, 21.

ture to speak of anything except what Christ has accomplished through me to win obedience from the Gentiles, by word and deed, by the power of signs and wonders, by the power of the Spirit of God, so that from Jerusalem and as far around as Illyricum I have fully proclaimed the good news of Christ (15:15-19).

His unique mission of bringing the gospel to the Gentiles, moreover, would lead to their inclusion with the Jews in one united church.[7] Thus he argues in chap. 4 that the Jews and Gentiles claim the same spiritual ancestor, Abraham. Further, he contends that the Gentiles who have accepted Christianity are "wild olive branches" that have been grafted into the Jewish root, so that they grow together as one plant (11:17-24). He describes the mission of Christ specifically in terms of the inclusion of the Gentiles alongside the Jews in the divine plan (15:8-12). From this perspective, Paul's collection for the Jewish Christians in Jerusalem had tremendous symbolic significance beyond being "simply a matter of charity; it was also about maintaining or even reestablishing the bond of unity, which the collection symbolized, between his largely Gentile Christian communities and the Jewish Christian community of Jerusalem."[8] Given the prominence of this theme throughout Romans and, indeed, the New Testament, Crafton is right to argue that Paul invites his audience to adopt a worldview at the center of which is God's plan to unite Jews and Gentiles together into one church:

> Paul creates a text which is a strategic and stylized naming of a situation, which invites the readers to participate in a specific world-view. Paul creates a rhetorical vision in which he and the Roman Christians are actors in a

---

7. Paul clearly views the Gentile Christians as joining a divine plan which was initially Jewish. Because of his work, the Gentiles are now able to join the "people of the Covenant" — the Jews — and become one "people of God." This idea, reflected in numerous places in the New Testament, finds its fullest expression in Ephesians, which, whether authentically Pauline or not, certainly reflects the same self-understanding that Paul demonstrates in Romans. See, particularly, Eph. 2:11-22, in which the death of Jesus is portrayed in terms of breaking down "the dividing wall of hostility" (i.e., between Jews and Gentiles); and 3:1-13, where the author, called Paul, describes his mission as "revealing the mystery made known to me by revelation" (3:3). The mystery, of course, is that now "the Gentiles have become fellow heirs [with the Jews], members of the same body, and sharers in the promise in Christ Jesus through the gospel" (3:6). For a discussion of how this vision is emphasized in Luke–Acts, see Jacob Jervell, *Luke and the People of God: A New Look at Luke–Acts* (Minneapolis: Augsburg, 1972).

8. Tobin, *Paul's Rhetoric*, 76. Tobin argued that the chasm had become sufficiently deep that Paul actually feared that the contribution would be rejected by the Jewish church.

larger divine purpose. It is his hope that they will perceive themselves, and his own person and ministry, in a new [w]ay, so that they might become active participants with him in the divine plan. Paul's intention is to involve the readers in his world as much as possible, through theological argument, through emotional and ethical appeal, and through demonstration of the ways in which he and the Romans are already participants in this world.[9]

At stake when Paul writes the epistle, then, is his fundamental understanding of God's plan for the nations, as well as that of his own unique place in that plan as the "apostle to the Gentiles."

This threat to Paul's vision was particularly acute among the Christians in Rome, as a result of events that had recently taken place there. Sometime around 49 C.E., Claudius expelled the Jews from Rome because of rioting among the Jews over a certain person whom Suetonius calls "Chrestus" (*Claud.*, 25.4). While it is impossible to be completely certain, this reference is likely to Christ, indicating that the riot was the result of the preaching about Jesus which took place among the synagogues in Rome.[10] Since at this point Christianity was considered a sect of Judaism,[11] Claudius's edict would have meant that all of the Jews in Rome — including Jewish Christians — had to leave the city.[12] The implications of this turn of events for the church in Rome can scarcely be overstated. Christianity in Rome undoubtedly started as a movement among the Jews of the city.[13] Before the edict of Claudius,

9. Jeffrey A. Crafton, "Paul's Rhetorical Vision and the Purpose of Romans: Toward a New Understanding," *Novum Testamentum* 32 (1990): 317-39, here 320.

10. This expulsion is also recorded in Acts 18:1ff. For reconstructions of this event and its impact on the Roman church, see Wiefel, "Jewish Community in Ancient Rome," 109; Bruce, "Romans Debate — Continued," 338-39. Witherington's discussion is particularly helpful (*Paul's Letter to the Romans*, 11-16). As Jewett explained, "Suetonius apparently believed that the disturbances were caused by a rabble-rouser named 'Chrestus,' a common slave name that could easily be confused with 'Christus' because of the tendency in Koine Greek to pronounce various vowels as i" (Robert Jewett, *Romans: A Commentary* [Minneapolis: Fortress, 2007], 60).

11. Neil Elliott, *The Rhetoric of Romans: Argumentative Constraint and Strategy and Paul's Dialogue with Judaism* (Minneapolis: Augsburg Fortress, 2000), 47-48.

12. A handful of scholars downplay the impact of this event on the character of the Roman church, among them Mark D. Nanos, *The Mystery of Romans: The Jewish Context of Paul's Letters* (Minneapolis: Fortress, 1996), 372-87. Witherington offers a cogent rebuttal (*Paul's Letter to the Romans*, 12-14).

13. See Wiefel ("Jewish Community in Ancient Rome," 93), who goes so far as to state that "expulsion of Jews from Rome also meant the end of the first Christian congregation in Rome which up until now had consisted of Jewish Christians." Cf. Bruce, "The Romans Debate — Continued," 340.

therefore, the flavor of Christianity in Rome, and more importantly, the leadership of the Roman church, would have been predominantly Jewish. As Tobin observed, "What distinguished Roman Christians from Roman Jews was the former's belief in Jesus as the Christ. But in other significant ways, Roman Christian belief and practice remained of a piece with Roman Jewish belief and practice."[14] Within this predominantly Jewish movement, the Gentiles would have constituted a minority, and those Gentiles who were part of the church would have been drawn largely from the category known as "God fearers," that is, Gentiles who had been sympathetic to Judaism and connected to the synagogue, but who had not officially converted to Judaism. The expulsion of the Jews, however, left the Gentile Christians to fend for themselves, and it is plausible to assume that the next five or so years witnessed the influx of more Gentiles into the Christian community, the development of a Gentile leadership, and the shift within the church toward a more Gentile atmosphere.[15] When Nero came to power in 54 C.E., he rescinded the edict and allowed the Jews to return.

It is not difficult to imagine the problems that would have arisen when the Jews began to return, finding what had now become a Gentile church. As Moo explained, the shift from "the earlier Jewish matrix of Roman Christianity to a more purely 'Gentile' framework (a process accelerated by the enforced exile of Jewish Christians under Claudius) . . . has given rise to a sense of inferiority on the part of the Jewish segment." Paul wrote Romans some four to five years later, at a moment

> when Jewish Christians, and in particular, their leadership, are just beginning to reestablish themselves in Rome. They have been marginalized by the expulsion, and Paul is addressing a largely Gentile Christian

14. Tobin, *Paul's Rhetoric*, 45.

15. Numerous texts in the New Testament indicate that since their first exposure to Christianity came through the synagogue, many of the earliest Gentile believers embraced a form of Christianity which included adherence to Jewish ceremonial and dietary regulations. (See, for example, Acts 15:1-35; Gal. 2:3-5; 5:1-12; Col. 2:6-23. This was, in fact, one of the major points of controversy within the early Christian church.) However, following the expulsion of the Jewish Christians and the movement of Christianity from the synagogue to private homes, Elliott argued, "It is reasonable to assume that careful observance of the Jewish Law would quickly have become dispensable for these Christians" (*The Rhetoric of Romans*, 51), and that the now predominantly Gentile Christianity would have developed "within an atmosphere of strong anti-Jewish sentiment in the city." See also William Horbury, "The Jewish Dimension," in *Early Christianity: Origins and Evolution to A.D. 600*, ed. Ian Hazlett (Nashville: Abingdon, 1991), 40-51.

audience which has drawn some erroneous conclusions about Jews and Jewish Christians.[16]

These historical events, fueled by the pervasive, historical animosity between Jews and Gentiles in the Roman world, thus created a situation in which Jews and Gentiles in the Christian church were deeply at odds with one another.[17] This explains Paul's focus on the Gentiles in the letter's opening (1:5-6), as well as the extended exhortation to unity in chaps. 12–14, which "reveals a split in the Roman community between Jewish and Gentile Christians," the mending of which many scholars see "as the key to the purpose of the letter."[18]

When Paul wrote Romans, then, he needed to win his audience over to his understanding of salvation by faith, clarifying for them where the Mosaic law and, indeed, the Jews themselves fit into salvation history. He had to do so, however, in a way that promoted unity in the church and, particularly, that gave Gentile Christians in Rome no reason to suspect that God had somehow discarded the "chosen nation." And he had to gain their support for his proposed mission to Spain. As Moo summarized,

> The various purposes share a common denominator: Paul's missionary situation. The past battles in Galatia and Corinth; the coming crisis in Jerusalem; the desire to secure a missionary base for his work in Spain; the need to unify the Romans around "his" gospel to support his work in Spain — all of these forced Paul to write a letter in which he carefully rehearsed his understanding of the gospel, especially as it related to the salvation-historical questions of Jew and Gentile and the continuity of the plan of salvation.[19]

Not surprisingly, Paul presents his gospel in chaps. 1–8 in a way that emphasizes the equality of Jews and Gentiles before God. His explanation for the Jewish rejection of Christianity in chaps. 9–11 predicts a large influx of Jews

---

16. Witherington, *Paul's Letter to the Romans,* 12. Jewett also observed that among the people named in chap. 16, several appear to be former members of the Christian community in Rome whom Paul met as Jewish refugees, and who are now being "treated as interlopers by the congregations of Rome, a situation that correlates with the argument about Gentile Christians accepting Jewish Christians in Romans 14–15" (*Romans,* 61).

17. Of course, this animosity is played out against a long history of hostility between Jews and Gentiles within Greco-Roman Society. This will be discussed at greater length in chap. 5.

18. Moo, *Epistle to the Romans,* 13, 19.

19. Moo, *Epistle to the Romans,* 20-21.

into the Christian church at some time in the future, and contains, as well, the stern warning to the Gentiles not to look with disdain toward the Jews who had not yet accepted Christ. Finally, the exhortation portion of the letter, in chaps. 12–15, centers overwhelmingly on unity and on the need for the believers in Rome to accept each other within the Christian community. Even Paul's personal comments in the closing chapter echo the theme of Jew and Gentile joined equally in one church. Clearly, then, Paul wrote his epistle with the aim of fostering unity among these estranged racial groups.

On a practical level, of course, it would have been difficult for Paul to seek support from a church embroiled in internal fighting. More devastating, however, was the threat that this racial hostility presented to Paul's self-understanding and sense of mission. His entire career as an apostle was driven by his vision of bringing together those who had traditionally been bitter enemies — Jews and Gentiles — into "one new person in Christ."[20] Thus, the problems in the Roman church presented Paul with the ultimate test case for his whole theology. If he could bring about the unity of Jewish and Gentile Christians in, of all places, the capital of the empire, he would have not only an excellent base of operations for his Spanish mission, but the confirmation of his entire life's work.

A central part of that overall rhetorical aim concerned his explanation of the purpose of the law in Rom. 7. Paul seems to have assumed that there are at least some in his audience quite familiar with the law — he addresses them as "those who know the law" (v. 1) — and who still placed a high value on the law. These may represent Jewish Christians or, as Stowers and Tobin assume, Gentile Christians who were originally drawn to Christianity through their association with Judaism, who highly esteemed the law for its ethical response to what they viewed as the decadence of Roman society.[21]

20. This is the phrase used in Eph. 2:15 which, although of questionable Pauline authorship, certainly represents Paul's understanding of God's plan for Jews and Gentiles.

21. Stowers argued that Paul's audience "consist[s] of gentiles who have great concern for moral self-mastery and acceptance by the one God and believe (or might be tempted to believe) that they have found the way to that goal through observing certain teachings from the Jewish law. These readers also might be tempted to consider themselves (or perhaps themselves and fellow Jewish followers of Christ) God's only true people, the mainstream of the Jewish people having rejected Jesus Christ and having been rejected by God. Against these assumptions of the readers encoded in the letter, Paul develops a rhetorical strategy to persuade them that the acceptance and self-mastery they seek is to be found not in following Jewish teachers who advocate works from the law but in what God has done and is even now doing through Jesus Christ" (Stanley K. Stowers, *A Rereading of Romans: Justice, Jews, and Gentiles* [New Haven: Yale University Press, 1994], 36). See also Tobin (*Paul's Rhetoric*, 44-46), who believes that the

In either case, Paul seems to have anticipated resistance to the understanding of the law that he advanced. At the very least, he took pains to show that the law was no longer binding, but without in any way lessening the value of the law or suggesting that, because it provoked human sinfulness, the law itself was somehow at fault.

Romans 7: An Overview

Beginning with a somewhat complex legal argument, the chapter takes up a claim introduced at several points in the epistle, that believers are free from the authority of the Mosaic law and, more radically, that the law, rather than providing a way out of sinfulness, actually made the situation worse — but that this outcome was actually the plan of God.[22] In this way, Paul attempts to show that Christians are free from the law, while also preserving a crucial place for the law in salvation history. Paul opens the chapter using a conversational mode of address: "Do you not know, brothers and sisters — for I am speaking to those who know the law — that the law is binding on a person only during that person's lifetime?" (v. 1). As Jewett pointed out, doing so would have given his audience "the impression that Paul is addressing them directly."[23] He follows this with the analogy that just as a woman whose husband has died is no longer bound by the law, so also — again addressing them directly as "my friends" — "you have died to the law through the body of Christ, so that you may belong to another, to him who has been raised from the dead in order that we may bear fruit for God" (v. 4). He follows this by briefly recounting their shared conversion experience, in the form of a "before and after" narrative that again touches on the place of the law. Before,

---

expulsion and later return of the Jews did not significantly change the culture of the Roman church, whose beliefs "included an emphasis on the superiority of the Mosaic law, specifically its ethical aspects, over what they saw as the degrading ethical practices of the Greco-Roman world" (45).

22. The chapter builds on his treatment in chap. 6 of another key question raised by his understanding of the law, that of ethics, which may be particularly aimed toward quelling the rumor that his view of the law removes the motivation for ethical living. There, he connects baptism to the death and resurrection of Christ, so that as Christ was raised from the dead, believers are raised from baptism "to newness of life" (v. 4). As a result, they are "dead to sin but alive to God" (v. 11), no longer living as "slaves of sin" (v. 17) but now as "slaves to righteousness" (v. 19). For an extensive treatment of how chap. 7 employs the language of chap. 6, see Tobin, *Paul's Rhetoric.*

23. Jewett, *Romans,* 430.

while we were living in the flesh, our sinful passions, aroused by the law, were at work in our members to bear fruit for death. But now we are discharged from the law, dead to that which held us captive, so that we are slaves not under the old written code but in the new life of the Spirit.

As Tobin observed, 7:1-6 contains an embedded syllogism:

The major premise is an uncontroversial legal principle (to which Paul had appended the equally uncontroversial example of Jewish marriage), and the minor premise is a restatement of Paul's interpretation of baptism in 6:3-4. The conclusion is that, as a result of baptism, the law no longer has any power over believers.[24]

In v. 7 Paul seems to continue that argumentative form when he asks the rhetorical question that might naturally rise from what he has just said: "What then should we say? That the law is sin?" which he answers with an emphatic "By no means!" (μὴ γένοιτο). But then, instead of continuing to argue using a process of logical deduction, he begins to interlace what appear to be autobiographical references with factual claims: "If it had not been for the law, I would not have known sin. I would not have known what it is to covet if the law had not said, 'You shall not covet.' But sin, seizing an opportunity in the commandment, produced in me all kinds of covetousness" (vv. 7-8).[25] This line of thought leads to his ironic conclusion that "the very commandment which promised life proved to be death to me. For sin, seizing

---

24. Tobin, *Paul's Rhetoric*, 223. For an extensive analysis of the syllogistic reasoning of 7:1-6, see Jewett, *Romans*, 428-39.

25. Stowers noted that the rhetorical question serves as a "transition from Paul's authorial voice, which has previously addressed the readers explicitly described by the letter in 6:1–7:6," constituting what rhetorical handbooks called "change of voice (*enallagē* or *metabolē*). These ancient readers would next look for *diaphōnia*, a difference in characterization from the authorial voice" (*Rereading of Romans*, 269). On Paul's use of personification to describe sin in this text, see Joseph R. Dodson, *The "Powers" of Personification: Rhetorical Purpose in the* Book of Wisdom *and the Letter to the Romans* (Berlin: de Gruyter, 2008): "So far in Romans, Paul has claimed that the Law increases trespass (5.20) and rules with Sin (6.14). From Paul's reasoning, one might question the relationship of the Law with Sin. Things become complicated as Paul tries to cast life under the Law as leading to both Sin and Death while maintaining that the Law is altogether good. Therefore, Paul creates a great tension, and a burning question: 'ὁ νόμος ἁμαρτία;' This is a relevant question indeed, in light of what Paul has said about the Law already in this letter, not to mention in previous letters. It is this question that Paul now addresses as he seeks to exonerate the Law by stressing the agency of personified Sin" (130).

an opportunity in the commandment, deceived me and through it killed me" (vv. 10-11). Although it is not entirely clear at this point whether Paul is speaking out of personal experience or simply speaking in what Kümmel called the "fictive I," his personal language is clearly subordinated to the argumentative form.[26] In other words, his "personal experience" substantiates the claim that "apart from the law, sin lies dead." To this point, then, Paul has argued based on an analogy to Jewish marriage drawn from within the law that the Mosaic code is no longer binding and that the law's purpose was to expose particular human attitudes and behaviors as being sinful. Indeed, the practical outcome of the law was to provoke even more sinfulness, since the presence of the commandment actually brought sin to life and inflamed him to commit even more sin.

In the next section (vv. 13-25), Paul at first appears to introduce yet another dimension of the unfolding argument, initiated with another rhetorical question much like the one posed earlier in v. 7: "Did what is good, then, bring death to me?" (v. 13). He answers with the same retort, "By no means!" (μὴ γένοιτο), which he follows with a prose explanation that continues the biographical form of the previous section: "It was sin, working death in me, through what is good, in order that sin might be shown to be sin, and through the commandment might become sinful beyond measure." Here, Paul restates what he has alluded to at several points in the epistle (e.g., 3:20; 5:20), that the purpose of the law was to demonstrate the true nature and power of sin. In one sense, his explanation adds little by way of new content to what he has just said in the previous verses, where he described sin as a demonic force that seizes the opportunity afforded by the law to produce all manner

---

26. Opinions vary on this question, although virtually everyone who examines the epistle from a rhetorical perspective follows the suggestion of Kümmel, that Paul is not speaking autobiographically, but instead, using *prosopopoeia*, or the "speech-in-character." Perhaps the strongest case is made by Stowers, who offers a detailed account of this figure from a variety of classical sources (*Rereading of Romans*, 16-21); see also Witherington, *Paul's Letter to the Romans*, 179-94. Others, such as Dunn and Middendorf, have argued that Paul's "I" language throughout Rom. 7 is autobiographical; see James D. G. Dunn, *Romans 1–8* (Dallas: Word, 1988); Michael P. Middendorf, *The "I" in the Storm: A Study of Romans 7* (St. Louis: Concordia, 1997). Jewett argues that "Paul's speech-in-character is artificially constructed in light of his preconversion experience as a zealot, but with an eye to the current situation in the Roman churches. It is formulated in such generic terms that persons outside of Paul's circle of experience can apply the argument to themselves" (*Romans*, 444). Moo, who leans toward the autobiographical explanation, nevertheless admits that "even those who see it not as a rhetorical figure but, instead, as autobiographical, still understand that he is speaking in some sense within a persona" (*Epistle to the Romans*, 448).

of sin. In the verses that follow, however, he takes up that same basic content and this time begins to dramatize the reality of sin becoming "sinful beyond measure" (ἵνα γένηται καθ᾽ ὑπερβολὴν ἁμαρτωλὸς ἡ ἁμαρτία, v. 13). To do so, he resorts not to further argument but, instead, to mimetic performance.

Performing Despair: Paul's "Speech-in-Character"

Paul's authorial voice shifts dramatically in v. 14, as he moves into what is now a highly personal mode of address. He no longer speaks to his audience directly; instead he speaks in soliloquy, as he vividly represents the outcome of sin's power, brought to its full fruition by the introduction of the law. In v. 13 Paul had employed the visual term, φαίνω (to "appear" or "be seen," from the same word group as *phantasia*, the human capacity for visualization), in order to describe the way that the law causes sin to be "seen" for what it is. Now, he actually embodies that reality in a way that brings the anguish of the law's curse "before the eyes" of his audience.

Scholars have been sharply divided, of course, over whether Paul is speaking autobiographically here, or whether this represents simply a theatrical creation designed to reinforce his earlier claims. When the text is viewed in terms of its persuasive intent, however, the answer to this question is immaterial, since the function is ultimately the same whether the "Paul" we encounter here is fictional or not. Therefore, as regards persuasive function, at least, Stowers is correct in arguing that Paul is speaking in the form of *prosopopoeia,* or what he terms the "speech-in-character."[27] Theon's *Progymnasmata* described *prosopopoeia* as "the introduction of a person to whom words are attributed that are suitable to the speaker and have an indisputable application to the subject discussed" (8). In other words, it is a dramatic performance in which the speaker takes on the persona of a historical or imaginary character, or even impersonates some abstract quality or concept, such as virtues or vices, meant to add "vividness and color and appeal to the emotions of the audience, often the emotion of pity."[28] In just this way, Paul in v. 14 launches into what Theissen described as "an inner dialogue that

---

27. Although Paul does not identify God directly here, his language clearly infers God's agency behind this function of the law. As Moo put it, "The two clauses [in v. 14] state the divine and ultimately positive purpose behind sin's destructive use of the law" (*Epistle to the Romans*, 452).

28. Tobin, *Paul's Rhetoric*, 227.

leads more and more deeply into destructive self-condemnation":[29] "For we know that the law is spiritual; but I am of the flesh, sold into slavery under sin. I do not understand my own actions. For I do not do what I want, but I do the very thing I hate."[30]

Several features underscore the passage's mimetic character. Clearly, we encounter a stark change in voice in v. 14, where Paul begins to speak exclusively in the first person. Although he had introduced the first person in the previous verses, in that case the audience still might have encountered that persona as Paul conversing with them directly, as he had done in v. 1. Now, however, it is clear that Paul has shifted from addressing them to taking on the voice of the victim of self-condemnation. Longinus noted the power of that kind of shift in voice, where the writer, talking *about* a person, "suddenly turns and changes into the person himself. A figure of this kind is a sort of outbreak of emotion" (*Subl.*, 21.1). Additionally, Paul's shift from past to present tense imbues the dramatic moment with a sense of presence, along the lines Longinus predicted when he said that by placing past events in the present, "the passage will be transformed from a narrative into a vivid actuality" (*Subl.*, 25.1). Longinus also observed that certain modes of sentence structure imitate how people actually communicate when they experience intense anger, fear, or indignation. Under the influence of such vehement emotions, they

> often put forward one point and then spring off to another with various illogical interpolations, and then wheel around again to their original

29. Gerd Theissen, *Psychological Aspects of Pauline Theology*, trans. John P. Galvin (Philadelphia: Fortress, 1987), 260.

30. Scholars differ as to whose experience, precisely, Paul is attempting to capture in this text, depending on whom they see as the audience of the epistle. Although Paul clearly envisions the Mosaic law, some see the passage as representing the experience of Gentiles whose introduction to Christianity came through their attachment to Judaism, and who therefore placed a high value in keeping the law. See Stowers, *Rereading of Romans*; also Emma Wasserman, "The Death of the Soul in Romans 7: Revisiting Paul's Anthropology in Light of Hellenistic Moral Psychology," *Journal of Biblical Literature* 126 (2007): 793-816, who found the background to Paul's argument in the Platonic ideas of conflict between the rational mind and the passions. Moo, based on his understanding that the epistle addresses a mixed audience, but one made up primarily of Gentiles, argued that "Paul speaks as a 'representative' Jew, detailing his past in order to reveal the weakness of the law and the source of that weakness, the *egō*" (*Epistle to the Romans*, 448). Whether directed explicitly toward Gentiles, or to a mixed audience, Witherington is correct to assert that the text captures "the general malaise of fallen humanity when it comes to sin, death, and the Law" (*Paul's Letter to the Romans*, 198).

position, while, under the stress of their excitement, like a ship before a veering wind, they lay their words and thoughts first on one tack then another (*Subl.*, 22.1).

Accordingly, Paul's style becomes increasingly frenetic, mimetically capturing the despair of a person in existential crisis, as he caroms from the admission, "I agree that the law is good," to the hyperbolic declaration, "I know that nothing good dwells within me." His language captures the increasingly vehement expression of self-loathing of one who "hates" (μισέω)[31] what he does, using vivid war metaphors to describe his struggle with sin — that part of himself wages war against his best intention, taking him captive to sin, so that he is "sold under sin." As Dunn observed,

> There is a strong existential edge to this sustained usage. . . . The metaphor is expressed in its most extreme form here since it speaks not only of warfare but of defeat (αἰχμαλωτίζεσθαι). This is consistent with the other most prominent metaphor in preceding sections, slavery, since defeat in battle usually resulted in the prisoners of war being sold as slaves.[32]

All of this leads to his cry of desolation in v. 24: "Wretched man that I am! Who will rescue me from this body of death?" Witherington described it well: "This person has reached the point of despair over human inability to please God and do his will and cries out for help."[33]

Taken together, the vehement language and frenetic style, along with the shifts in tense and person, artfully transform a line of rational argumentation into a dramatic performance that brings before the eyes of Paul's audience a vision of a tortured soul, torn, frantic, at war with itself, and finally, overcome with despair. No longer is the audience the direct target of Paul's logical persuasion; instead, they now overhear an anguished inner dialogue.[34] To

---

31. Dunn, *Romans 1–8*, 389. Dunn noted, "The use of μισέω as the antithesis to θέλω is striking: he 'hates, abhors, detests' what he does. The disowning is much sharper here: he wholly destests what he does, as one 'sold under sin' (v 14)."

32. Dunn, *Romans 1–8*, 295.

33. Witherington, *Paul's Letter to the Romans*, 204-5; so clearly does this exclamation draw on a common dramatic form that Stowers went to far as to claim that it "reads almost as a parody of the tragic outcry" (*Rereading of Romans*, 271).

34. As Jewett observed, "By maintaining the first person possessive μου ('my'), Paul maintains the 'speech-in-character' that dramatizes his own experience with the law, thus avoiding any direct accusation against the groups in Rome" (*Romans*, 471).

what end does Paul create this dramatic performance? Clearly, it reinforces the claims he made earlier that the law functioned to expose sin for what it is and even to cause a full flowering of sin, as a prelude to the coming of grace. But rather than simply explaining or proving that point logically, Paul instead brings his hearers into a vicarious experience of the reality that his argument was advancing. Indeed, beyond merely proving that the law is no longer in force (an especially important aim for those in his audience who still placed a high value on the law), Paul brings them symbolically into the existential crisis in which the setting aside of the law now becomes a source of relief, so that they go from resisting the argument to eagerly welcoming the argument's conclusion. As Longinus put it, "Besides developing his factual argument, the orator has visualized the event and consequently his conception far exceeds the limits of mere persuasion" (*Subl.*, 15.10). In short, that mimetic experience was more powerful than any argument could ever be.

Paul's Drama and the "Argument" of Romans

Paul's dramatic performance of the anguished sinner takes up the position for which he had offered logical arguments and recasts that understanding of the law as a mimetic performance in which the anguished sinner experiences self-condemnation, despair, and finally, the freedom of forgiveness. In doing so, he invites his audience to experience extrarationally both the purpose of the law and the release from the law's authority, both of which lie at the heart of his understanding of salvation history. But of course, more is at stake for Paul than simply proving his claim about the role of the Law in salvation history. His understanding of salvation by grace through faith, rather than by law, has raised urgent questions about Christian behavior, which he addresses explicitly in chap. 6: If the Law no longer has power over the believer, what motivation will there be to pursue righteousness? Or as he puts it in 6:15, "Should we sin because we are not under law but under grace?" Related and equally pressing is Paul's concern for unity between Jews and Gentiles in the Christian church, an issue that represents a central aim of the entire epistle and, indeed, lies at the heart of Paul's entire sense of calling to be an apostle.

For Paul the answer to all three questions lay in their common experience of what might be called "radical conversion." As his story is told three times in Acts (chaps. 9, 22, and 26), and alluded to at other points in his writings (e.g., Gal. 1:11-17), Paul's conversion to Christianity constituted nothing less than a dramatic and total reorientation of his entire life. In Gal. 1:13-14, he reminds the Galatians of "how intensely I persecuted the church of God and tried to destroy it. I was advancing in Judaism beyond many Jews of my own age and was extremely zealous for the traditions of my fathers." So dramatic was the change in his life that his conversion sent shock waves through the church as they received this report: "The one who formerly was persecuting us is now proclaiming the faith he once tried to destroy" (1:23). Later, in 1 Cor. 15:9-10, Paul will describe the motivation that grew out of his experience of conversion: "I . . . do not even deserve to be called an apostle because I persecuted the church of God. But by the grace of God I am what I am, and his grace to me was not without effect. No, I worked harder than all of them — yet not I, but the grace of God that was with me."[35] Thus, for Paul, the motivation for righteous living lies in a deep sense of gratitude for grace, an understanding that is clear in the primary petition with which he opens the paraenesis of Rom. 12–14: "I appeal to you therefore, brothers and sisters, by the mercies of God, to present your bodies as a living sacrifice, holy and acceptable to God, which is your spiritual worship." As Romans makes clear, Paul also assumes that the common experience of conversion would also serve as the foundation for unity between Jews and Gentiles in the Christian community. Thus, he offers a lengthy argument that all, Jews and Gentiles alike, are in sin and under God's wrath (1:18–3:20), but now, by God's grace, have had revealed to them "the righteousness from God" that is "apart from law," leading to the "redemption that is in Christ Jesus"(3:21, 24). That common experience allowed him to assert, "There is no distinction [i.e., between Jew and Gentile; cf. 10:11, where the identical construction is used], since all have sinned and fall short of the glory of God; they are now justified by his grace as a gift" (3:22-24).[36]

---

35. As Tobin argued, the same understanding underlies Paul's response to the so-called "Judaizers" in Phil. 3:2-11, who sought to impose observance of the Mosaic law on the Christians there. "On the basis of his own experience of knowing Christ . . . all else is in comparison rubbish. He includes the Mosaic law in this. . . . Put rather scholastically, if the surpassing worth of knowing Christ is sufficient, then the law is no longer necessary" (*Paul's Rhetoric*, 250).

36. In fact, as Tobin pointed out, it was Paul's own experience and his "conviction that righteousness was a gift of God received through faith by Jews and Gentiles alike apart from observance of the law" that raised the problem of the law in the first place. As he put it, Paul could not live out his calling as apostle to the Gentiles "and at the same time continue observance of the Mosaic law, the institution that was the basis for the distinction between Jews and Gentiles" (*Paul's Rhetoric*, 246, 250).

Paul indicates at several points in the epistle his understanding that the process of conversion follows a predictable path — a path much like that of his own conversion — from a desperate awareness of one's utter sinfulness and abject helplessness to attain one's own righteousness, which opens one to the reception of God's grace and forgiveness. Thus, his catalog of Gentile *and* Jewish sinfulness in chaps. 1–3 reaches its devastating climax in the catena of quotations from the Hebrew Scriptures:

> There is no one who is righteous, not even one;
> there is no one who has understanding,
> there is no one who seeks God.
> All have turned aside, together they have become worthless;
> there is no one who shows kindness,
> there is not even one.
> Their throats are opened graves;
> they use their tongues to deceive.
> The venom of vipers is under their lips.
> Their mouths are full of cursing and bitterness.
> Their feet are swift to shed blood;
> ruin and misery are in their paths,
> and the way of peace they have not known.
> There is no fear of God before their eyes (Rom. 3:10-18).

This leads directly into his pronouncement, "But now, apart from law, the righteousness of God has been disclosed . . . the righteousness of God through faith in Jesus Christ for all who believe" (Rom. 3:21-22). Later, in 7:5-6, Paul offers a second brief summary of the conversion experience that reflects the same process, similarly cast as a "before and after" narrative:[37]

> While we were living in the flesh, our sinful passions, aroused by the law, were at work in our members to bear fruit for death. But now we are discharged from the law, dead to that which held us captive, so that we are slaves not under the old written code but in the new life of the Spirit.

Thus, for Paul, the key to both motivation and unity in the church is the common experience of conversion and the visceral sense of gratitude for

---

37. As Tobin stated, "The temporal character of the contrast is emphasized by the 'then' and 'now' contrast at the beginning of each verse" (*Paul's Rhetoric*, 223).

having received as a gift what one could never have achieved on one's own: liberation from sin and death.

But Paul also seems to understand that rational argument by itself can never create the kind of deep, indelible memory of redemption that would be needed to undergird both the mutual forbearance and the commitment to righteous living which both lie at the heart of Christian faith. Instead, what his hearers need is a vivid, phenomenological consciousness of actually going through that process in their own experience. And this, ultimately, he provides them in the *prosopopoeia* of 7:14-25. Having given them an extended argument about the role of the law, he now transports them into a dramatic experience that takes them from past (7:7-11) to present (7:14-23), leading to the climactic cry of despair in the future tense, "Who will rescue me from this body of death?" (7:24). For his answer, Paul "breaks forth in a 'joyful shout' that reiterates the ecstatic cry of 6:17, thanking God for deliverance that would otherwise be impossible":[38] "Thanks be to God through Jesus Christ our Lord!" (v. 25).

As Witherington concluded,

> We need to take seriously that Paul is describing a crisis experience that leads to a crying out for help here. . . . What we have then in 7:14-25 and continuing into the next argument in ch. 8 is a narrative of a conversion and its theological and spiritual implications seen after the fact and from a Christian perspective.[39]

In this way, when Paul declares in 8:1, "There is therefore now no condemnation for those who are in Christ Jesus," and later when he asks, "Who will bring any charge against God's elect? . . . Who is to condemn?" (8:33-34), the Romans are prepared to hear a confident response, because they have already experienced it subjectively. But likewise, when they are challenged to "offer their bodies as living sacrifices," living ethically and seeking unity in the church, all out of a sense of gratitude for the "mercies of God," they are also prepared to meet the challenge, since they have known those mercies not simply as an abstract idea but as a visceral experience.

---

38. Jewett, *Romans*, 472.
39. Witherington, *Paul's Letter to the Romans*, 198.

Conclusion

A number of scholars have suggested that the language with which Paul casts his tortured expression of despair might reflect the influence of the tragic figure of Medea, who anguishes over her love for Jason.[40] For example, Ovid's *Metamorphoses* (7.18) has her say, "Love urges one thing; reason another. I see, and I desire the better; I follow the worse." Seneca's Medea cries out to herself, "What, wretched woman, have I done?" (*Med.*, 92). Each example derives from a persona in the poetic and not the rhetorical tradition. Yet commentators typically describe Rom. 7:14-25 in argumentative terms, as an "explanation" or, perhaps, an "analysis" of the human condition, terms that reflect highly rationalistic assumptions about the nature both of Paul's discourse and of religious faith in general.[41] Such an approach fails to do justice to the imaginative power through which this passage's content is conveyed.

In this chapter, I have argued for an altogether different understanding of this text, highlighting it as a prime example of the kind of mimetic performance embedded within an otherwise logical train of reasoning, a type of discourse which Longinus viewed as the pinnacle of oratorical excellence. Such deft activation of the audience's imagination in support of factual argument, he said, "not only convinces the audience, it positively masters them" (*Subl.*, 15.9). Paul dramatically performs the helplessness, self-condemnation, and despair of the person who longs to keep the law but finds himself powerless to do so. By virtue of their common experience, as well as the human propensity toward empathy, he hopes his hearers will be compelled to share that experience vicariously. By doing so, they will grasp "in their guts" the claims that he had earlier directed toward their "minds," that the law's purpose was actually to increase sin as a way of ending once and for all any human claim to self-righteousness, and that with the coming of Christ, the law was no longer binding on God's people. At the same time, by taking the audience through that common experience of self-condemnation and despair and then into a state of blissful relief brought on by the sudden awareness of grace, he seeks to transport all of the members of his audience,

40. Stowers, *Rereading of Romans*, 271-72. Stowers also notes that just before he introduces the example of Medea, Epictetus employs what Stowers calls the "fictive I": "Who is more wretched than I?" (*Discourses* 2.17.18). See also Witherington, *Paul's Letter to the Romans*, 195; and Moo, *Epistle to the Romans*, 452.

41. Moo (*Epistle to the Romans*, 453) sees Paul in this text as "explaining" concepts related to sin and the law. Witherington describes this passage as an "*analysis* of the general malaise of fallen humanity" (*Paul's Letter to the Romans*, 198, emphasis added).

Jew and Gentile, into a shared phenomenological consciousness of the kind of religious conversion experience that he believes is a prerequisite to unity in the church. Finally, he hopes that the experience of gratitude that his audience feels in response to their newfound freedom from condemnation will provide the motivation for ethical living that will become the focus of his exhortation in chaps. 12–14.

CHAPTER FOUR

Rhapsody on Love (1 Corinthians 13)

In his discussion of digression (*eggressio*), which he understands as any point in a speech where an orator departs from the speech's prescribed argumentative form in order to "express indignation, pity, hatred, rebuke, excuse, conciliation," and the like, Quintilian cites as an example a moment when Cicero is preparing to extol the virtues of the Roman general Pompey the Younger: "The divine orator" is suddenly "stopped in his tracks as if it were by the general's name, breaks off the topic on which he had embarked and plunges straight into his digression" (*Inst.* 4.3.13). Such departures from the proper *stasis* of an argument, Quintilian believes, represent opportunities to

> amplify or abridge a topic, make any kind of emotional appeal or introduce any of those topics which add such charm and elegance to oratory, topics that is to say such as luxury, avarice, religion, duty: but these would hardly seem to be digressions as they are so closely attached to the arguments on similar subjects that they form part of the texture of the speech (*Inst.* 4.3.15).

This kind of display, he admits, might help keep the oration from appearing "cold and repulsive." But as Walton pointed out, Quintilian also believes that such diversions are ultimately irrelevant to judging the argumentation of the speech itself and, indeed, such violations of the prescribed argumentative form could actually be misleading because of their appearance of relevance.[1] Quintilian's treatment is notable for the ambivalence he shows toward

---

1. Douglas N. Walton, *Relevance in Argumentation* (Mahwah, NJ: Erlbaum, 2004), 32-33.

digression. Although effective pragmatically, in a conceptual framework where the aim of discourse is the critical judgment of logical arguments, such flights of oratorical fancy hardly seem appropriate.

NT scholars have shown a similar ambivalence toward Paul's rhapsody on love in 1 Cor. 13. Compared to its immediate context, chaps. 12 and 14, the markedly different style and language with which it was written have led some to question its connection with the rest of the epistle altogether. Conzelmann called it a "self-contained unity" with "ragged" links to the rest of chaps. 12–14, and Walker asserted that it was a non-Pauline interpolation.[2] Fee, on the other hand, spoke for a number of scholars when he argued that the passage was "fully relevant to the context, and without it the succeeding argument would lose much of its force."[3] Commentators frequently analyze the passage in terms of its "argument," as if Paul were simply advancing propositions for his audience's assent.[4] As other scholars have long recognized, however, this "poem of praise" possesses such a lyrical quality that many early interpreters argued that it was actually a hymn — a proposal that, although no longer seriously entertained, underscores its poetic character.[5]

In this chapter, I argue that although in form and function 1 Cor. 13 perhaps can be explained more easily in terms of traditional rhetoric than the other passages examined in this study, even here, Paul aims for more than simply securing the audience's agreements to claims regarding the

2. Hans Conzelmann, *1 Corinthians*, trans. James W. Leitch (Philadelphia: Fortress, 1975), 217; William O. Walker, "Is First Corinthians 13 a Non-Pauline Interpolation?" *Catholic Biblical Quarterly* 60 (1998): 484-99; for a point-by-point refutation of Walker's argument, see Jeremy Corley, "The Pauline Authorship of 1 Corinthians 13," *Catholic Biblical Quarterly* 66 (2004): 256-74.

3. Gordon D. Fee, *The First Epistle to the Corinthians* (Grand Rapids: Eerdmans, 1987), 626.

4. Mitchell, for example, labels chap. 13 a "sub-argument" within a larger deliberative discourse on spiritual gifts; Margaret M. Mitchell, *Paul and the Rhetoric of Reconciliation: An Exegetical Investigation of the Language and Composition of 1 Corinthians* (Louisville: Westminster John Knox, 1993), 270-73.

5. "Poem of praise" is Ryken's designation (Leland Ryken, *Words of Delight: A Literary Introduction to the Bible* [Grand Rapids: Baker Books, 1992], 474). For a brief discussion of the history of the interpretation of 1 Cor. 13 as a hymn, see D. A. Carson, *Showing the Spirit: A Theological Exposition of 1 Corinthians 12–14* (Grand Rapids: Baker Books, 1987), 52-53. Of the three examples from Greek and Jewish literature that Conzelmann offers as parallels to 1 Cor. 13, two have strong connections to the poetic tradition. The first is a poem from the 7th-century poet, Tyrtaeus, and the second, a passage from Plato, is an "ironical imitation of the style of the tragedian Agathon" (*1 Corinthians*, 219 n. 17).

superiority of love over all other forms of religiosity.[6] Rather, he uses poetic style and structure to create a mimetic performance that, he hopes, will imaginatively transport his hearers into an experience of love's grandeur, as a way of provoking the kind of self-awareness and emotional disposition that are needed to employ spiritual gifts with a sense of humility and proportion. Rather than being a diversion, then, Paul's encomium of love is actually a crucial centerpiece in his treatment of spiritual gifts, providing powerful motivation for pursuing unity in the Corinthian church. In what follows, I first summarize the rhetorical situation to which Paul addressed the epistle and analyze the larger context of the passage, which consists of his treatment of spiritual gifts in the church in chaps. 12–14. This provides the context for the following close examination of Paul's rhapsody of love.

Spiritual Gifts and Interpersonal Conflict in the Corinthian Church

If 1 Corinthians is any indication, Paul faced few more serious challenges to his work as an apostle than those presented by the church in Corinth, a church that he had personally founded.[7] Both 1 and 2 Corinthians show his

---

6. As Joop F. M. Smit ("The Genre of 1 Corinthians in the Light of Classical Rhetoric," *Novum Testamentum* 33 [1991]: 193-216) pointed out, writers in the classical tradition struggled with the place of epideictic rhetoric (of which the encomium is a species) in relation to the other two clearly argumentative forms, deliberative and judicial, as well as in its distinctiveness from poetic: "In this genre . . . speaking is made an art, . . . [like] literature, even poetry" (p. 198). In this connection he cited the observation of Perelman and Olbrechts-Tyteca: "In epideictic oratory every device of literary art is appropriated, for it is a matter of combining all of the factors that can promote this communion of the audience. It is the only kind of oratory which immediately evokes literature, the only one that might be compared to the libretto of a cantata." These observations about the close connection between poetry and the epideictic genre of rhetoric support my contention for the appropriateness of exploring the function of an epideictic passage such as 1 Cor. 13 from a poetic as well as a rhetorical perspective. See also Chaim Perelman and Lucie Olbrechts-Tyteca, *The New Rhetoric: A Treatise on Argumentation* (Notre Dame: University of Notre Dame Press, 1969), 51.

7. With the exception of Ephesus, in which he spent three years immediately following his work in Corinth, Paul appears to have remained longer in Corinth than in any other city in which he established a church, a total of eighteen months. For a discussion of the chronology of Paul's mission work, see W. H. C. Frend, *The Rise of Christianity* (Philadelphia: Fortress, 1984), 85-117; and Williston Walker, *A History of the Christian Church*, rev. Cyril C. Richardson, Wilhelm Pauck, and Robert Handy (New York: Scribners, 1970), 24-29. For a historical reconstruction of Paul's involvement with the Corinthian church, see F. F. Bruce, *Paul: Apostle of the Heart Set Free* (Grand Rapids: Eerdmans, 1977), 248-79; Donald Guthrie, *New Testament*

relationship with the Corinthians to have been frequently tumultuous and, at times, openly hostile and combative.[8] With no other church did Paul face as many theological aberrations, ethical lapses, or threats to his authority as an apostle than with the Corinthian church. Indeed, a cursory reading points to 1 Cor. as an *ad hoc* response to a whole succession of problems and questions brought to Paul's attention by at least two sources, and possibly as many as four.[9] The first of these was a letter from the Corinthians to Paul, perhaps carried by a delegation consisting of three persons, Stephanus, Fortunatus, and Achaicus.[10] Some of these questions had likely come in

Introduction (Downers Grove: InterVarsity, 1970), 424-39; Richard A. Horsley, *1 Corinthians* (Nashville: Abingdon, 1998), 28-33; Joseph A. Fitzmyer, *First Corinthians: A New Translation with Introduction and Commentary* (New Haven: Yale University Press, 2008), 38-45. For an account that focuses particularly on the way that Roman society emphasized social status, with its implications for the Corinthian community, see Ben Witherington III, *Conflict and Community in Corinth: A Socio-Rhetorical Commentary on 1 and 2 Corinthians* (Grand Rapids: Eerdmans, 1995), 22-29.

8. In addition to 1 and 2 Cor., Paul appears to have written two other letters to the Corinthians, which are not preserved in the NT. In 1 Cor. 5:9 he mentions a previous letter in which he urged them "not to associate with sexually immoral persons." Then, in 2 Cor. 2:4, he refers to a letter written "out of much distress and anguish of heart and with many tears." Some scholars have argued, however, that 2 Cor. is actually a composite of as many as three separate Pauline letters, including at least a portion of the two "lost" letters. According to this theory, 2 Cor. 6:14–7:1 is identified with the "previous letter" referred to in 1 Cor. 5:9 and 2 Cor. 10–13 contains the "sorrowful" letter referred to in 2 Cor. 2:4. For discussion, see Luke Timothy Johnson, *Writings of the New Testament: An Interpretation* (rev. ed.; Minneapolis: Fortress, 2002), 274-75; Guthrie, *New Testament Introduction*, 421-49; Everett F. Harrison, *Introduction to the New Testament* (Grand Rapids: Eerdmans, 1971), 282-98; and Werner Georg Kümmel, *Introduction to the New Testament*, trans. Howard Clark Kee (Nashville: Abingdon, 1996), 269-79.

9. Dunn suggests that Paul may have received information about the Corinthian church from Apollos himself; see James G. D. Dunn, *1 Corinthians* (London: T & T Clark, 2003), 18.

10. The portion of the letter that begins in 1 Cor. 7:1 is introduced by the phrase, "Now concerning the matters about which you wrote." In the closing of the letter (16:17-18), Paul specifically mentions the coming of Stephanus, Fortunatus, and Achaicus. On this basis it is usually assumed that the delegation brought the Corinthians' letter to Paul. See, for example, Kümmel, *Introduction to the New Testament*, 272; F. F. Bruce, *1 and 2 Corinthians* (Greenwood: Attic, 1971), 24; Fee, *First Epistle to the Corinthians*, 7. However, Elisabeth Schüssler Fiorenza has offered a different reconstruction, arguing that while the Corinthians' letter represented a hostile reaction to Paul's teaching, the delegation led by Stephanus was apparently supportive of his influence among the Corinthians, judging from Paul's favorable mention of them in 16:17-18; see Schüssler Fiorenza, "Rhetorical Situation and Historical Construction in 1 Corinthians," *New Testament Studies* 33 (1987):386-403. Schüssler Fiorenza wrote, "It appears that he [Stephanus] arrived later and gave Paul a more positive view of the situation at Corinth, so that Paul could rely on him to present his response to the community and to see to it that his

response to a letter Paul had written to the church sometime earlier (referred to in 1 Cor. 5:9), while others may simply have arisen among the Christians themselves. Around the same time, or perhaps subsequent to the arrival of the delegation, he received the distressing news from persons associated with a woman named Chloe, an individual acquainted with the Corinthian church, that serious problems had arisen among the congregation — among them, severe divisions in the church, an occurrence of incest, and instances of Christians taking one another to court.[11] In addition to these problems, Paul also became aware (from which source we cannot be sure), that at least some among the Corinthians were openly rejecting the doctrine of the resurrection of the dead. Finally, complicating Paul's ability to address these problems was the fact that some among the community had begun to resist Paul's authority, either because of what they perceived as his lack of skill as an orator — by his own admission, he proclaimed the Gospel "not with wisdom of words" (οὐκ ἐν σοφίᾳ λόγου, 1 Cor. 1:17, KJV)[12] — or because

---

instructions were followed, for the community is told to subordinate itself to Stephanus and his co-workers" (394).

11. Regarding the issue of division, a number of scholars have argued that a core problem in the Corinthian church had to do with a rivalry between those who professed allegiance to Paul versus Apollos, which occupies much of the first part of the epistle. For two detailed treatments of this problem, see Joop F. M. Smit, "'What Is Apollos? What Is Paul?' In Search for the Coherence of First Corinthians 1:10–4:21," *Novum Testamentum* 44 (2002), 231-51; and Maria Pascuzzi, "Baptism-based Allegiance and the Divisions in Corinth: A Reexamination of 1 Corinthians 1:13-17," *Catholic Biblical Quarterly* 71 (2009): 813-29.

12. Paul goes on to admit that he had come to the Corinthians οὐ καθ' ὑπεροχὴν λόγου ἢ σοφίας ("not . . . [with] lofty words or wisdom") as he proclaimed to them "the mystery of God" (1 Cor. 2:1). To the contrary, he presented the gospel to them "in weakness and in fear and in much trembling" (2:3). In 2 Cor. 10:10, Paul quotes opponents who have gone so far as to make this accusation against him: "His letters are weighty and strong, but his bodily presence is weak, and his speech contemptible." For some among the Corinthians, this lack of eloquence raised serious doubts about his credibility, as they evaluated Paul and other Christian teachers in terms of the itinerant orators and philosophers known as the sophists, for whom influence and authority were determined by oratorical eloquence. So common was sophistic oratory in the ancient world, Winter argues, that an audience could be expected to respond to a speaker out of a set of expectations informed by this rhetorical tradition: "Perceptive audiences noted whether the structure of a particular oration conformed to the canons laid down in the rhetorical handbooks. It was also their expectation that an orator would have a charismatic presence, including a striking physique, a well-resonated voice, an impressive wardrobe, and a commanding presence" (Bruce W. Winter, "Is Paul among the Sophists?" *Reformed Theological Review* 53 [1994]: 28-38, here 28-29). See also C. K. Barrett, *The First Epistle to the Corinthians* (San Francisco: Harper and Row, 1968), 49; Fee, *First Epistle to the Corinthians*, 94; Simon J. Kistemaker, *Exposition of the First Epistle to the Corinthians* (Grand Rapids: Baker, 1993), 72-73.

of the fact that he had supported himself as a tradesperson,[13] or for other reasons that elude us.[14]

A number of scholars have sought to discover a single underlying cause of this array of problems, as a way both to explain the situation in Corinth and also to demonstrate the unity of the epistle.[15] At one point, it was common for scholars to see behind the various problems in Corinth a fundamental misunderstanding of Christian eschatology — what some termed an "over-realized eschatology."[16] More recently, however, scholars have viewed

13. For at least some of the Corinthians, the fact that Paul supported himself through his work as a tradesman, rather than accepting their financial support of his ministry in Corinth, represented a further reason to reject his authority. Apparently, as Fee put it, "they were either offended by his not accepting their patronage or they questioned the apostleship of one who acted thus — or perhaps both" (*First Epistle to the Corinthians*, 27). So vexing was this "festering sore" between Paul and the Corinthians that he addresses it no less than three different times in the two Corinthian epistles (1 Cor. 9:3-18; 2 Cor. 11:7-11; 12:11-18). The combative tone with which he addresses this subject, moreover, indicates that it was quite a point of contention between them (Fee, *First Epistle to the Corinthians*, 9; see also his discussion of the sociological background in which such a practice would have been considered both demeaning and offensive; *First Epistle to the Corinthians*, 398-400). See also Gerd Theissen, *The Social Setting of Pauline Christianity*, trans. and ed. John H. Schütz (Philadelphia: Fortress, 1982), 44-46, which treats extensively both Paul's refusal to accept financial support and his desire to work at a trade. Another excellent treatment of the background to this issue is Peter Marshall, *Enmity in Corinth: Social Conventions in Paul's Relations with the Corinthians* (Tübingen: Mohr Siebeck, 1987), 165-258.

14. Nils Dahl, in his historical reconstruction, argued that the circumstances which occasioned Paul's writing of 1 Cor. may have brought their ambivalence toward Paul to a point of crisis. As he described the situation, there were a number of areas of controversy among the Corinthians, many of them in response to the instructions Paul had given in the "previous letter." Stephanus, as the head of the delegation bringing the letter to Paul, was "quite an advocate of writing a letter to Paul to ask for his opinion on controversial questions" ("Paul and the Church at Corinth according to 1 Corinthians 1:10–4:21," in *Christian History and Interpretation: Studies Presented to John Knox*, ed. William R. Farmer, C. F. D. Moule, and R. R. Niebuhr [Cambridge: Cambridge University Press, 1967], 324-25). Thus, the very fact that Paul was to be consulted may have brought their opposition to Paul to a head.

15. As Thiselton noted, scholars have suggested the presence of as many as nine different letters making up the present epistle. See Anthony C. Thiselton, *The First Epistle to the Corinthians: A Commentary on the Greek Text* (Grand Rapids: Eerdmans, 2000), 36-41. Although the position is not unanimous, the majority opinion more recently has tended to accept the letter's integrity, influenced by the strong case made from a rhetorical-critical perspective by Mitchell.

16. The classic study of this phenomenon among the Corinthians is Anthony C. Thiselton, "Realized Eschatology at Corinth," *New Testament Studies* 24 (1977-78): 510-26. As Barrett described it, "The Corinthians are behaving as if the age to come were already consummated, as if the saints had already taken over the kingdom . . . ; for them there is no 'not yet' to qualify the

the problems as resulting from socioeconomic divisions, and especially from the emphasis on values related to status and power in Roman society. As Witherington put it, most of the Corinthians' problems, with the possible exception of their misunderstanding of the resurrection addressed in chap. 15, "were social, not theological in origin."[17] Mitchell went so far as to argue that all of the problems in the Corinthian church were the result of factionalism:

> 1 Corinthians is throughout an argument for ecclesial unity, as centered in the πρόθεσις, or thesis statement of the argument, in 1:10: "I urge you, brothers and sisters, through the name of our lord Jesus Christ, to all say the same thing, and to let there not be factions among you, but to be reconciled in the same mind and in the same opinions."[18]

While Mitchell's position has been influential, others have questioned whether she overplayed this problem, and have instead attributed the prob-

---

'already' of realized eschatology" (*First Epistle to the Corinthians*, 109). Noting both the roots of the problem and its ethical implications, Käsemann and Leitch argue that the Corinthians were operating out of a "sacramental realism which sees complete redemption to have already been effected, in that by baptism a heavenly spiritual body has been conferred and the earthly body has been degraded to an insubstantial, transitory veil. This is the root of all that has gone wrong in Corinth; the contempt for discipline and decency, the want of consideration for the weaker brother at the Lord's Supper and in daily life; the rise of women ecstatically gifted and the over-valuing of glossolalia and sexual asceticism, which are being regarded as the outward expressions of angelic status" (Ernst Käsemann and James Waterson Leitch, "On the Topic of Primitive Christian Apocalyptic," *Journal for Theology and the Church* 6 [1969]: 99-133, here 126). More generally, "realized eschatology" is the name which NT scholars frequently use to describe the tension clearly present in the New Testament between "the mission of Jesus in history" and the inauguration of the "new age" and its consummation at the parousia. Thus, the NT writers can speak of a sense in which the new age is somehow realized in Christian experience in the present, even as its completion is anticipated in the future. As Ladd put it, "The fulfillment occurs in this age; the consummation awaits the eschatological age to come"; see Gerhard E. Ladd, "Eschatology," in *The International Standard Bible Encyclopedia*, ed. Geoffrey W. Bromiley (Grand Rapids: Eerdmans, 1979-88), 2:133-40.

17. Witherington, *Conflict and Community*, 74. Although he concurs with a similar position as that of Witherington — that the problems in Corinth were the result not of a "Corinthian heresy" but of factions in the church — Grindheim nevertheless argued that they still risked "grave theological error": "By attempting to excel by worldly standards the Corinthians were running the risk of defining themselves as those for whom the gospel was hidden and thus forfeiting their salvation"; see Sigurd Grindheim, "Wisdom for the Perfect: Paul's Advice to the Corinthian Church (1 Corinthians 2:6-16)," *Journal of Biblical Literature* 121 (2002): 689-709, here 689-90.

18. Mitchell, *Paul and the Rhetoric of Reconciliation*, 1.

lems more generally to the Corinthians' lack of maturity and their background in paganism, a position reflected in Lee's assessment:

> In dealing with the situation at Corinth, Paul was faced not only with the immediate problems in the congregation, such as the abuse of tongues, but with the greater problem of how to bring a young, formerly pagan people to maturity in Christ. For Paul, the issue was not simply how to change their present behavior, but how to bring the congregation to a deeper understanding of how to live out the implications of their new life in Christ.[19]

Aasgaard supported this possibility in his attention to the imagery of the immature child that occurs at several points in the epistle, including 1 Cor. 13.[20] Regardless of whether Paul is addressing one underlying crisis or simply a set of problems "that rose in the life of a particular community at a certain point toward the beginning of its development,"[21] Paul found himself called upon to employ every possible weapon in his rhetorical arsenal in an effort to bring about the Corinthians' adherence to what he believed to be the theological claims and ethical demands of orthodox Christianity. Among the problems that he sought to address had to do with the misunderstanding and abuse of spiritual gifts, especially glossolalia.

---

19. Michelle V. Lee, *Paul, the Stoics, and the Body of Christ* (Cambridge: Cambridge University Press, 2006), 198. Among those who endorsed Mitchell's position are Witherington, *Conflict and Community*; and Dunn, *1 Corinthians*. Against that position, see Thiselton, *First Epistle to the Corinthians,* who pointed out that "Paul does more than address a series of issues which arise as a result of factions and discord" (34). See also José Enrique Aguilar Chiu, *1 Cor 12–14: Literary Structure and Theology* (Rome: Pontifical Biblical Institute, 2007). See also Kistemaker, *Exposition of the First Epistle to the Corinthians*, who argued that Paul was responding to a succession of problems related to leadership, morality, cultural religious practices, worship, and doctrine.

20. For example, in his discussion of 1 Cor. 2:6–3:4, where Paul chides the Corinthians because he could not speak to them "as spiritual people, but rather as people of the flesh, as infants in Christ" (3:1), he writes, "Here infancy is employed as an illustration of religious inadequacy: the Corinthians have fallen down to a stage below what is required" (Reidar Aasgaard, "Paul as a Child: Children and Childhood in the Letters of the Apostle," *Journal of Biblical Literature* 126 [2007]: 129-59, here 144). On the Corinthians' immaturity as the core problem, see also David A. Ackerman, *Lo, I Tell You a Mystery: Cross, Resurrection, and Paraenesis in the Rhetoric of 1 Corinthians* (Eugene: Pickwick, 2006).

21. Horsley, *1 Corinthians*, 22.

1 Corinthians 12–14: An Overview

Although the problem of divisiveness may not lie behind every issue addressed in the letter, it certainly seems to be a crucial factor in 1 Cor. 12–14, as it was manifested in the Corinthians' misunderstanding and abuse of spiritual gifts. Apparently, they were engaging in a pattern of spiritual "one-upmanship," viewing their possession of particular gifts, especially glosso-lalia, or "speaking in tongues," as opportunities to advance their standing relative to their fellow Christians. Their determination to use these gifts for self-aggrandizement had introduced chaos and divisiveness in their public gatherings which, as Paul put it earlier, "do more harm than good" (11:16, NIV). Dunn suggested that the problem may have been linked to the popularity of ecstatic experiences within Roman religious culture:

> Charismatic phenomena and ecstatic behavior were common features of many cults of the time. 12.2 almost certainly refers to such cultic madness, such as was a feature of the Dionysiac festivals familiar throughout Greece ("carried away to dumb idols"). It is therefore a fair inference from 12.2 that at least some of the Corinthian believers had personally participated in such uninhibited celebrations.[22]

At the same time, he pointed out, the Corinthians' behavior was also rooted in the problem of "social status and stratification," with the result that "those of higher status regarded a leading role in the Dionysiac-like festivals as a matter of prestige and honor, so that the manifestation of the Spirit's gifts was a much-coveted experience among the well-to-do."[23] In particular, it seems that the Corinthians viewed tongue-speaking as the prerequisite for possessing the status of πνευματικός ("spiritual"), an adjective that Paul uses in the substantive form repeatedly in the epistle to describe individuals (lit. "spiritual ones," 2:13, 14; 3:1; 14:37). As Eriksson observed, some among the Corinthians seem to have adopted the label as a reference to their own status within the church, a "label Paul denies them."[24] The result was that some

---

22. Dunn, *1 Corinthians*, 80. See also Eriksson, who likewise noted the high value given to ecstatic speech in ancient cultures; see Anders Eriksson, *Traditions as Rhetorical Proof: Pauline Argumentation in 1 Corinthians* (Stockholm: Almqvist & Wiksell, 1998), 201.

23. Dunn, *1 Corinthians*, 80-81.

24. Anders Eriksson, " 'Women Tongue Speakers, Be Silent': A Reconstruction through Paul's Rhetoric," *Biblical Interpretation* 6 (1998): 80-104, here 84. Fee likewise argued that πνευματικοί was a technical term some within the Corinthian church used to denote their

among the Corinthians had come to value more sensational and ecstatic gifts — particularly, glossolalia — over more seemingly mundane gifts (e.g., administration and "forms of assistance," 12:28), and to scorn those who were not so gifted.[25]

Paul responds to this problem with a lengthy discourse cast, most rhetorical scholars argue, in the deliberative mode. He emphasizes the diversity of spiritual gifts granted "for the common good" (12:7), inverting the status hierarchy for spiritual gifts and subordinating all of them to the "still more excellent way" of love. Finally, he severely regulates the practices of glossolalia and prophetic utterance in the gatherings of the church.[26]

Paul begins chap. 12 with the introductory formula, περὶ δὲ τῶν πνευματικῶν (lit. "concerning the spirituals"), signaling the start of a new topic. Interestingly, his use of the term πνευματικοί rather than χαρίσματα ("gifts," 12:4), may be an intentional indication that he is not only addressing the topic of spiritual gifts, but also those who have taken on the term as a designation of their own status. He will similarly use the term at the end of the passage (14:37) where, in something of an *inclusio*, he says, "Anyone who claims . . . to have spiritual powers [lit. "to be spiritual," εἶναι ἢ

---

status as "people of the Spirit, whose present existence is to be understood in strictly spiritual terms" (Fee, *First Epistle to the Corinthians*, 12). Eriksson went on to argue that the problem in Corinth centered particularly on a group of women pneumatics who are not explicitly identified until the end of chapter 14, reflecting Paul's use of *insinuatio*, or the "subtle approach" ("Women Tongue Speakers," 85; see also idem, *Traditions as Rhetorical Proof*, 201-4).

25. Although he sees the problem as more one of a lack of knowledge over against factionalism, Chiu concurs that "the Corinthians valued the gift of tongues above the other gifts, and consequently looked down on those who did not have the gift of tongues. Surely there is a situation of division, but this is only the consequence of a problem of ignorance about the spiritual gifts" (*1 Cor 12-14*, 115).

26. Although, in my view, she downplays the poetic character of chap. 13 in general, Mitchell's argument that 1 Cor. 12 and 14 reflect deliberative argumentation is compelling (*Paul and the Rhetoric of Reconciliation*; so also Witherington, *Conflict and Community*; Dunn, *1 Corinthians*). See also Joop F. M. Smit, "Argument and Genre of 1 Corinthians 12-14," in *Rhetoric and the New Testament: Essays from the 1992 Heidelberg Conference*, ed. Stanley E. Porter and Thomas H. Olbricht (Sheffield: Sheffield Academic Press, 1993), 211-30, esp. 223-24. Chiu, on the other hand, questions that designation, noting that the end of chap. 14 does not reflect deliberative rhetoric; there, "Paul gives rules to them. He does not attempt to convince" (*1 Cor 12-14*, 114). See also Lee, who notes that "the presence of rhetorical categories or forms in 1 Corinthians does not necessarily mean that the entire work was conceived as a formal epideictic, forensic, or deliberative rhetorical discourse" (*Paul, the Stoics, and the Body of Christ*, 25). Lee's position is that the passage represents the genre of paraenesis, patterned after the form as it was used in Stoic philosophy.

πνευματικός] must acknowledge that what I am writing to you is a command of the Lord."[27] He follows that introductory formula in v. 2 by reminding them of their past, noting that they had been "enticed and led astray to idols that could not speak," which leads him to distinguish true spiritual gifts from pagan ecstasies (v. 3).[28] Smit suggested that this might reflect a use of *insinuatio*, reflecting Paul's awareness that he is about to "call the Corinthians to order in the question of glossolalia," at a point when his audience values tongue-speaking and questions Paul's authority. In response, he critiques "unrestrained enthusiasm" under the guise of "an apparently innocent reminder of the past," and then somewhat subtly reminds them of his authority ("I want you to understand . . ." v. 3).[29]

He follows this with an extended discussion in 12:4-30 on the nature of spiritual gifts and their role in the church, which he begins in vv. 4-6, with what a number of observers have seen as a thesis statement for the entire chapter regarding the principle of "unity in diversity." He carefully articulates this in the form of three parallel antitheses that contrast the variety (διαιρέσεις) of gifts, services, and activities with "the same Spirit" (v. 4), "the same Lord" (v. 5), and "the same God who activates all of them in everyone" (v. 6). As Mitchell observed, the parallelism "reverberates back to 8:6 in its emphasis on Corinthian unity in the same spirit, the same Lord, and the same God. How can there be discord in the church when there is unity in these strongest of forces?"[30] Paul then states that "to each is given the manifestation of the Spirit for the common good." His use of the singular, manifestation (ἡ φανέρωσις τοῦ πνεύματος), is striking for the way that it highlights the unity of the source of these gifts, over against the diversity of the gifts themselves. Paul proceeds to enumerate a series of gifts, among them special dispensations of wisdom, knowledge, and faith, and the ability to heal and perform miracles. At the end of the list come the gifts that were most highly valued among his audience, namely prophecy, the "discernment of spirits" (a gift likely related to prophecy), and finally, "various kinds of tongues" and its related gift, "the interpretation of tongues." Paul thus re-

---

27. Eriksson, "Women Tongue Speakers," 84.

28. Regarding Paul's reference to someone saying, "Let Jesus be cursed" (v. 3), Fitzmyer noted that it is unclear whether Paul is addressing a specific practice and, if so, who is involved and in what situation, whether it involves uttering a curse under the threat of persecution or even using Jesus' name to curse someone else (*First Corinthians*, 456-57).

29. Smit, "1 Corinthians 12–14," 214. See also Chiu (*1 Cor 12–14*), who sees an additional *inclusio* in the parallel use of ἀγνοεῖν (ignorant) in 12:1 and 14:38.

30. Mitchell, *Paul and the Rhetoric of Reconciliation*, 268.

verses the hierarchy against which the Corinthians were evaluating their own status as πνευματικοί ("spiritual").

In vv. 12-30, Paul elaborates on the unity-in-diversity principle by means of an extended analogy comparing the church to a body, introduced with the declaration, "Just as the body is one and has many members, and all the members of the body, though many, are one body, so it is with Christ" (v. 12). In the physical body, each organ is important, each is organically connected to the whole, and each functions in harmony with the others (12:12-26). Witherington pointed out that this was a common analogy in Greek thought, although it was typically used to justify rather than challenge social hierarchy:

> Instead of using it to support an existing social hierarchy where lesser members of society serve the greater, Paul uses it to relativize the sense of self-importance of those of higher status, making them see the importance and necessity of the weaker, lower-status Corinthian Christians. Paul questions the usual linking of high social status and honor by saying that God gives more honor to the "less presentable members."[31]

Paul then applies his analogy to the Corinthian "body," connecting that analogy to the enumeration of specific gifts offered earlier in vv. 7-10, again placing tongues at the end of the list. Mitchell noted, "It is no accident that here the gift of tongues comes last (12:8; cf. 12:10), for it is the spiritual gift which has caused the most friction in the group, due to its public and separatist nature."[32] Finally, Paul concludes the chapter with a series of sharp rhetorical questions (vv. 29-30): "Are all apostles? Are all prophets? Are all teachers? Do all work miracles? Do all possess gifts of healing? Do all speak in tongues? Do all interpret?" Of course, those questions, in light of the analogy, demonstrate the rank absurdity of all members of the "body" pursuing the same spiritual gift. As with the earlier lists, Paul again places tongues in the last position, implying its inferiority relative to the other manifestations of the spirit. But this series of questions also raises the emotional tone of the passage to a level almost of outright confrontation, bringing the argument to something of a climax. Whereas in the opening verses of the chapter, Paul appears to employ a more

31. Witherington, *Conflict and Community,* 259. On the use of the body as an analogy in Greek thought, see also Mitchell, *Paul and the Rhetoric of Reconciliation,* 268-69; and Lee, *Paul, the Stoics, and the Body of Christ,* who explored its usage in Stoic philosophy.

32. Mitchell, *Paul and the Rhetoric of Reconciliation,* 270.

indirect and cautious approach, by the end, with these sharp questions, Paul is figuratively "in their face," his voice raised, as he ridicules the self-proclaimed "spiritual ones" for so grossly misunderstanding the work of the Spirit.

In chap. 14, following the encomium of love, Paul will return to the discussion of spiritual gifts, focusing on the nature and relative importance of tongues compared to prophecy, and giving explicit regulations govern- ing the use of prophecy and, especially, tongues in the assembly. His tone there will become, once again, argumentative and hortatory, pervaded by imperative verbs, as he delivers to the Corinthians his instructions for how they are to behave. He exhorts them, first and foremost, to "pursue love," after which he urges them to value prophecy over tongues, since the former has the potential to edify the community (14:1). His argument in chap. 14, as several have noted, revolves around the utility of the various gifts: "If I come to you speaking in tongues, how will I benefit you unless I speak to you in some revelation of knowledge or prophecy or teaching?" (v. 7).[33] In support of that argument he mentions several musical instruments (the flute and harp in v. 7, and the bugle in v. 8), which must produce clear and definite notes in order for their tunes to be discernible. In two parallel questions he asks, "If they do not give distinct notes, how will anyone know what is being played? And if the bugle gives an indistinct sound, who will get ready for battle?" (vv. 7-8). Applied to the Corinthians, he continues, "If in a tongue you utter speech that is not intelligible, how will anyone know what is being said?" (v. 9). So apparently obvious is the conclusion that Paul chides the Corinthians for thinking like children (μὴ παιδία γίνεσθε ταῖς φρεσίν, 14:30), which, of course, recalls his earlier statement about their lack of maturity (3:1-3). Then, in v. 26, he brings the discussion to an end with a series of fifteen imperatives in which he "tells" the Corinthians what to do. Chiu de- scribed the tone with which Paul delivers his "rules" to the audience in these words: "He does not attempt to convince (this he does in chaps. 12-13, as well as in 14:1-25). There is no room for discussion."[34] Paul allows for two or three

---

33. Fee saw a strongly apologetic undercurrent in Paul's references to his own use of spiritual gifts, particularly glossolalia (tongue speaking), in 14:6, 15, and 18. He inferred from these statements that Paul had not made the demonstration of this spiritual gift a prominent element of his own ministry among the Corinthians, causing them to experience "considerable doubt, based on their own criteria, whether he is truly *pneumatikos* (spiritual) or a prophet" (*First Corinthians*, 8, see also 709).

34. Chiu, *1 Cor 12–14*, 114. He observed that in her effort to make the text fit precisely the deliberative genre of oratory, "Mitchell's notion that the rules given in 14:26-36 are mere counsels seems to deprive them of their real force."

tongue speakers to express themselves, but only if someone is present who can interpret the message, and similarly, permits two or three prophets to speak provided they speak in turn and all conduct themselves in a way that promotes decorum and order (vv. 26-32). His overriding concern is that the Corinthians strive to excel in the gifts that build up the church (14:3-5, 12, 17). As noted above, he concludes the argument by declaring that anyone claiming "spiritual" status will acknowledge that what he is telling them "is a command of the Lord" (v. 37).

As the foregoing discussion makes clear, both chapters reflect Paul's careful attention to the rhetorical dimensions of his communication. His use of *insinuatio* in the opening of chap. 12, his attention to form (e.g., the parallel antitheses of 12:4-5 and the *inclusio* centered on πνευματικός ["spiritual"] in 12:1 and 14:37), his invocation of a common metaphor for unity in Greek philosophy, that of the "body" in 12:12-30, his listing of spiritual gifts in a way that reverses the value hierarchy with which his audience has viewed them, his argument from utility, supported by vivid metaphors of tuneless music and an uncertain trumpet attempting to call the troops to arms — all of these reflect his strategic efforts to offer a convincing argument for his understanding of spiritual gifts and a compelling reason for them to follow the orders with which he concludes chap. 14. Yet for all of his effort to offer unassailable argumentative support for his claims and commands, Paul seems to understand that something more is needed to accomplish his persuasive goal. This he attempts to fulfill not with more argument, but with poetry.

Paul's Rhapsody of Love

In the midst of this long argumentative passage, Paul abruptly interrupts the flow of thought to offer what Kennedy called an "encomium of love."[35] As noted above, throughout chap. 12, Paul addresses his audience directly and explicitly (e.g, "Now concerning spiritual gifts, brothers and sisters, I

35. George A. Kennedy, *New Testament Interpretation Through Rhetorical Criticism* (Chapel Hill: University of North Carolina Press, 1984), 18, 156. Several scholars have made detailed and convincing arguments in support of Kennedy's assessment. See Smit, "Genre of 1 Corinthians 13"; and James G. Sigountos, "The Genre of 1 Corinthians 13," *New Testament Studies* 40 (1994): 246-60. Smit's essay is especially helpful for the way that the author highlights the core dimensions that characterized the encomium in the classical rhetorical tradition, and he exhaustively demonstrates their presence in 1 Cor. 13.

do not want you to be uninformed . . . , 12:1), a direct mode of address cul-minating in the staccato series of strident rhetorical questions in 12:29-30. All of this leads to the imperative in 12:31, where Paul issues this command to the Corinthians: "Strive [ζηλοῦτε] for the greater gifts," an order that will be repeated in 14:1 in a way that continues his argument focused on tongues and prophecy — only now, shaped by the experience of the soaring poetry of chap. 13.

In the second half of v. 31, however, Paul signals a shift in both tone and theme, as he tells his audience, "And I will show you a still more excel-lent way." His turn from second to first person signals that movement, as does his use of the term δείκνυμι ("show" or "demonstrate") to characterize what he is about to do — not to argue, but to offer a depiction. Pointing out that this is the only instance where Paul uses this verb, Smit asserted that its occurrence "is no accident" and "should be taken as a reference to the γένος ἐπιδεικτικόν [epideictic genre]."[36] In other words, Paul is deliberately signaling a shift to an epideictic or demonstrative form of discourse which, as Smit noted, "gives precedence to the technique of amplification and min-imization. In eulogy it is necessary to enlarge on the merits of the person in question and to reduce the defects to a minimum; in vituperation it is just the other way round."[37] Further, whereas in chap. 12 he places the gifts of the Spirit in something of a hierarchy and ended with the command that they pursue the greater (μείζονα) gifts, now he presents his forthcoming topic, love, not as a gift to be evaluated in comparison to other gifts, but as a "way" (ὁδός) — the "still more excellent" (καθ᾽ ὑπερβολήν, lit. the "hyperbolic") way. His language begins the process not simply of changing "themes" but, as Chiu suggests, changing "levels":

> It is intended to lead the Corinthians, preoccupied with and zealous for spiritual gifts (ζηλωταὶ πνευμάτων, cf. 14:12) as they are, to a differ-ent level of thinking, and of seeing things, to an "extraordinary" (καθ᾽ ὑπερβολὴν ὁδόν) level, which indicates a qualitative leap. This level or path καθ᾽ ὑπερβολὴν ὁδόν, Paul calls ἡ ἀγάπη.[38]

Crucial to his aim of "showing" the more excellent way will be his use of poetic form and language.

36. Smit, "1 Corinthians 12–14," 226.
37. Smit, "Genre of 1 Corinthians 13," 210.
38. Chiu, 1 Cor 12–14, 285.

As chap. 13 opens, Paul has clearly taken on a different voice from the kind of direct mode of address that he has been using to this point and that he will resume in chap. 14. He drops the direct form of address and instead now speaks in the voice of what Smit calls the "rhetorical 'I'."[39] His language contains none of the imperatival verb forms that characterize chaps. 12 and 14 ("Strive for the greater gifts," 12:31; "Pursue love and strive for the spiritual gifts, and especially that you may prophesy," 14:1). Instead, the leading verbs in vv. 1-3 are all in the subjunctive mode, giving the language a hypothetical cast. These features give the chapter the character of soliloquy, "a dramatic speech uttered by one character speaking alone while on the stage (or while under the impression of being alone)," through which he "reveals his or her inner thoughts and feelings to the audience."[40] Paul thus shifts his persona from that of the prosecutor hammering away at the Corinthians to one of a poet rhapsodizing the virtues of love, in a way that allows his audience to "overhear" his lyrical performance. In this fictive guise, he turns the gaze of his audience away from himself to the personification of love.

The first part of the encomium, vv. 1-3, which Sigountos labeled a "prologue," consists of three carefully crafted parallel stanzas or periods, each comprised of three segments: (1) a conditional positive protasis containing an imaginative description of a spiritual gift or action (e.g., "speaking in the tongues of mortals,") that includes a hyperbole related to that gift or action (e.g., "even of angels," καὶ τῶν ἀγγέλων); (2) a conditional negative protasis that highlights the contrasting lack of love ("but do not have love,"

---

39. Smit, "Genre of 1 Corinthians 13," 197. So also Fitzmyer, *First Corinthians*, 492. By contrast, based on parallels between 1 Cor. 8–10 and 12–14, Collins and Harrington argued that Paul is advancing an ethos argument here, offering autobiographical reflections in support of his claims about the necessity for love; see Raymond F. Collins and Daniel J. Harrington, *First Corinthians* (Collegeville: Liturgical, 1999), 472-73. Holladay offered a similar argument, which puts him at pains to show how Paul's hyperbolic statements in vv. 1-3 can in any sense be hypothetical; see Carl R. Holladay, "1 Corinthians 13: Paul as Apostolic Paradigm," in *Greeks, Romans, and Christians: Essays in Honor of Abraham J. Malherbe*, David L. Balch, Wayne A. Meeks, and Everett Ferguson, eds. (Minneapolis: Fortress, 1990), 80-98. However, this position overlooks several important differences between chaps. 9 and 13. Whereas chap. 9 is clearly autobiographical, chap. 13 is highly abstract and poetic, and takes a form that is in marked contrast to the chapters that frame it. (See also Mitchell, *Paul and the Rhetoric of Reconciliation*, 53-54, 58, who made a similar argument, but one which is subject to the same criticism of ignoring the more abstract and poetic character of chap. 13.)

40. Christopher Baldick, "Soliloquy," in *The Concise Oxford Dictionary of Literary Terms* (Oxford: Oxford University Press, 1996; accessed via *Oxford Reference Online*).

ἀγάπην δὲ μὴ ἔχω); and (3) a negative apodosis (e.g., "I gain nothing").[41]
Each stanza has its own features that mimetically represent the contrast Paul
hopes his audience will experience between the gifts they value so deeply
and the "more excellent way" of love. In the first (v. 1), the tongues of men
and even of angels, without love, are degraded to "a noisy gong or a clanging
cymbal," a description that Spicq characterized in this way: "The onomatopoetic effect is striking. In Greek . . . the word cymbal reproduces the sharp,
heavy sound of clashing."[42] Additionally, the adjective translated "clanging,"
ἀλαλάζον, is also likely onomatopoetic, but in this case, it mimics the actual
sound of the tongue speaker while at the same time presenting an ironic
contrast to the word used to describe the act of "speaking" (λαλῶ) in the
tongues of men.[43] The effect of that contrast may also have been enhanced
by its familiarity in Greco-Roman thought. As Spicq pointed out,

> the description of an "empty" sophist or rhetor as a gong, lyre, cymbal,
> or trumpet became a commonplace of literature and philosophy. St. Paul
> undoubtedly borrows the expression, but where the cynics used it to con-
> trast the verbose arrogance of the orators with the emptiness of their
> thought, Paul uses it to contrast the utterances of the speaker in tongues
> with manifestations of charity.[44]

The second stanza (v. 2) depicts gifts related to prophecy in a complex
structure that begins with a conditional statement, "If I have prophetic powers" (ἐὰν ἔχω προφητείαν), followed by an elaboration that presents two
related gifts in the form of a reverse parallelism (καὶ εἰδῶ τὰ μυστήρια πάντα
καὶ πᾶσαν τὴν γνῶσιν, e.g., structured in a verb-object-adjective-adjective-
object, a–b–c–c'–b' format), and ending with a description of the gift of

41. Sigountos, "Genre of 1 Corinthians 13," 251-55. See also Smit, "Genre of 1 Corinthians
13," 201-2.

42. Ceslaus Spicq, *Agape in the New Testament*, 2 vols., trans. Marie A. McNamara and
Mary H. Richter (St. Louis: Herder, 1965), 2:145.

43. Although he does not elaborate, Kistemaker viewed ἀλαλάζον as onomatopoeia (*Exposition of the First Epistle to the Corinthians*, 457). On the significance of the term λαλεῖν, to
speak, which Paul evokes with the onomatopoetic adjective ἀλαλάζον here, Eriksson wrote:
"It is important to note the 28 occurrences of λαλεῖν in these chapters. The first occurrence is
ἐν πνεύματι θεοῦ λαλῶν in 12:3, and henceforth, λαλεῖν denotes communal tongue speaking,
the use of tongues in prayer and public prophesying" (*Traditions as Rhetorical Proof*, 199).

44. Spicq, *Agape in the New Testament*, 2:146. See also Smit ("Genre of 1 Corinthians 13,"
200), who pointed out that "in classical antiquity the comparison of a garrulous orator with a
hollow-sounding instrument like a gong or a cymbal occurs regularly."

faith that parallels the opening part of the stanza, καὶ ἐὰν ἔχω πᾶσαν τὴν πίστιν ὥστε ὄρη μεθιστάναι ("and if I have all faith, as to remove mountains"). As Smit pointed out, the all-encompassing character of these gifts is enhanced not only by the complex structure in which they are presented, but also by the repetition of various forms of the word "all" (πάντα, πᾶσαν). Of course, Paul's mention of "removing mountains" recalls Jesus' reference to the "faith as of a mustard seed," where it is clearly presented hyperbolically as the ultimate feat of religiosity (Matt. 17:20).[45] Taken together, the form and language of the protasis of the second stanza seem to imbue these gifts with grandeur and magnificence, setting the stage for Paul's statement of their benefit to him without love, which presents a shocking contrast to that amplification. Absent love, so gifted an individual is described in two words: οὐθέν εἰμι ("I am nothing"). As Smit eloquently put it, "The gifts, presented in the first protasis as being all-embracing . . . are reduced to 'nothing' in the apodosis."[46]

The third stanza (v. 3) brings the opening section to its culmination with a depiction not simply of the exercise of gifts or faith, but acts of great sacrifice. Paul paints two possibilities, again, in parallel phrases. The first poses the possibility that one might give away — literally "parcel out" — "all my possessions" (καὶ ἐὰν ψωμίσω πάντα τὰ ὑπάρχοντά μου). The second presents the ultimate self-sacrifice and the climactic "religious act" of the entire section: "If I hand over my body to be burned" (καὶ ἐὰν παραδῶ τὸ σῶμά μου ἵνα καυθήσομαι).[47] Without love, he tersely summarizes the final state of affairs, again, in two words: οὐδὲν ὠφελοῦμαι ("I gain nothing"). Here,

---

45. Smit adds that "Paul uses this metaphor to further enhance his hyperbolic presentation of the charismata of which the repeated 'all' is a clear indication" ("Genre of 1 Corinthians 13," 200).

46. Smit, "Genre of 1 Corinthians 13," 203.

47. Author's translation. Scholars are divided over whether the reading in v. 3 should be καυθήσομαι, "to be burned," or καυχήσωμαι, "that I may boast." Most modern translation adopt the latter reading. As Sigountos ("Genre of 1 Corinthians 13," 253-54) argues, while there is textual support for both, the primary reason why καυχήσωμαι has been preferred is simply that it is the more difficult reading, reflecting one of the axioms of traditional textual criticism. However, Paul's use of hyperbole in vv. 1-3 strongly supports καυθήσομαι. Sigountos explains, "Because the apodosis is οὐδὲν ὠφελοῦμαι, the issue is *self*-aggrandizement — do *I* profit from fiery suicide? Paul here envisions an individual who believes that the sacrifice of one's body (in the flames) accrues some kind of profit or merit to himself. . . . The traditional καυθήσομαι 'I may be burned,' is a fine hyperbole. Intrinsically, self-immolation is an extremely powerful image" ("Genre of 1 Corinthians 13," 254). See also Fitzmyer (*First Corinthians*, 494), who took an alternative view.

as with the first two stanzas, the same pattern prevails, as Sigountos noted: "The apodosis in verse 3 answers the hyperbole with crushing force — even if one surrenders one's body to the flames, without love, the ultimate sacrifice is meaningless because 'no profit accrues to my account.'"[48]

The second major division (vv. 4-7) consists of praise for love's noble deeds, again in a carefully structured poetic form. Here, Paul turns the attention from the fictive "I" to personifying love itself, which becomes the subject of fifteen different verbs enumerating its attributes. Of these, seven are positive, while eight represent the negative qualities that love is not, with the seven positive attributes divided into a set of two and a set of five, which frame the eight negative qualities. The first two ("love is patient; love is kind," v. 4), as Smit notes, are presented as a chiasm (ἡ ἀγάπη μακροθυμεῖ, χρηστεύεται ἡ ἀγάπη, in a verb-object-object-verb, a-b-b'-a', pattern).[49] Next come the negative qualities, introduced with the statement, οὐ ζηλοῖ ἡ ἀγάπη ("love is not jealous"), which presents the first of eight cola that begin with the negative (οὐ) and present a verb in the third-person singular (οὐ περπερεύεται, "is not boastful"; οὐ φυσιοῦται, "does not become conceited"; οὐκ ἀσχημονεῖ, "does not behave unseemly"; οὐ ζητεῖ τὰ ἑαυτῆς "does not seek its own way"; οὐ παροξύνεται, "does not become angry"; οὐ λογίζεται τὸ κακόν, "does not keep a record of wrongs"; οὐ χαίρει ἐπὶ τῇ ἀδικίᾳ, "does not rejoice at unrighteousness"). The final colon is balanced by a positive counterpart, "but rejoices with the truth" (συγχαίρει δὲ τῇ ἀληθείᾳ), which leads into a succession of four cola which each begin with a verb ending in -ει followed by the word "all" (πάντα): "bears all things, believes all things, hopes all things, endures all things." As Smit observed, "The fourfold repetition of 'everything' (πάντα) forms a climax which concludes the series." In the middle section of the encomium, then, we find an extended amplification of love, a "heaping up" of terms that magnify love's true grandeur and mimetically represent its eternal character. This, of course, provides the counterpart to the supposed grandeur of the gifts and religious acts, particularly glossolalia and prophecy, which, without love, are starkly devalued in the first part of the encomium and are shown to be merely temporary in the section that follows.

In the final section, Paul offers an extended and, again, highly structured comparison between love and the passing spiritual gifts, introduced with

---

48. Sigountos, "Genre of 1 Corinthians 13," 254.

49. Smit, "Genre of 1 Corinthians 13," 201. I am especially indebted to Smit's careful analysis for my account of Paul's artistry in this section of 1 Corinthians 13.

a declaration that builds on the preceding enumeration of love's qualities, while also introducing the temporal dimension that will characterize this final portion of the encomium: "Love never fails." This section, Collins and Harrington argued, reflects the ancient poetic form of *priamel*, "a literary form in which something that is of most value is measured against things of lesser value."[50] In this final section, Paul pursues that contrast in four parallel antitheses that poetically contrast the imperfect, incomplete "now," a period characterized by the presence of the spiritual gifts that the Corinthians value so greatly, with a future time of perfection, when those gifts will have passed away.

The first of these three antitheses builds on Paul's declaration from the first half of v. 8 regarding love's permanence, "love never fails." He contrasts this with prophecy, tongues, and knowledge, in three parallel clauses, each introduced with the conjunction "if" (εἴτε), followed by a reference to one of three gifts, and finally, a future-tense verb signaling the cessation of that gift, ending in -αι ("if there are prophecies, they will pass away, if there are tongues, they will be stilled, if there is knowledge, it will cease" [author's translation]; εἴτε δὲ προφητεῖαι, καταργηθήσονται, εἴτε γλῶσσαι, παύσονται, εἴτε γνῶσις, καταργηθήσεται). The second temporal antithesis occurs in vv. 9-10, where Paul sets the "now" in opposition to that which is to come, in a way that mirrors in reverse form the contrast he has just made in v. 8. Using present-tense verbs in two parallel clauses in v. 9 he says, "For we know only in part and we prophesy only in part" (ἐκ μέρους γὰρ γινώσκομεν καὶ ἐκ μέρους προφητεύομεν), but "when the complete [τὸ τέλειον, lit. 'the perfect'] comes, the partial will come to an end."[51] He rounds out the contrast using the same verb that he had applied to prophecy and knowledge in v. 8 (καταργηθήσεται, "will pass away"). In v. 11, he offers the third temporal antithesis, this time invoking the image of the child, which recalls his reproach for their lack of maturity in 3:1-4, where he scolded them for being, not spiritual (πνευματικοῖς), but infants in Christ (νηπίοις ἐν Χριστῷ, 3:1), and anticipating his reproach for thinking

---

50. Collins and Harrington, *First Corinthians*, 483.

51. It is unclear exactly what Paul has in mind when he sets up a dichotomy in 13:9-10 between that which is "in part" and "the perfect/complete." There are at least two possibilities, a contrast between immaturity and maturity, or between this age and the age to come. Either possibility would fit the immediate context as well as the larger argument of the epistle. For discussion, see Fee, *First Corinthians*, 644-46; William E. Orr and James Arthur Walther, *1 Corinthians* (New York: Doubleday, 1976), 296-97; Conzelmann, *1 Corinthians*, 226; Kistemaker, *Exposition of the First Epistle to the Corinthians*, 467-68; Fitzmyer, *First Corinthians*, 494.

like children (παιδία) in 14:30. This time, however, he casts that language in the poetic voice of the "rhetorical 'I',"[52] describing the childlike behavior in three parallel clauses consisting of an imperfect past tense verb, the preposition "as" (ὡς), and a repetition of the word "child": "When [ὅτε] I was a child, I spoke like a child, I thought like a child, I reasoned like a child" (ἐλάλουν ὡς νήπιος, ἐφρόνουν ὡς νήπιος, ἐλογιζόμην ὡς νήπιος).[53] In contrast to the childlike phase of his development (introduced with the temporal conjunction ὅτε, which parallels the first half of the antithesis), the narrator completes the antithesis by declaring, "When I became an adult, I put an end to childish ways," using the same verb, καταργέω (lit. "to abolish, nullify") that he used to describe the cessation of prophecy and knowledge (v. 8) as well as the demise of the "partial" (v. 10). For the fourth and final antithesis, Paul shifts to a "general we"[54] as the subject of a contrast between seeing and knowing in the present versus seeing and being known fully in the age to come. Again, the antithesis is marked by the repetition of the parallel formula, ἄρτι . . . τότε . . . (now . . . then . . .). Finally, the encomium ends with the summary, introduced with the formula "but now" (νυνὶ δέ), followed by three enduring virtues that appear to continue beyond and surpass the gifts addressed in the encomium: "Now faith, hope, and love abide, these three." Recalling the command to strive for the "greater" gifts (τὰ χαρίσματα τὰ μείζονα, 12:31), the poem concludes with an *inclusio*, "The greatest (μείζων) of these is love."[55]

Viewed in terms of its content, the foregoing analysis underscores the integral thematic relationship that numerous scholars have found between the encomium on love and its broader argumentative context and, indeed, the overall epistle. On the one hand, of course, if chap. 13 were removed, along with the transition statements in 12:31 and 14:1, chaps. 12 and 14 would form a continuous, uninterrupted line of thought, which has led scholars to view chap. 13 as an excursus or digression and prompted some

52. Smit, "Genre of 1 Corinthians 13," 197.

53. Aasgaard ("Paul as a Child") noted the connection between the state of childhood and the former imperfect age, contrasted with the future, perfect age to come, as well as the imagery of the immature child used at other points in the epistle, highlighting the negative character of that imagery.

54. Smit, "Genre of 1 Corinthians 13," 197.

55. Fitzmyer (*First Corinthians*, 494) noted the interpretive problem raised by the triad of faith, hope, and love, relative to the gifts mentioned in vv. 10-12. He concluded, simply, that "faith, hope, and love remain in this life for the Christian, even if all other *pneumatika* fall away. They are essential to Christian life."

to posit that it was not even in the original letter at all.[56] Yet, as Mitchell observed, chap. 13 treats many of the same issues addressed elsewhere in the letter. The behaviors that Paul cites in chap. 13 (tongues, prophecy, knowledge, and boasting) "make reference to the precise issues dividing the church at Corinth."[57] Additionally, the list of love's attributes enumerated in vv. 4-7 "bears a one-to-one correspondence with Paul's description of the Corinthians' factional behavior." Chiu also pointed out that "the eulogy on love envelops the comparison with the gift of glossolalia (13:1, 8) and that of prophecy (13:2, 8, 9). This comparison of love with those two gifts is not by chance, since chap. 14 focuses the attention on prophecy and glossolalia."[58] Those indications and others like them led Horsley to conclude that chap. 13 is "an integral step in a deliberative argument in which Paul shifts into the praise of a virtue as an illustration of his exhortation."[59]

Yet, as Horsley's observation also implies, and as the above analysis makes abundantly clear, Paul presents that content in a dramatically different form than he does in the surrounding context. In chaps. 12 and 14, he uses didactic explanation and logical argumentation in order to correct the Corinthians' misunderstandings, to convince them of the correctness of his position, and to persuade them to institute appropriate reforms to their current practice. His approach in those chapters is self-consciously rhetorical in the sense that Aristotle and others in the classical tradition would have understood it, offering evidence in support of judgment. In the encomium of love, by contrast, Paul eschews rational argumentation and instead offers his readers a highly structured, poetic experience of love. The passage functions mimetically on several levels. As already noted, the opening stanzas in vv. 1-3 use language and syntax to evoke the grandeur of the gifts, depicting each with hyperbole and crescendo, leading to a climax — as Sigountos observed, from human to angelic tongues, from prophecy to omniscience, and from giving away one's possessions to self-immolation — in a way that captures the

---

56. Witherington's assessment is representative of those who identify chap. 13 as a digression that is nevertheless closely related to the surrounding argument: "Chapter 13 is a digression. Though it is an epideictic piece exalting love, it is used in a deliberative argument to exhort the Corinthians to let love be their guiding principle in all they say and do. . . . It was not uncommon for a rhetor to insert in the middle of a forensic argument an epideictic excursus or digression focusing on presentation, not argumentation" (*Conflict and Community*, 264).

57. Mitchell, *Paul and the Rhetoric of Reconciliation*, 58.

58. Chiu, *1 Cor 12–14*, 135.

59. Horsley, *1 Corinthians*, 174.

value the Corinthians placed on them.[60] But then, in each case, the language and form depicts their abrupt deflation, in the first case by means of an onomatopoetic imitation of jarring, discordant noises, and in the second two using terse, two-word declarations to express their utter uselessness. In each case, the effect is one in which Paul symbolically inflates the Corinthians' most highly valued signs of "true spirituality" and then, as it were, abruptly bursts the bubble.

If Kennedy is correct in his sense of the flow of the tone in the encomium as a whole, Paul may be employing mimesis in another way as well. In a comment made almost in passing, Kennedy notes that "Paul's encomium of love is personal and nervous, emotional at the beginning, but quieter at the end as the emotional energy is dissipated."[61] His perceptive observation is especially interesting when viewed in light of the fact that the Corinthians seemed to place particular value on ecstatic religious experiences, perhaps even approaching something like emotional frenzy, which could lead to the kind of display that would cause an outsider visiting the Corinthian assembly to proclaim, "You are out of your mind" (14:23).[62] Paul seems in the opening stanzas to capture something of that heightened enthusiasm in the effusive and hyperbolic language he uses to describe the charismata. But as he moves to the middle section, where he enumerates the attributes of love, Paul's language, while highly structured, nevertheless becomes much less extravagant. Finally, as the encomium comes to an end, the emotional fury resolves entirely as he depicts tongues being stilled and prophecy and knowledge coming to an end. In a way that mirrors the content of chap. 14, where he attempts to argue and exhort the Corinthians to mature from chaos to order, his encomium poetically enacts the same movement.

Of course, most importantly, the encomium attempts to capture the grandeur of love itself. As noted above, Paul aims in 1 Cor. 13 not simply to convince the Corinthians that the other gifts are of less value than love. Rather, his purpose is to show that in comparison to love, the gifts they hold in such high esteem are nothing. Contrasted with love they are utterly worthless. As Chiu put it, he seeks to take them to "a different level of thinking," to effect a "qualitative leap."[63] Smit captured the difference between the way Paul compares the gifts of tongues and prophecy with *each other,* in contrast

---

60. Sigountos, "Genre of 1 Corinthians 13," 253.

61. Kennedy, *New Testament Interpretation,* 156.

62. See Smit, "1 Corinthians 12–14," 214.

63. Chiu, *1 Cor 12–14,* 285.

to the way he places both of them against the ultimate grandeur of love. He commented that in chaps. 12 and 14, Paul offers an argument that presents "two different phenomena as species of one and the same genus, thus making comparison possible, and reach[es] the conclusion that the one [prophecy] ranks far higher than the other [tongues]." By contrast, he pointed out, "The passage on love does not exhibit such reasoning. It simply places the species of one genus, the charismata, over against a singular and unique reality: love. This antithesis is not argued, but posited without further discussion."[64] To be sure, Paul certainly had the rhetorical skill to offer an explicit argument that advanced that claim logically. What is striking, of course, is that he instead chose to create that sense of contrast between love and the charismata by shifting to a different form of discourse, one that mimetically captured the grandeur of love. In other words, by shifting to a poetic form, Paul signals that when it comes to love, we have encountered a different level of spiritual reality altogether.

What might the Corinthians have experienced as this passage was read in their hearing? They would have noted the sudden change in tone marked by Paul's shift in voice as well as in his turn to a poetic style and structure. They would likely have recognized the familiar form of the encomium through which the speaker praises worthy people and deeds, only in this case, the object of praise is an abstract quality, love.[65] The result would have been a mimetic performance through which, far more than logically proving the superiority of love, the poetic form would have created an emotional experience of love's grandeur. After a succession of arguments culminating in a series of sharp rhetorical questions with the force of a stinging accusation, the Corinthians are suddenly taken out of that argumentative flow and transported to a state of consciousness in which they feel the presence of the sublime. Having imaginatively and emotionally experienced the sublimity of love, Paul seems to expect that his audience will see themselves and their own petty behaviors in a new light and aspire to a higher plane of living. Only then are they prepared once again for a direct mode of address that instructs them about how to exercise spiritual gifts in the assembly "for the building up of the church" (14:12).

---

64. Smit, "1 Corinthians 12–14," 222.

65. On the stability of the encomium form within Greek literature as well as its presence in Jewish and early Christian writings, see Sigountos, "Genre of 1 Corinthians 13," 247-50.

Conclusion

Of all the passages examined in this study, Paul's rhapsody on love seems more properly "rhetorical" in the traditional sense, as a digression from his main argument in which he extols the superiority of love over all other signs of religiosity and "argues" that religious activity unmotivated by love is ultimately futile. In this chapter, I have argued that Paul's poetic treatment of love actually held a central place in his overall treatment of the abuses and divisive exercise of ecstatic spiritual gifts in the Corinthian church. His response to their competition for the possession of ecstatic manifestations of the Holy Spirit is to transport them into an ecstasy of another kind, one produced by the careful use of poetic language and form.

Paul speaks to a community of Christians that seems hopelessly divided; they grasp for spiritual gifts as a way of advancing their own status over their fellow Christians, leading Paul to inspire them to pursue the "still more excellent way" of love. Part of his response, of course, is to explain the nature of the church as a body and the various gifts as "organs" that work together. Part of that response is also to regulate particular practices that are currently disrupting the assembly. But a central element in Paul's treatment of the problems in Corinth is a poetic expression of praise for love, an expression aimed not so much at convincing his hearers intellectually of its superiority as it is at providing for them an imaginative, transcendent experience of its grandeur and sublimity. Having participated in the mimetic representation of love and been stirred by its grandeur, the Corinthians are then, Paul hopes, ready to hear his command that they "pursue love" (14:1).

CHAPTER FIVE

United in Worship (Ephesians 1:3-14)

As chap. 3 of this study emphasizes, the Christian church in its earliest years faced few problems as difficult or as threatening to its future as that of the hostility between Jewish and Gentile converts to the movement. Both groups clearly brought to their experience of Christianity the long-standing history of antagonism and suspicion that had characterized their relations in the ancient world. As Dodd poignantly observed, the peoples of the Greco-Roman world viewed the Jews as "a people apart, characterized, as it seemed to them, by *hostile odium adversus omnes,* and they reciprocated this hatred with an anti-Semitism which smoldered for long periods and broke out in violence from time to time."[1] Not surprisingly, the issue of Jew–Gentile relations dominates much of the early Christian writings, reflecting early church leaders' commitment to the vision of one united church, transcending racial boundaries. Their commitment to that vision presented them with a difficult persuasive dilemma: How does one overcome longstanding racial hostility? How does one even gain a hearing in order to address the issue?

The purpose of this chapter is to examine one particularly creative response to this pressing issue, the blessing that opens the epistle to the Ephesians (1:3-14). As I shall argue, the issue of Jew–Gentile unity pervades the epistle as a whole. In chaps. 2–3, Paul offers an extended discussion explaining how the inclusion of Gentiles within the "commonwealth of Israel" was both a central part of God's plan for the world from before

---

1. C. H. Dodd, *Christianity and the New Humanity: Two Essays* (Philadelphia: Fortress, 1965), 11.

creation, as well as being at the core of Paul's own call to apostleship.[2] Likewise, the epistle's exhortation section, which begins in 4:1, is dominated by the call to maintain the unity that God, through the Holy Spirit, has already established. For all his concern with fostering racial harmony, however, Paul does not at first address the issue explicitly. Instead, he begins the epistle by offering a carefully composed liturgy, an extended, formulaic expression of praise to God. This expression of worship will play a crucial role in the overall persuasive design of the epistle, for it invites the audience to celebrate a constellation of values, among them one the author expects will be met with antagonism and resistance — that of unity in the church. As with the other mimetic texts examined in this study, the blessing of Eph. 1 takes up material presented elsewhere in the epistle as explicit argumentation and exhortation, and it casts that material in a poetic form that offers the audience a mimetic performance of the themes that Paul will later address more directly. In this way, when the audience confronts explicit challenges to pursue unity later in the epistle, they will be pursuing values and acting out of attitudes that, Paul hopes, they have already glimpsed in their own experience. Before examining the liturgy itself, the chapter begins with a reconstruction of the epistle's rhetorical situation.

2. The question of the authorship of Ephesians continues to be a topic of debate among NT scholars, although that question is of minimal importance to the argument being advanced in the present study. For this reason, I have adopted the traditional way of referring to the author as Paul, with the understanding that the actual author may be unknown. For discussions regarding authorship, see Everett F. Harrison, *Introduction to the New Testament* (Grand Rapids: Eerdmans, 1971), 331-39; and Paul Feine, Johannes Behm, and Werner Kümmel, *Introduction to the New Testament* (Nashville: Abingdon, 1966), 248-58. For a lengthy discussion of the evidence against Pauline authorship, see Rudolf Schnackenburg, *Ephesians: A Commentary*, trans. Helen Heron (Edinburg: T & T Clark, 1991), 24-33. As Lincoln points out, although many NT scholars still hold to Pauline authorship, a number have argued that the epistle was written by a later follower of Paul who wrote in Paul's name and "was responsible for the portrait of Paul that can be constructed from the letter by the reader" (Andrew T. Lincoln, *Ephesians* [Dallas: Word, 1990], lxii). A somewhat more nuanced account of this later position holds that while this letter and the related epistle, Colossians, do not come literally from Paul's hand, "they exhibit sufficient continuity with his letters to warrant the conclusion that they were written by followers of his who saw themselves as carrying on his work and writing under his authority" (Charles H. Talbert, *Ephesians and Colossians* [Grand Rapids: Baker Academic, 2007], 6-11). Witherington, on the other hand, offers a spirited defense of the traditional view of Pauline authorship; see Ben Witherington III, *The Letters to Philemon, the Colossians, and the Ephesians: A Socio-Rhetorical Commentary on the Captivity Epistles* (Grand Rapids: Eerdmans, 2007), 217-24.

Gentiles, Jews, and the Plan of God

Unlike 1 Thessalonians, Romans, or 1 Corinthians, the epistle to the Ephesians has been the subject of much disagreement among scholars regarding such basic questions as its authorship, audience, and occasion. Regarding the exact circumstances to which the epistle was directed, Thielman noted that suggestions "could be easily multiplied," but none "is convincing."[3] Talbert similarly concluded that, given the absence of an explicitly identified problem, "all attempts to find a purpose for Ephesians in the correction of or defense of a single problem have failed." Instead, he observed, many scholars have concluded that the epistle's purpose had to do with "identity formation in a more general sense than the correction of a specific problem."[4]

What most scholars do accept, however, is that the epistle's central goal was to seek the unity of Jewish and Gentile believers in the early Christian church. Working back from the text itself, Talbert focused on the author's choices in the areas of "language, style, arguments, and *topoi*" in order to develop a provisional identification of the circumstances of the audience, and included first among his list of issues the problem of Jew–Gentile division.[5] Hoehner similarly noted the emphasis throughout the epistle on "reconciliation between Jews and Gentiles who believe in Christ."[6] As Thielman pointed out, that conclusion "rests firmly on 2:11-22 (cf. 3:6)," which "emphasizes the plight of unbelieving Gentiles in their position outside Israel and the reconciliation that Gentile believers now experience with believing Jews and with God."[7] Verhey and Harvard, who hold to the Pauline authorship of Ephesians, situate that emphasis within the broader context of Jew–Gentile relations within the early church as a whole, seeing it as the dominant issue in the background of early Christianity:

---

3. Frank Thielman, *Ephesians* (Grand Rapids: Baker Academic, 2010), 19. Thielman offered an extended treatment of the authorship (pp. 11-19), arguing that the epistle is Pauline, written during his two year imprisonment in Rome in A.D. 62. See also his discussion of the various options offered to explain the audience and their circumstances (pp. 19-28); cf. also Harold W. Hoehner, *Ephesians: A Critical Exegetical Commentary* (Grand Rapids: Baker Academic, 2002), 98-106; and Talbert, *Ephesians and Colossians*, 6-13.

4. Talbert, *Ephesians and Colossians*, 12-13.

5. Talbert, *Ephesians and Colossians*, 16-17.

6. Hoehner, *Ephesians*, 113.

7. Thielman, *Ephesians*, 24.

The mission of Paul to the Gentiles had prompted more than one contro-versy about the relations of Jews and Gentiles in the church. Paul con-sistently insisted on the full inclusion of the Gentiles and on the unity and equality of Jew and Gentile in the church. For the Galatians and the Romans the relation of Jew and Gentile had been, in different ways, the occasion for Paul's letters.[8]

When the historic relationship of Jews and Gentiles in the Roman Em-pire is considered, it is not difficult to understand why this was the case. The customs and beliefs of the Jews were strange to Greek society and, ironically, they were often perceived as irreligious. Their rejection of Greek culture caused Jews to be viewed as misanthropic.[9] Consequently, Jews in the an-cient world were often met with suspicion and disdain, attitudes reflected in numerous writings of the period. For example, Cicero derided the Jewish religion as a *superstitio barbara* (*Flac.*, 28.67) and Horace, the great Roman satirist, ridiculed the Jews for such things as their zealous efforts to prosely-tize, their superstitious beliefs, and their strange customs of Sabbath-keeping and circumcision (*Sat.*, 1.4.143; 1.5.100; 1.4.70). Perhaps most derisive was Tacitus's account of the origins of the Jewish people, which accused Mo-ses, their founder, of introducing "new religious practices, quite opposed to those of all religions. The Jews regard as profane all that we hold sacred; on the other hand, they permit all that we abhor" (*Ann.*, 5.4).[10]

As might be expected, such anti-Semitism was met with equally hostile attitudes by many Jews toward the "uncircumcised pagans." These attitudes are reflected, for example, in such popular non-canonical Jewish writings as the Wisdom of Solomon, where the long-awaited Messiah becomes God's in-strument of punishment upon the Gentiles, destroying "the godless nations with the word of his mouth" (17:17).[11] The NT gives voice to similar attitudes,

8. Allen Verhey and Joseph S. Harvard, *Ephesians* (Louisville: Westminster John Knox, 2011), 27-28. See also Thomas R. Yoder Neufeld, *Ephesians* (Scottdale, PA: Herald, 2002), 26.

9. For example, as early as the fifth century B.C.E., the Greek historian Hecataeus asserted that Moses, the leader of the Jews, "initiated a form of life encouraging seclusion from human-kind and hatred of aliens" (cited in V. Tcherikover, *Hellenistic Civilization and the Jews* [New York: Atheneum, 1974], 360-61).

10. See also W. Wiefel, "The Jewish Community in Rome and the Origins of Roman Christianity," in *The Romans Debate*, ed. Karl P. Donfried (Minneapolis: Augsburg, 1977), 100-119. For an account of how these attitudes were later crystallized in Roman law, see Amnon Lindar, *The Jews in Roman Imperial Legislation* (Detroit: Wayne State University Press, 1987).

11. See also *1 Enoch*, where, in frequently depicted judgment scenes, God destroys the enemies of the Jews (38:4-5: 46:4-8; 48:8-10; 62:1-16; 63:1-12). These attitudes are also reflected

as when Jesus depicts a Greek woman's request that he heal her daughter as throwing "the children's food . . . to the dogs" (Mark 7:27), and when Peter hesitates even to enter the home of — much less preach to — Cornelius, a Gentile who desires to know the Gospel (Acts 10–11).

Within this climate of longstanding prejudice and animosity, then, the writers of the New Testament faced the Herculean task of uniting the members of these traditionally hostile racial groups, newly converted to Christianity, into one new movement, the Christian church. New Testament writers persistently found themselves called upon to address tension between Jews and Gentiles.[12] But that racial hostility may have loomed especially large for the author of Ephesians. Verhey and Harvard explain that in A.D. 66, after years of seething animosity that "periodically prompted efforts at appeasement on both sides," tensions erupted in a full-scale revolt by the Jews. "The war that followed was no polite reassurance of Roman authority. It was a bloodbath. Moreover, the enmity of war spilled over in anti-Jewish riots in Alexandria, Caesarea, and Antioch."[13] Dodd concurred: "It was one of the most atrocious wars recorded in ancient history. . . . It ended in A.D. 70 with the total defeat of the Jews, the destruction of their capital city, and the end of a Jewish state in Palestine for nineteen centuries."[14] As Verhey and Harvard went on to argue, this political situation "threatened a central accomplishment of Paul's mission; the unity of Jew and Gentile was in jeopardy. It was this political crisis, we think, that prompted the encyclical we call Ephesians."[15]

Not surprisingly, then, the epistle to the Ephesians is dominated by

---

in a number of places in the Hebrew Bible. See, for example, Isaiah's parody of pagan religion (44:9-20; 46:1-13), predictions of the fall of Babylon (47:1-15), and graphic descriptions of God's punishment of Israel's traditional enemies (63:1-6; cf. 34:1-17): "I trampled down peoples in my anger, I crushed them in my wrath, and I poured out their lifeblood on the earth." See also Ezek. 38–39; Dan. 1–5; Joel 3; Nahum; and Ezra 9–10. Of course, although not a dominant voice, other writings represent a more gracious attitude toward the Gentiles. For discussion, see D. S. Russell, *The Method and Message of Jewish Apocalyptic* (Philadelphia: Westminster, 1964), 297-303.

12. See, for example, Acts 8:4-40; 10–11; 21:20-25; Romans 1:16–4:25; 7:1-25; 9–11; 14:1–15:13; 1 Corinthians 1:18-25; 8:1–11:1; 2 Corinthians 8–9; Gal.2:1–4:7; and Phil.3:2-4. For a discussion of how this emphasis is particularly reflected in Romans, see Jeffrey A. Crafton, "Paul's Rhetorical Vision and the Purpose of Romans: Toward a New Understanding," *Novum Testamentum* 32 (1990): 317-39.

13. Verhey and Harvard, *Ephesians*, 29.

14. Dodd, *Christianity and the New Humanity*, 11.

15. Verhey and Harvard, *Ephesians*, 29.

concerns for unity between Jews and Gentiles in the Christian church,[16] concerns that Dodd argued were linked to the rhetorical situation outlined above:

> It may have been actually during the war — in any case it was very near to it in time — that a remarkable pamphlet upon the subject of reconciliation was issued from Christian sources: the pamphlet which we call the Epistle to the Ephesians. . . . Its dominant theme is the unity designed by God for mankind, and its realization in and through the catholic church.[17]

Even a cursory examination of the epistle as a whole underscores this focus. Paul begins chap. 2 by offering a generic conversion narrative that initially hints at the ethnic divide, depicting believers' pre-conversion state as one of separateness by using alternating first- and second-person pronouns ("*you* were dead through . . . trespasses and sins," v. 1; "all of *us* lived among them," v. 3).[18] He then describes God's action on behalf of sinful humanity, shifting entirely to an inclusive first-person plural from that point on: "God, who is rich in mercy . . . made *us* alive together with Christ" (vv. 4-5) so that now "*we* are . . . created in Christ Jesus for good works" (v. 10). The conversion narrative thus highlights the pre-conversion division, presumably between Jews and Gentiles, even as it emphasizes their common experience of sin, grace, and new life in Christ.

16. For discussion, see John Pohill, "An Introduction to Ephesians," *Review and Expositor* 76 (1977): 465-80, esp. 477; Jack T. Sanders, "Hymnic Elements in Ephesians 1–3," *Zeitschrift für die neutestamentliche Wissenschaft* 56 (1965): 214-32, esp. 230; Carol B. Hock, "The Significance of the SYN-Compounds for Jew–Gentile Relations in the Body of Christ," *Journal of the Evangelical Theological Society* 25 (1982): 175-83; Calvin J. Roetzel, "Jewish Christian–Gentile Christian Relations: A Discussion of Ephesians 2:15A," *Zeitschrift für die neutestamentliche Wissenschaft* 74 (1983): 81-89; Lincoln, *Ephesians*, lxxiii-lxxxiii; and Edna Mouton, "The Communicative Power of the Epistle to the Ephesians," in *Rhetoric, Scripture and Theology: Essays from the 1994 Pretoria Conference*, ed. Stanley E. Porter and Thomas H. Olbricht (Sheffield: Academic Press, 1996), 290-91.

17. Dodd, *Christianity and the New Humanity*, 11; see also Pohill ("Introduction to Ephesians," 477), who asserted that the key to the epistle "is to be found in the theme of unity which runs throughout . . . of Jew and Greek bound together into one body in Jesus Christ."

18. Some hold that the distinction here is clearly one being made between Jews and Gentiles. Although he is not convinced, Lincoln admitted that its proximity to the explicit distinction made in 2:11-12 renders "such a distinction . . . more plausible here." For discussion, see Lincoln, *Ephesians*, 88.

Then, in 2:11-21, Paul again recounts his audience's conversion experience, but this time the narrative focuses explicitly on the exclusion of Gentiles from the salvation history of Israel, introduced with the conjunction διό, "therefore" ("so then," NRSV), which indicates that what follows is an elaboration of the account just provided. The Gentiles, formerly considered the "uncircumcision" (v. 11), were "without Christ, being aliens from the commonwealth of Israel, and strangers to the covenants of promise" (v. 12). But now, he continues, "You who were once far off have been brought near by the blood of Christ" (v. 13). The work of Christ was thus to "create in himself one new humanity," so that now "you are no longer strangers and aliens, but you are citizens with the saints and . . . members of the household of God" (v. 19).

Paul follows this in chap. 3 with a brief account of his own commission to preach to the Gentiles, noting how God had revealed to him a mystery, hidden from former generations but now revealed to God's "holy apostles and prophets" (v. 5), that "Gentiles have become fellow heirs" with the Jews (v. 6). Thus, God's "eternal purpose" is now "made known to the rulers and authorities in the heavenly places" (v. 10). All of this leads up to Paul's prayer in 3:14-19, that they be "rooted and grounded in love," followed by a brief doxology (vv. 20-21), which serves as a transition into the epistle's exhortation (chaps. 4–6), where Paul again focuses on harmony in the Church by urging the Ephesians to make "every effort to maintain the unity of the Spirit in the bond of peace" (4:3).

In this extended discourse on God's plan for the Gentiles within the "commonwealth of Israel," as well as in the exhortations to unity that grow out of it, Paul uses the didactic and hortatory modes of address that we might naturally associate with rhetoric. He carefully explains that God's long-hidden mystery is the gathering of Gentiles with Jews into one church. Even when he offers a prayer on his audience's behalf, his mode of discourse is one of direct address. In other words, rather than addressing God in a prayer that the Ephesians would be allowed to "overhear" or join in with, Paul instead explains to them directly the content of his prayer for them: "I pray that you may have the power to comprehend . . . the love of Christ" (3:18-19). Finally, when he turns to admonition (chaps. 4–6), Paul's mode of address becomes imperatival, filled with imperatival verbs that function as direct commands regarding appropriate Christian behavior.

What is striking, however, is how Paul introduces all of this in the opening blessing of 1:3-14. As we shall see, that introductory passage anticipates the primary ideas and even the language that will be used throughout the rest of the epistle — the themes of predestination and election, God's grace and wisdom, the revealing of God's mystery, and especially the unity of "all things together in Christ" (1:10) to which God is taking the cosmos. But rather than explaining or arguing in support of these ideas or exhorting his hearers to live in accord with them, Paul instead embeds them within a communal expression of praise to God. He thus invites the Ephesians to engage in a mimetic performance of the values and ideas that he will take up in the rest of the epistle.

The Blessing's Form and Language

At first reading, even in translation, this "monstrous sentence conglomeration,"[19] as Hoehner called it — a single sentence in the original — appears to the modern reader to be an almost hopelessly tangled mass of participial phrases and relative clauses thrown together in haphazard fashion. Scholars have long recognized, however, that the text is actually a carefully constructed liturgical eulogy crafted in the tradition of the Jewish *berakah*, or blessing, perhaps even incorporating hymnic language from other early Christian worship settings.[20] Lincoln's observation captured this consensus: "The heaping up of words and phrases in this profuse and effusive style are [*sic*] a deliberate attempt to express the riches of which he speaks in an appropriate way. This is the language of prayer and worship."[21] The passage's intricate arrangement, and particularly the author's copious use of parallel words, clauses, and grammatical forms, has led to numerous attempts to discover the blessing's precise poetic structure, with no clear consensus.[22]

Despite their lack of consensus on the passage's precise syntactical structure, many scholars do share a common understanding of the passage's thematic organization or "movement of thought."[23] At the broadest

---

19. Hoehner, *Ephesians*, 153.

20. Sanders, "Hymnic Elements."

21. Lincoln, *Ephesians*, 12.

22. As will be clear, however, I take Sanders's ("Hymnic Elements," 227) oft-quoted assertion that "formal elements in 1:3-14 cannot even with a minor degree of precision be related to the subject matter" to be an overstatement.

23. Talbert, *Ephesians and Colossians*, 43; Talbert argues that "the structure of 1:3-14 is to be sought first of all in its content rather than in a formal pattern" (42). This concurs with Best's assertion that "we must seek the structure of the eulogy in its content rather than in a

level, this thematic movement is signaled by the passage's three participial phrases, "having blessed us" (ὁ εὐλογήσας ἡμᾶς), "having predestined
us" (προορίσας ἡμᾶς), and "having made known to us" (γνωρίσας ἡμῖν).[24]
The first phrase, as Talbert points out, introduces the main thought of the
blessing, the call to bless God for having "blessed us with every spiritual
blessing."[25] The content that follows, introduced by the conjunction καθώς
(lit. "just as"), is syntactically linked to that main statement, which it elaborates. The second two phrases introduce two broad categories of God's
blessing, the first, God's having "predestined us for adoption," culminating
in the "redemption through his [Christ's] blood" and "the forgiveness of sins"
(v. 7). The second broad category has to do with God's revealing "the mystery of his will" (v. 9), a mystery that has to do with the unity toward which
God has taken the entire cosmos, the joining of "all things together . . . in
heaven and . . . on earth" (v. 10). Within that broader thematic organization,
scholars have also noted a temporal movement, from God's election prior to
creation to the working out of God's plan within history, and leading to the
conclusion of God's salvation history at the eschaton, when God will bring
about the unity of all things in Christ.[26] To this temporal movement might
also be added a spatial progression as well, where God's blessings originate
"in the heavenly places," move down to the arena of human activity with the
blessing's allusion to the cross ("redemption through his blood," v. 7), and
culminate in the bringing together of all things "in heaven and . . . on earth"
in Christ. Regardless of the precise structure, then, the passage represents
a communal expression of worship to God intended to move an audience
along a spatial-temporal narrative framework from praising God for the gracious outworking of God's plan, from God's preordination before creation,
to the outpouring of God's grace and redemption within human history, to
its final consummation with the bringing of all things together "in heaven
and on earth" at the end of time.

Turning to the syntactical organization of the text itself, when the

---

formal pattern" (Ernest Best, *A Critical and Exegetical Commentary on Ephesians* [Edinburgh:
T & T Clark, 1998], 110).

24. Best, *Ephesians*, 109; Lincoln, *Ephesians*, 15-16; Neufeld, *Ephesians*, 38; and Thielman,
Ephesians, 41.

25. Talbert, *Ephesians and Colossians*, 43. Thielman similarly notes that "εὐλογήσας is a
substantival participle and is not only the chief syntactical element in verse three but arguably
in the entire passage" (*Ephesians*, 41).

26. See Best, *Ephesians*, 129; Talbert, *Ephesians and Colossians*, 44; Hoehner, *Ephesians*,
175.

passage is divided along the thematic lines noted above, the possibility of discerning a more exact organizational pattern becomes clearer. The blessing opens with an introductory expression of praise in vv. 3-4, beginning with the typical *berakah* formula, "Blessed be the God and Father of our Lord Jesus Christ," and the reason for that praise, the fact that God "has blessed us with every spiritual blessing in the heavenly places in Christ," specifically, "having chosen us from the foundation of the world to be holy and blameless in his sight." This basic content is then amplified in the remainder of the blessing in two distinct, parallel units of thought which are structured, as Dibelius, Käsemann, and others noted,[27] around the prepositional phrases "in love" (ἐν ἀγάπῃ) and "in all wisdom and insight" (ἐν πάσῃ σοφίᾳ καὶ φρονήσει), each of which introduces the two prepositional phrases ("having predestined us," προορίσας ἡμᾶς, and "having made known to us," γνωρίσας ἡμῖν), that articulate the themes of the two main sections, as shown in the following translation (by the author):

Opening

[3]Blessed be the God and Father of our Lord Jesus Christ, who has blessed us with every spiritual blessing in the heavenly places in Christ, [4]having chosen us from the foundation of the world to be holy and blameless in his presence;

---

27. Cited in Sanders, "Hymnic Elements," 225. The question of whether the prepositional phrases "in love" (ἐν ἀγάπῃ, v. 4) and "in all wisdom and insight" (ἐν πάσῃ σοφίᾳ καὶ φρονήσει, v. 8) should be connected with the clauses that precede or that follow them remains a subject of dispute. Larkin offered a compelling argument for taking them as *introducing* the actions of God described in the phrases that *follow* them. In the first instance he explained, "Given the focus of the passage's argument on God's actions, and the phrase's contribution to the text's cohesion when linked to the following participle, it is best to take it with what follows." Concerning the second phrase, "in all wisdom and insight," he pointed out that "parallels in discourse structure where an ἐν PP precedes a participle . . . are strategically present elsewhere in the eulogy (1:4-5, 10-11), and support linking this phrase to the participle that follows." He went on to argue, "Thus, these are not qualities that God gives, but rather qualities that he exercises in making known the mystery to us" (William J. Larkin, *Ephesians: A Handbook on the Greek Text* [Waco: Baylor University Press, 2009], 4, 7). See also Best, *Ephesians*, 127, 133; Thomas B. Slater, *Ephesians* (Macon: Smyth & Helwys, 2012). For an alternative view see Hoehner (*Ephesians*, 182-83, 213) who, though he places the prepositional phrases with the content that precedes them, nevertheless acknowledged strong support in the commentary tradition as well as in a number of translations for the structure advocated in the present study.

Body

A1 In love
   ⁽⁵⁾having predestined us for adoption unto him through Jesus Christ

A2 according to the good pleasure of his will
   ⁽⁶⁾unto the glory of his grace which he lavished on us in the one he loves

A3 ⁽⁷⁾in whom we have redemption through his blood, the forgiveness of sins according to the riches of his grace ⁽⁸⁾which he caused to overflow unto us;

B1 In all wisdom and insight
   ⁽⁹⁾having made known to us the mystery of his will

B2 according to his good pleasure which he displayed in him
   ⁽¹⁰⁾unto the working of his plan in the fullness of time, to bring all things together in Christ
      both things in heaven and things on earth, in him

B3a ⁽¹¹⁾in whom we were chosen, having been predestined according to the plan of him who works in all the purpose of his will, ⁽¹²⁾in order that we might be for the praise of his glory, we who were the first to believe in Christ,

B3b ⁽¹³⁾in whom you also [were chosen], who heard the word of truth, the gospel of our salvation, in whom having believed, you were sealed with the promised Holy Spirit,

Conclusion

⁽¹⁴⁾who is the guarantee of our inheritance, unto the redemption of our possession, unto the praise of his glory.

Schematized in this way, one can readily observe an almost line-by-line parallel structure built into the text, achieved grammatically and syntactically, as well as by the writer's lexical choices. The sequence of phrases in stanza A, "in love," "according to the good pleasure of his will," and "in whom we have redemption," is grammatically and syntactically parallel to the sequence in stanza B, "in all wisdom and insight," "according to his good pleasure," and "in whom we were chosen/in whom you also were chosen." The phrases "having predestined us" and "unto the glory of his grace" in stanza A are similarly parallel to the phrases "having made known to us" and "unto the working of his plan" in stanza B.

Finally, within stanza B, part 3, a structurally parallel relationship exists between the phrases "in whom we also were chosen" (v. 11) and "in whom you also were chosen" (v. 13). These verses mark a significant shift in the blessing's mode of address, signaled most obviously by the alternation of the first- and third-person pronouns. Verse 11 begins, "in whom we were chosen," which at first sight appears to continue the theme of extolling God for the blessings given to *all* Christians. But as O'Brien pointed out, "the *we* is restricted, for in the following verse the same people are spoken of as those who 'first hoped in Christ' (v. 12)."[28] Then, in v. 13, the pronoun shifts to the first-person plural, "you also . . . who heard the word of truth . . . believed . . . [and] were sealed with the Holy Spirit." This alternation of pronouns suggests a change in the voice of the author or narrator from that of addressing God on behalf of a congregation of worshippers to addressing the worshippers more directly. Additionally, the language moves from broad abstract theological categories to more historically grounded events, represented in the temporal distinction between "we who were the first to believe" and "you also who heard the word of truth." Also significant is the way that these verses take up words and ideas expressed earlier in the blessing — chosen, predestined, the working of God's plan, the praise of God's glory, etc. All of this indicates that in these verses, the author recalls broad themes for which God has been praised in the blessing up to this point, but now they are applied to the concrete historical situation of the author and audience.

Of course this alternating use of pronouns raises the question of to whom, exactly, vv. 1-13 refers, a question that has been the subject of some debate among scholars. At the outset, it should be noted that regardless of the precise identity of the "we" and "you" here, the overall theme of this section is clearly that of unity between the groups represented by these designations, so that the concrete instantiation of God's plan to bring "all things together . . . in heaven and . . . on earth" is to be found in fellowship enjoyed by those "who were the first to believe" and "you [who] also heard the word of truth." In other words, the suasory function of the liturgical form and language remains the same regardless of whether we can identify the precise audience for whom it is intended. Nevertheless, there is strong evidence and

---

28. Peter T. O'Brien, *The Letter to the Ephesians* (Grand Rapids: Eerdmans, 1999), 116.

support for the traditional position that the two groups referred to here are Jews and Gentiles.[29] The passage clearly anticipates the longer discussion of the revelation of the "mystery of Christ" (3:3-4), that "the Gentiles have become fellow heirs, members of the same body, and sharers in the promise in Christ Jesus through the gospel" (3:6).[30] As Ernst put it, "If one considers the general theme of Ephesians to be the 'one church from Jews and Gentiles,' then the appearance of the accented 'we' (v 11) and 'you' (v 13) makes clear sense."[31] This understanding moreover fits the broader conception of the "priority" of the Jews in salvation history that we find elsewhere in the NT (e.g., Rom. 1:6, "to the Jew first and also to the Greek"). The description that follows the "you also" in v. 13 (e.g., "were sealed with the promised Holy Spirit"), even seems to recall the key elements of the first recorded Gentile conversion, that of Cornelius and his household, who, according to the account in Acts 10, heard the gospel, believed, and were filled with the Holy Spirit — which signaled to Peter and his Jewish companions that God had indeed welcomed Gentiles into the church.[32] Finally, this understanding helps to explain the return to an inclusive first-person plural in the final verse of the blessing. Neufeld asserted,

> The return in verse 14 to a clearly inclusive *our* expresses the vision in Ephesians of God's people made up of both *we* and *you*, the *near* and *far* — Jews and Gentiles, old and new, first and second (and third) generation believers. *We* and *you together* constitute the community of the *chosen*.[33]

29. See O'Brien, *Letter to the Ephesians*, 116 n. 114, for a listing of scholars who take this position. See also Margaret Y. MacDonald, *Colossians and Ephesians* (Collegeville: Liturgical, 2008), 203; John Muddiman, *The Epistle to the Ephesians* (Peabody, MA: Hendrickson, 2004), 64; Neufeld, *Ephesians*, 54-55; Slater, *Ephesians*, 29; and Talbert, *Ephesians and Colossians*, 43. Alternative explanations can be found in Thielman, *Ephesians*, 75-76; Lincoln, *Ephesians*, 13; Hoehner, *Ephesians*, 213; and Best, *Ephesians*, 147-48.

30. Against those who note that the theme of Jew–Gentile unity has not yet been introduced in the epistle, O'Brien asserted, "It may be questioned as to whether the theological significance of the Jew–Gentile question in the letter and its relation to the mystery have been taken sufficiently into account. One should not be surprised at its anticipation in vv. 3-14. Many of the important themes of the letter are prefigured in the introductory eulogy" (*Letter to the Ephesians*, 117).

31. J. Ernst, *Die Briefe an die Philipper, an Philemon, an die Kolosser, an die Epheser* (Regensburg: Pustet, 1974), 278, cited in O'Brien, *Letter to the Ephesians*, 117 n. 116.

32. Acts 10:44-48. See also O'Brien, *Letter to the Ephesians*, 117.

33. Neufeld, *Ephesians*, 55. See O'Brien's response to Lincoln's claim that the return to the first-person plural in v. 14 "tells overwhelmingly against such a proposal" (Lincoln, *Ephesians*,

When viewed in light of the epistle's rhetorical situation and, I shall argue, the blessing's persuasive function, it seems clear that the author here treats separately what may already have been commonly acknowledged as separate religious communities. He addresses each explicitly and finally rejoins them using the inclusive language with which the blessing concludes.

The blessing of Eph. 1, then, is a highly structured ceremonial or ritual expression of praise to God which can be divided in this way:

> **Opening:** states the basic content concerning our having been chosen by God ("Blessed be . . . in his sight")

> **Body:** develops the basic content, in two structurally parallel stanzas, each consisting of three well-defined thought units ("In love . . . Holy Spirit")
> > **Stanza One:** Praise for God's love and grace, reflected in our predestination, adoption, and redemption through Christ
> > **Stanza Two:** Praise for the revelation of the mystery of God's will, to bring all things together in Christ

> **Conclusion:** recalls the concept of "chosenness" introduced in the opening and developed in the body ("who is the guarantee of our inheritance"), and closes with a final, formulaic expression of praise ("unto the praise of his glory")

Within this structure, moreover, the author uses traditional formulaic, possibly hymnic, thought and phraseology, much of which is likely familiar to his audience. When viewed in light of the rest of the epistle's content, and particularly its exhortations to unity, however, it becomes clear that the liturgy's purpose goes beyond simply expressing gratitude to God. Rather, the blessing is persuasive, intended to transport its hearers into a symbolic *experience* of unity as a way of preparing them for the explicit doctrinal explanations and exhortations that will come later in the epistle.

---

13): "It is entirely appropriate for Paul to assert that *the promised Holy Spirit* is the guarantee of our inheritance, that is, of Jew and Gentile alike" (O'Brien, *Letter to the Ephesians*, 117).

Liturgy as Persuasion

Although he did not discuss liturgy explicitly, Longinus's description of the sublime seems to have anticipated the kind of suasory potential — as he put it, the possibility of being "elevated and exalted by true sublimity" (*Subl.*, 7.2) — inherent in that discursive form.[34] He especially highlighted the sense of participation that hearers might feel in the performance of the discourse, as if they were no longer merely the audience but were now co-creating the poetic expression: "Filled with joy and pride, we come to believe that we have created what we have only heard." As a number of scholars have noted, liturgy uniquely brings about the kind of experience Longinus seemed to be describing, since by its very nature it provides a communicative form through which a congregation expresses its praise to God.

Scholars have especially noted the power of liturgy to make theological reality "present" for a congregation of worshippers in a way that mere description or explanation of that reality never can. Ladrière, for example, draws on speech-act theory to explore what he sees as the three performative functions of liturgy.[35] First is what he calls "existential induction," which has to do with the power of liturgy to evoke certain affective states in the worshipper. He notes that the performative verbs — ask, pray, bless, give thanks

34. On the most basic level, of course, the blessing accords with what classical theorists understood about epideictic rhetoric. As Aristotle conceived it, the purpose of epideictic rhetoric was the praise or blame of the values addressed by the rhetor or the persons or deeds held up as examples of those values (*Rhet.*, 1.9). On this basis, according to Perelman and Olbrechts-Tyteca, epideictic rhetoric "has significance and importance for argument because it strengthens the disposition toward action by increasing adherence to the values it lauds." In epideictic rhetoric, they continue, "The speaker tries to establish a sense of communion centered around particular values recognized by the audience" (Chaim Perelman and Lucie Olbrechts-Tyteca, *The New Rhetoric: A Treatise on Argumentation*, trans. John Wilkinson and Purcell Weaver [Notre Dame: University of Notre Dame Press, 1969], 50-51). So in a general sense, the blessing does serve to knit the community together around a common set of values. Central among those values held up for the audience to consider is the unity to which God has brought them. But at least as the handbook tradition seems to indicate, even in a eulogy one still had a rhetor speaking directly to an audience, albeit in a grand style, "arguing" why the subject was worthy of their admiration or vituperation. In the blessing in Ephesians, by contrast, the audience actually symbolically performs the act of praising God themselves, which potentially takes them into a phenomenological experience of the values for which they bless God.

35. Jean Ladrière, "The Performativity of Liturgical Language," in *Liturgical Experience of Faith*, ed. Herman Schmidt and David Power, trans. John Griffiths (New York: Herder and Herder, 1973), 50-62, here 56-59. See also Richard D. McCall, *Do This: Liturgy as Performance* (Notre Dame: University of Notre Dame Press, 2007).

— all "express illocutionary acts presupposing certain attitudes: trust, veneration, gratitude, submission, contrition, and so on. These attitudes come into effect at the very moment when, by virtue of the enunciation of the sentence, the corresponding act takes place." In other words, the function of liturgical language is not so much to express a preexisting attitude as it is to create that attitude in the act of its enunciation — in Ladrière's words, "to dispose souls to welcome that which it suggests." Second, he emphasizes the role of liturgy not simply to describe or express a community that exists prior to its expression, but actually to constitute that community through the very act of its performance: "In so far as it gives to all participants — as co-locuters — the chance to take on the same acts, it establishes between them that operative reciprocity which constitutes the reality of a community." Finally, and most importantly, Ladrière underscores the power of liturgy to imbue the reality that it expresses with actuality and concreteness, making that reality "present for the participants, not as a spectacle, but as a reality whose efficacy they take into their very own life, that about which it speaks." Viewed from the perspective of classical poetics, liturgy thus represents mimesis *par excellence*. Rather than explaining theological ideas or offering evidence for their veracity, it draws worshippers into a consciousness of the reality that it proclaims.

In this way, as a liturgy, the blessing of Eph. 1 invites the audience into a performance in which they celebrate the values that they will later be encouraged to adopt as their own. Paul's consistent use of the first-person plural pronoun to describe both himself and his audience symbolically constitutes, out of both, one congregation united in praise: "We praise God for what he has done for us." In its expression of praise, moreover, the blessing symbolically reconfigures the entire discursive exchange from what might be expected in a typical rhetorical event. Viewed dramatistically, the blessing places Paul, the "rhetor," in the position of a fellow worshipper instead of an orator explicitly attempting to persuade his audience to believe or to act in some way. Indeed, the hearers are no longer even "addressed" by the discourse — no one is explaining to them why God should be blessed or exhorting them to bless God. Now they become the performers, whose focus is directed not at the speaker or even at each other, but at their true "audience," who is God. Most importantly, the blessing draws its audience into the communal act of voicing praise and thanksgiving for the works of God that it proclaims — election, grace, redemption, and unity — treating both the works themselves and the emotions of awe and gratitude that it expresses toward those acts as present reality. Along the lines Longinus suggested, no longer are the worshippers simply hearing about God; now, they are talking to God. They do not merely hear theological ideas but, rather, they apprehend realities about God in their direct experience.

Among the factors that create sublimity or elevation in a poetic work, Longinus (*Subl.*, 39.1-3) especially underscored form or arrangement, an insight that has special relevance to the blessing of Eph. 1. Using the analogy of music, he noted how harmony and rhythm are instruments not only of pleasure but also of "grandeur and emotion." Musical instruments fill the hearers "with certain emotions" and make them "somehow beside themselves and possessed." The music "sets a rhythm, it makes the hearer move to the rhythm and assimilate himself to the tune, 'untouched by the Muses though he be'" (e.g., even if the hearer has no natural musical talent). The notes of the lyre, for example, are meaningless in isolation. Arranged together, however, they "often cast a wonderful spell of harmony with their varied sounds and blended and mingled notes." In the same way, within poetic discourse, form or arrangement creates "a harmony of words, man's natural instrument, penetrating not only the ears but the very soul. . . . The combination and variety of its sounds convey the speaker's emotions to the minds of those around him and make the hearers share them."

In his own writings on artistic form, Kenneth Burke built on the understanding articulated by Longinus in order to describe more precisely the way that arrangement or structure within an artistic work can move an audience toward assent to its content. Burke linked the power of artistic form to what he believed were certain "potentialities of appreciation" for various processes of arrangement or development that were simply part of the human brain's neurological structure.[36] These "innate forms of the mind" enable an audience to appreciate such formal features as crescendo, balance, repetition, disclosure, reversal, contradiction, expansion, magnification, and series. He argued, for example, that the formality of beginnings and endings, "such procedures as the greeting of the New Year, the ceremony of laying cornerstones, the 'housewarming,' the funeral, all indicate that the human

---

36. Kenneth Burke, *Counter-statement* (Berkeley: University of California Press, 1968), 46-49, 139. Burke conceived of the mind's appreciation for crescendo, for example, in this way: "If we wish to indicate a gradual rise to a crisis, and speak of this as a climax, or a crescendo, we are talking in intellectualistic terms of a mechanism which can often be highly emotive. There is in reality no such thing as a crescendo. What does exist is a multiplicity of individual artworks each of which may be arranged as a whole, or in some parts, in a manner which we distinguish as climactic. And there is also in the human brain the potentiality for reacting favorably to such a climactic arrangement" (45).

mind is prone to feel beginnings and endings as such." Consequently, for Burke, artistic form is no mere embellishment to content. Much more, it readily awakens

> an attitude of collaborative expectancy in us. For instance, imagine a passage built about a set of oppositions ("we do this, but they on the other hand do that; we stay here, but they go there; we look up, but they look down," etc.). Once you grasp the trend of the form, it invites participation regardless of the subject matter. Formally, you will find yourself swinging along with the succession of antitheses, even though you may not agree with the proposition being presented in this form.[37]

"Participation" in the form invites assent to the content of that form, or at least "prepares for assent to the matter identified with it." Thus, for Burke, the potential of poetic discourse to engage an audience, to invite symbolic participation by means of artistic form, explains its power to move or persuade an audience.[38]

The blessing of Eph. 1 reflects just such a conception of the nature of form. Of course, each of the blessing's poetic features would individually have been expected to evoke the kind of response described by Lincoln:

> Repetition and redundance are the essence of liturgy and here the repetition of certain words and phrases, the repeated genitives, and the collection of synonyms not only have the effect of intensifying the force of the concepts involved, but also serve to provide the sentence with a certain rhythm. In addition, the succession of long syllables in a number of places periodically slows down the flow of words so that a chant-like effect is produced as the eulogy is spoken.[39]

37. Kenneth Burke, *A Rhetoric of Motives* (Berkeley: University of California Press, 1969), 58.

38. Burke's conception of the power of the artistic act to bring the audience into "participation" with the act underlies the distinction he makes between the audience's watching a performance and the audience's experiencing the act (*Counter-statement,* 59-60). As an example, he describes the experience of feeling suspense as one watches a rubber band being stretched: "It is the suspense of certain forces gathering to produce a certain result. We know that it will be snapped — there is thus no ignorance of the outcome. *Our satisfaction arises from our participation in the process, from the fact that the beginnings of the dialogue lead us to feel the logic of its close*" (145, emphasis added).

39. Lincoln, *Ephesians,* 17.

But equally important as the effect of those formal features by themselves is the fact that, as noted above, they come together in a complex structure that conveys a discernible line of thought reflecting the epistle's overall rhetorical aim of uniting Jewish and Gentile believers into one Christian community. In part A, Paul invites the audience to praise God for the richness of his love, expressed in his act of having predestined "us" for adoption unto Him. This was accomplished "according to the pleasure of his will" through the outpouring of "his grace," resulting in "our redemption through his blood" and "the forgiveness of sins." Using language and concepts with which his audience was no doubt familiar, Paul engages the Ephesians in praise for the acts of God, which constituted the "core" of their Christian experience and for which they no doubt felt genuinely thankful. This content is then connected, by means of the parallel grammatical and syntactical structure, with the ideas in part B of the body, ideas which the audience likely resisted. As Burke suggested, the blessing's form invites the audience's "collaboration" with the content in this second half of the blessing — in his words, to continue "swinging along with the succession" of parallel phrases that capture the content that they were reluctant to embrace.

In part B, Paul invites the audience to praise God for his wisdom and insight, demonstrated in the revelation of "the mystery of his will," again according to his good pleasure. This will of God, long a mystery but now made known, was "to bring all things together in Christ, both things in heaven and things on earth."[40] In this way, the audience praises God for the ultimate, cosmic unity toward which, in the fullness of time, he is taking all things, a unity that will later be described as the creation in Christ of "one new humanity in place of the two," that is, of Jews and Gentiles (2:15).

Having praised God for this ultimate, cosmic unity, the audience is then led to praise God for the concrete expression of that unity in their own experience. That concrete expression of cosmic unity, of course, is the gathering together of "we who were the first to believe" (i.e., Jewish Christians), with "you also . . . who heard the word of truth" (i.e., Gentile Christians). Here, we encounter a grammatical feature that may have especially served to draw them into the blessing's content. The parallel structure in the opening clauses of vv. 11 and 13 ("in whom we were chosen" and "in whom you also"), and the absence of a verb in the latter clause, may indicate that the phrase "in whom you also" is an ellipsis for which the words "were chosen"

40. Here and in the following paragraphs, translations of Ephesians 1 are the author's, as provided above.

would have been supplied by the audience.[41] This would reflect the kind of persuasive strategy that Aristotle saw at work in the enthymeme, which he described as having the power to engage an audience by inviting them to "assume" one of its key premises (*Rhet.*, 1.2; 2.1). If this is the case, then the audience is here being invited to participate in the act of blessing even more profoundly by "filling in the blank," as it were, supplying the language that brings the parallelism of both phrases to complete symmetry and thus reinforcing the blessing's central idea, that the Jews and the Gentiles are equally chosen within the eternal plan of God.

By means of this complex structure, then, the blessing begins by leading the audience to praise God for the elements of their Christian experience with which they are both comfortable and familiar, and then moves them to continue praising God for that which they are reluctant to accept — the fact that although they are from traditionally hostile ethnicities, they now form one new community. All of this is accomplished in a traditional *berakah,* which, as a liturgical form, possessed unique power to make ideas present and actual in the experience and emotions of the worshipper. Even apart from its content, the liturgy constituted as a united community the disparate individuals who would join together in its performance. Having symbolically enacted and existentially experienced their unity through their participation in the blessing of Eph. 1, the audience is thus prepared to accept the more explicit doctrinal exposition and moral exposition on Christian unity that follow.

Conclusion

One of the characteristics of the NT epistles' poetic texts is the way that, rather than presenting new information, they instead typically take up ideas and dispositions explained or argued elsewhere in the epistle and cast them as mimetic representations. As this chapter has shown, the blessing of Eph. 1 reflects this same pattern, presenting poetically the same themes that will be addressed in more explicitly rhetorical ways later in the epistle. In crafting this text, Paul seems to appreciate the fact that racial hostility, like most

41. As Blass and Debrunner point out, ellipsis in the New Testament commonly takes a form in which "the repetition of a grammatical element is left to be supplied." For discussion, see F. Blass and A. Debrunner, *A Greek Grammar of the New Testament and Other Early Christian Literature,* trans. and rev. Robert W. Funk (Chicago: University of Chicago Press, 1961), 253-55.

deeply held attitudes and personality traits, is extremely difficult to change, and may not be altered simply through explicit, logical argumentation. Instead, he seems to assume that change at this level may only come about by giving his audience the kind of visceral experience that can "overwrite" the experiences that shaped their attitudes and personalities in the first place. At the very least, he understands that any attempt to lead out by directly charging the audience to accept each other will meet stiff resistance.

In response, Paul creates a liturgy in which the audience symbolically enacts that unity, in a sense, in their own voices. Simply by virtue of its form as a communal expression of praise, the blessing has the potential to unite the worshippers. But even more, the structure of the discourse itself moves the audience from a position of praising God for the blessings that they truly enjoy, to those "blessings" which they resist — which turn out to be centered on God's plan to bring Jew and Gentile together into one body. By celebrating these values through liturgy — in Burke's words, by participating in the form of the discourse — Paul hopes that they will actually come to possess them. Remarkably, when he gives them his explicit challenge to be unified in 4:3, he tells them not to seek, but rather to maintain the unity of the Spirit. His choice of terms suggests that they have already glimpsed the reality that they will now be urged to practice.

CHAPTER SIX

Reconfiguring the Rhetorical Encounter, Part One: Placing Hearers "in" the Content

In a radio talk that he did for the BBC in October 1962, C. S. Lewis harshly berated the anonymous artist (Lewis identified him only as "the imbecile") who illustrated his nursery edition of Bunyon's classic allegory, *Pilgrim's Progress*. Lewis took exception to the way the artist had depicted the scene where the character Christiana comes to the edge of the river, bids farewell to her friends who have traveled with her to the water's edge, and, with a wave, begins her journey to the other side. The artist responded by drawing "a picture of an old lady on her deathbed surrounded by weeping relatives in the approved Victorian manner." Lewis retorted with irritation, "But if Bunyon had wanted a literal deathbed scene he'd have written one." Lewis then explained that "this stupidity" derives from the pernicious tendency, once we have grasped what an image means, to throw the image away and to think of "the ingredients in real life which it represents," when in fact

> the right process is really the exact reverse. We oughtn't to be thinking, "This green valley where the shepherd boy is singing represents humility." We ought to be discovering, as we read, that humility is like that green valley. That way, moving always into the book, not out of it, from the concept to the image, enriches the concept. And that's what allegory is for.[1]

Lewis's broadside hints at the theme of this book, that there is a crucial difference between contemplating ideas as abstract concepts and actually experiencing those ideas as they are captured in verbal images and other

---

1. C. S. Lewis, British Broadcasting Service audio recording (no date), *C. S. Lewis Speaks His Mind*, Episcopal Media Center. Transcribed by the author.

poetic forms. Lewis highlights the power of the imaginative experience over against the mere abstraction to profoundly shape our understanding.

Some nineteen centuries earlier, the Roman rhetorical theorist Quintilian captured the same distinction between thinking *about* some action or condition and actually imagining oneself *in* that condition or performing that action, as if one were actually there:

> When the mind is idle or occupied with wishful thinking or a sort of daydreaming, images (*imagines*) . . . seek us out, and we think we are traveling or sailing or fighting a battle or addressing a crowd or disposing of wealth which we do not possess, and not just to think about but actually to do (*nec cogitare sed facere*) these things (*Inst.*, 6.2.30).[2]

Quintilian then goes on to ask, "Can't we give this mental vice some utility? Surely we can." As the passages examined in this study show, Paul answered his question with a resounding "yes."

In contrast to the practice of traditional rhetoric, which offered arguments and evidence aimed at bringing about a critical judgment between competing alternatives, Paul sought to create a holistic worldview — to use Charles Taylor's language, a "social imaginary" — that would determine Christians' fundamental self-identity and ways of seeing and acting in the world.[3] He hoped, with his discourse, not only to influence the audience's cognitive understanding but, much more, to "reprogram" their visceral reactions to the world. In Paul's efforts to shape early Christians' beliefs and behaviors, he offered abundant explanation and argument, as well as explicit exhortation. But as this study has emphasized, at strategic moments in his writing, he shifted his mode of discourse from argument and exhortation to a form of poetic discourse that used mimesis to create imaginative representations of the ideas they sought to advance, transporting their hearers, as Longinus put it, "out of themselves," exploiting poetic language's "irresistible power and mastery" in order to create memories that would be "stubborn and indelible" (*Subl.*, 1.4; 7.3-4).

This chapter and the one that follows explore the implications of this use of poetic form, arguing that the shift from argumentation to poetic form

---

2. The translation of Quintilian here is from Michele Kennerly, "Getting Carried Away: How Rhetorical Transport Gets Judgment Going," *Rhetoric Society Quarterly* 40 (2010): 269-91, here 269-70.

3. See above, p. 10.

radically reconfigured the overall rhetorical encounter from the way it had been conceived in the classical tradition. Specifically, Paul's use of poetic form altered the three fundamental relationships of the rhetorical encounter, the relationships of audience to content, rhetor to audience, and audience members to one another. For example, his turn in Rom. 7 from speaking *in propria persona* to using the voice of dramatic soliloquy altered the traditional relationship of rhetor to audience by symbolically removing the "empirical Paul" from the persuasive encounter. Likewise, his vivid depiction of the parousia in 1 Thess. 4 potentially altered the auditors' relationship with one another by taking them through an emotional shared experience. But perhaps the most important change in the audience's position effected by this use of poetic form was the shift in the audience's relationship to the content itself, from that of contemplating it as an abstract idea to encountering it as a subjective experience.

In this chapter, I examine what I take to be the most important implication of the turn from argument to mimesis, which has to do with the way that mimesis placed the hearers "in" the content, along the lines Quintilian suggested above. The succeeding chapter explores two implications that grow out of this shift from "thinking about" to "being in" the imaginative experience, which have to do with how these poetic texts altered the audience's relationship with the rhetor and the audience members' relationship with one another. As a starting point for examining the altered relationship of audience to content, we begin by exploring contemporary research into the problem of "counterargument" and its parallel in the classical tradition, represented in Aristotle's advice for overcoming the natural barriers between the audience and the arguments they were being asked to accept.

Rhetoric and the Problem of Counterargument

Contemporary social scientists who study persuasion and social influence recognize that any direct attempt at persuasion faces the inevitable problem of "counterargument," that is, the tendency of individuals to respond to explicit arguments by resisting their influence, meeting them with critical judgment, alternative explanations, rationalizations, etc. This research has shown, for example, that auditors respond to direct evidence such as statistical data with much greater levels of counterargument than they do to exemplars such as stories, illustrations, and personal testimony, a reaction that has been explained in terms of Csikszentmihalyi's "flow theory," which holds that "individuals find it rewarding and enjoyable to identify and develop patterns in something like exemplars and follow the flow in those patterns."[4] As Limon and Kazoleas explained,

> When people are in the flow of a story, they find . . . disrupting the flow of that story to critically analyze it highly undesirable. . . . When a receiver listens to an exemplar they [*sic*] are apt to get caught up in the flow of the exemplar in terms of sequencing and the images invoked therein. Once receivers move into the flow of information they are apt to counterargue less.[5]

Other researchers have similarly accounted for that effect in terms of an audience's experience of "transportation," that is, the degree to which they become absorbed or immersed in an artistic work. Moyer-Gusé and Nabi concluded, "Because transportation is an enjoyable and immersive process . . . [the audience is] less motivated and less able to interrupt this process to counterargue."[6] Whereas direct argument tends to put the auditor in a position as a judge or critic of the evidence, which inherently undermines the argument's power to convince, certain other kinds of discourse have the power to draw the listener *into* an immersive experience, a stance that tends to lower their resistance to being persuaded.

Because of its focus on logical argument, classical rhetoric likewise understood the auditor as being, in some sense, "removed from" the content of discourse, as an observer or critic judging the evidence from the "outside," that is, from a position of inherent skepticism and even defensiveness. Despite his focus on logical argument, Aristotle recognized the auditor's

4. M. Sean Limon and Dean C. Kazoleas, "A Comparison of Exemplar and Statistical Evidence in Reducing Counter-Arguments and Responses to a Message," *Communication Research Reports* 21 (2004): 291-98, here 292.

5. Limon and Kazoleas, "Comparison of Exemplar and Statistical Evidence," 292. See also Glen R. Hass and Darwyn E. Linder, "Counterargument Availability and the Effects of Message Structure on Persuasion," *Journal Of Personality & Social Psychology* 23 (1972): 219-33; Mike Allen, "Meta-Analysis Comparing the Persuasiveness of One-sided and Two-sided Messages," *Western Journal Of Speech Communication* 4 (1991): 390-404; and Kitae Kim, Shinil Moon, and Thomas Feeley, "Transportation Lowers Resistance to Narrative Persuasion Messages: Testing Three Explanations," paper presented at the annual meeting of the International Communication Association, Boston, MA, May 5, 2011.

6. Emily Moyer-Gusé and Robin L. Nabi, "Explaining the Effects of Narrative in an Entertainment Television Program: Overcoming Resistance to Persuasion," *Human Communication Research* 36 (2010): 26-52, here 31.

position relative to the discourse content as a problem, and much of what he says in his treatise is actually aimed at overcoming that barrier. Certainly, his emphasis on proofs related to emotion reflects his sense of the need to reduce barriers to an audience's reception of the argument. As he writes in the opening of Book 2, "When people are feeling friendly and placable, they think one sort of thing; when they are feeling angry or hostile, they think either something totally different or the same thing with a different intensity" (*Rhet.*, 2.1). Because emotional states influence cognitive processes, effective rhetors will know how to put their hearers "into the right frame of mind" (2.1). Likewise, his focus on ethos reflects his understanding that the audience's attitude toward the rhetor shapes their experience of the argument, so that "when they feel friendly to the man who comes before them for judgment, they regard him as having done little wrong, if any; when they feel hostile, they take the opposite view" (2.1). For this reason, orators must not only make their arguments "demonstrative and worthy of belief," they must also make their character "look right" (2.1). Even in his discussion of logical proofs, Aristotle understands and at times seems to endorse what appear to be manipulative efforts to bring the auditor "closer" to the content. His famous explanation of the enthymeme emphasizes the importance of not explicitly stating a premise that is already familiar to the audience: "There is no need even to mention it; the hearer adds it himself" (1.2). That advice hints, at least, at his awareness that by supplying the assumed premise, the auditor will be drawn into the argumentative process. We see the same concern in his instruction to place enthymemes before examples, because to reverse them "will give the argument an inductive air, which only rarely suits the conditions of speechmaking" (2.20). Perhaps nowhere is his awareness of the need to bring the audience "into" the content more obvious than in his discussion of the effectiveness of the maxim as an enthymematic premise: "Even hackneyed and commonplace maxims are to be used, if they suit one's purpose: just because they are commonplace, every one seems to agree with them, and therefore they are taken for truth" (2.21). As a result, hearers will perceive the rhetor to be expressing "as a universal truth the opinions which they hold themselves about particular cases" (2.21). As with his instructions regarding ethos and pathos, Aristotle's advice here points to his attempt to overcome the difficulty created by the fact that rhetoric, as a process of presenting logical arguments that auditors judge by means of rational processes of critical evaluation, inevitably places them outside the content.

Writers in the rhetorico-poetic tradition such as Gorgias and Longinus demonstrate an acute appreciation for the way that mimesis shifts the hearer's position from being an outsider (to a logical argument) to being an insider (to a phenomenological experience). Longinus captures the distinction between the two positions when he observes the following about a passage from Demosthenes, cited at the outset of this study:

> There, besides developing his factual argument the orator has visualized the event and consequently his conception far exceeds the limits of mere persuasion. In all such cases the stronger element seems naturally to catch our ears, so that our attention is drawn from the reasoning to the enthralling effect of the imagination, and the reality is concealed in a halo of brilliance. And this effect on us is natural enough; set two forces side by side and the stronger always absorbs the virtues of the other (*Subl.*, 15.10-11).

Like the contemporary scholars who describe audience involvement with narrative using the metaphor of "transportation," Gorgias described the audience's experience using spatial metaphors that represented a change in the audience's location. As he put it, in the presence of such language, auditors found themselves "seized" and "carried off" (*Hel.*, 6-7). He immediately followed his notorious claim that the "inspired incantations" of language transport "by means of [their] wizardry" with a discussion of the "persuasions by fictions" that offer a way of recollecting the past or knowing the future. Gorgias implies that language offers a means, as if by magic, to travel to the past or the future (*Hel.*, 10-11). Kennerly summarized how this sensation of "transport" serves to overcome the natural position of the auditor as a critic of argument who stood "outside" of the discourse:

> According to the Gorgianic vision of rhetoric, words and images share the capacity to "stamp the soul," thereby restricting their recipients' range of judgment. It is through such restriction that rhetorical transport carries people away with shockingly or shamefully little resistance. . . . Persuasion and visualization do not necessarily take us to ugly places, but they do take us places, and the destination often is not up to us.[7]

In this way Gorgias saw "persuasion by speech" as the "equivalent to abduction by force" (*Hel.*, 12).

Longinus also clearly reflects the same understanding in his choice of "transport" (ἔκστασις, *Subl.*, 1.4) as his titular word for the power of the

---

7. Kennerly, "Getting Carried Away," 276-77.

sublime. Like Gorgias, Longinus understood the power of rhetoric to move an audience "from an alteration of an emotional state . . . to one that transitions into an alteration of location."[8] In the *Iliad's* description of the battle of the gods, for example, hearers do not merely hear *about* the battle; rather they are imaginatively "in" the scene, able to "see . . . the earth split to the foundations, . . . the whole universe sundered and turned upside down" (*Subl.*, 9.6). Through the genius of "great prose writers and poets of the past . . . many are carried away by the inspiration of another" (13.2). Similarly, through his judicious use of figures was Demosthenes "enabled to carry the audience away with him" (16.3), even to the point that he "drags his audience along with him" (22.3).

When it comes to the New Testament, of course, early Christian writers sought to "convince" their audiences of things that those hearers, in most cases at least, actually *wanted* to believe, or to foster traits and states of emotion that their audience *actually valued*. As noted in this study's introduction, Kirkwood's insightful study of the rhetoric of parables emphasizes that most religions seek to cultivate such personal traits as devotion and selflessness, traits which would be considered valuable to devotees. He also pointed out that most traditions of spirituality place high value on sustained affective states such as hopefulness or affectionate regard for one's fellow believers. Commenting on the well-known observation that stories have the power to arouse emotions in support of broader persuasive goals, he asserted that it would be a mistake to view the impact of parables on feelings and states of awareness only in this light. Indeed, in many religious traditions, "certain moods and states of mind (e.g., equanimity, mental quietude, awe, devotion) are not just the means, but the ends of spiritual discipline." But even here, when the devotees welcome the beliefs and attitudes, they still face their own form of counterargument, which Kirkwood describes as the "habitual mental process — i.e., an internal, verbal dialogue and an underlying rational activity — which must be suspended temporarily if other states of awareness desired by the aspirant are to occur."[9] In other words, the same resistance to direct persuasion that scholars identify — the tendency to rationalize — also represents a serious obstacle to the kind of "social imaginary" that the

8. Kennerly, "Getting Carried Away," 274. See also Kennerly's discussion of the same language in Quintilian (*Inst.*, 6.2.32.1-3), who observed that through vivid language activating *phantasia*, "one . . . is able to carry off (*rapere*) the judge with him [by means of *enargeia*], and put him in whatever frame of mind he wishes."

9. William G. Kirkwood, "Storytelling and Self-confrontation: Parables as Communication Strategies," *Quarterly Journal of Speech* 69 (1983): 58-74, here 65-66.

early Christian writers were inviting their audiences to share. In Kirkwood's study, parables represented one important rhetorical form with the power to bring about either a kind of self-confrontation that would give rise to new states of self-awareness, or a momentary glimpse of a mood or trait valued in the spiritual tradition. As this study has shown, that is precisely the aim that lies behind Paul's use of a broad array of different poetic forms. In each case, what they have in common is their potential for suspending processes of rationalization and counterargument by placing audiences "in" the content that they advance.

Placing Hearers "in" the Content

Each of the texts examined in this study attempts to promote a crucial element of the Christian worldview for which the desired response is not just critical judgment or mental assent, but a complete, holistic adoption, so that it becomes the believer's personal, "natural" response to the world — the sense of deep gratitude for having been rescued from sin and death by the grace of God, the unity of believers brought together by God in "one body," the Church, and the expectation of the return of Christ and the resurrection of the dead. In each case, it was understood that these were foundational to how believers felt and acted, how they treated each other, and how they lived in the world. Further, each of the four paradigmatic texts examined in this study conveys ideas and concepts that might have been expected to meet with resistance or even defensiveness from the audience.

In Rom. 7, Paul challenges long-held beliefs about the purpose of the Torah, which held that it functioned to set Israel apart as being more righteous and more privileged than the rest of humanity. Instead, Paul sought to show that the Torah's ultimate function was actually to underscore the absolute sinfulness and helplessness of all people and so to eliminate any basis for self-righteousness. In 1 Cor. 13 and Eph. 1, as in Rom. 7, Paul responds to division and hostility in the church. He attempts to overcomes these rifts, which were rooted in deep-seated attitudes and perspectives from the Christians' various cultural backgrounds. In 1 Thess. 4, Paul offers a vision of reality that is flatly contradicted by the Thessalonians' own experiences of suffering and grief. In each case, Paul meets the persuasive challenge by providing strong arguments and often painstaking explanations and exhortations in support of the theological understanding he advances. But in each case, he also takes up that theological content and presents it mimetically, so that the audience does not simply consider the argument as outside observers or judges. Rather, these poetic texts shift the symbolic location of the auditors so that they are transported "into" an experience of that theological understanding.

In the case of 1 Thessalonians, Paul seeks to advance the claims of Christian faith in the face of experiences that flatly contradict those claims. He writes to an infant congregation made up primarily of Gentiles converted to Christianity out of pagan lifestyles that included idol worship and sexual promiscuity. Perhaps as a result of Paul's untimely departure, they have faulty or inadequate knowledge of the nature of the parousia and the resurrection of the dead. They face the challenge of remaining faithful in the face of continued, intense persecution, Paul's seeming abandonment, and now, the deaths of several of their fellow Christians. Together, these circumstances call into question the legitimacy of the gospel and their faith that the God Paul proclaimed to them is truly the "living and true God," and they underminine their ability to "wait for his Son from heaven, whom he raised from the dead — Jesus, who rescues us from the coming wrath" (1:9-10).

Paul responds to that urgency in a number of ways. Using the brief apocalyptic citations that function as thematic discourse markers punctuating the epistle as a whole, he structures the entire letter within an eschatological framework. Rather than arguing for such an eschatology, he treats it as knowledge already shared by himself and his hearers, reflecting the kind of persuasive tactic Aristotle advocated in his discussion of the enthymeme. This strategy, of course, brings the audience "closer" to embracing the content by presenting it as something they already believe. But it still represents ideas that they hold conceptually, rather than being truly their "second nature" way of seeing the world, a fact made clear by Paul's need to remind them of it. Then, in 4:13 Paul explicitly addresses the question of those who "sleep" in Christ, using a typical Pauline disclosure formula, "But we do not want you to be uninformed." He offers them a logical argument that begins with a shared premise, "We believe that Jesus died and rose again." From this he deduces, "Even so, through Jesus, God will bring with him those who have died," which he follows with a prose explanation of the order in which those events will unfold. Throughout all of this, Paul's audience stands "outside" of the content of his discourse, considering the merits of his arguments and deciding whether or not to give assent to his claims.

Paul disrupts that position, however, when in vv. 16-17 he launches into the eschatological vision that (re)presents in mimetic form the content for which he has just argued. Using poetic structure and multisensory language that mimics the events it proclaims — the "cry of command," the "archangel's call," and the "sound of God's trumpet" — and drawing on language to which the audience, by virtue of previous associations, would likely have brought a rich set of emotional and visual meanings, Paul brings the Second Coming and the resurrection before their very eyes. No longer are they considering whether it will happen. Now, they are caught up in a momentary glimpse of that reality. In marked contrast to the position they held when Paul was offering them logical argumentation, they are now "in" the content, undergoing it as if it were really happening. Only after they have had the phenomenological experience of the resurrection and parousia are they prepared to "encourage one another with these words" and to hear the explicit ethical and moral exhortations of 5:1-11, which function as the natural outgrowth of the fervent expectation aroused in them by their glimpse of the eschaton.

Likewise, in his epistle to the Romans Paul faces the rhetorical challenge of trying to hold Jewish and Gentile Christian communities together in one Christian church in the face not only of the immediate clash of religious sensibilities, but also of centuries of severe ethnic hostility. Paul's entire vision of God's salvation history, as well as his own sense of calling as an apostle, seem to hinge on this challenge. A central part of his effort to meet this challenge is reframing his audience's understanding of the Torah as being God's tool not only to expose sin as sin, but to bring about a full flowering of sin in order to expose the utter propensity toward evil that exists in human nature — in his words, so that sin "might become sinful beyond measure" (Rom. 7:13). Again, his aim runs starkly counter to the traditional way that both Jews and God-fearing Gentiles would have viewed the law. Beneath all of this, finally, is what Paul sees as the central dynamic behind the Christian life, a radical conversion brought about by the experience of utter helplessness and despair in the face of one's inability to live up to God's standard. For Paul, the common experience of despair leading to the acceptance of salvation as God's gift was both the key to unity in the church and the source of gratitude that would provide the motivation for righteous living apart from the law.

The way that Paul advances his understanding of the law in Romans 7 indicates that he anticipates resistance to that position, and he attempts to defuse it in a number of ways. He grounds his claim using a deductive argument grounded in a legal principle drawn from the Torah itself (7:1-4). He uses the diatribe form to raise and then answer questions that represent extreme implications of the point he is making (7:7, 13). He even explains the effect of the law in his own experience, using an autobiographical form to explain how the introduction of a commandment like "You shall not covet" not only identified the sin of covetousness as such, but also "produced in me all kinds of covetousness" (7:7-8). As was the case with the arguments he made regarding the eschaton in 1 Thessalonians, Paul's audience stands outside the content, weighing the merits of his claims from a position of critical judgment.

The symbolic position of the audience, however, shifts dramatically in 7:14 from objectively weighing argument to subjectively undergoing an intense emotional experience, as Paul moves into his dramatic performance of existential despair over his failure to keep the law. Shifting verb tense and person and employing vehement language and frenetic style, Paul brings before the eyes of the audience a vision of the tortured soul caught in the despair of guilt and self-condemnation. The result is the potential, at least, for the audience members to go from considering the merits of his argument to vicariously experiencing — being "in" — the crisis of coming face to face with the glaring reality of their own sinfulness.

In Rom. 7, then, Paul's climactic strategy for overcoming the resistance to his argument, as well as for arousing in his hearers the emotions of humility and gratitude toward God and, by extension, affection toward each other, is not more logical reasoning, but rather a mimetic performance that places his audience *inside* the experience of the reality he has been describing. He takes up the claim for which he had offered logical arguments in 7:1-14 and recasts that understanding of the law as a drama in which the audience is invited to feel the anguished sinner's self-condemnation, despair, and, finally, the freedom of forgiveness, as if those feelings were their own. In doing so, Paul allows his audience to experience extrarationally both the purpose of the law and the release from the law's authority, both of which lay at the heart of his understanding of salvation history.

When Paul writes 1 Corinthians, he addresses a congregation embroiled in strife and controversy, one that questions his authority as an apostle and operates out of gross misunderstandings of the nature and work of the Holy Spirit, and whose worship assemblies have apparently degenerated into chaotic shouting matches between rival Christians seeking to display their own spiritual giftedness as a way to advance their social status. His response to the immediate problem of division and the abuse of spiritual gifts, which occupies chaps. 12–14, includes some of the strongest language that we ever encounter in Paul's writings. Using a broadly deliberative form, Paul argues that the diversity of gifts are given by "the same Spirit . . . the same Lord . . . [and] the same God" (12:4-5) for the common good, a position he reinforces with an extended analogy of the church as a human body. He ends chap. 12

with a series of sharp rhetorical questions that underscore the absurdity of the Corinthians' behavior and attitude toward spiritual gifts. Then, in chap. 14, Paul explains the specific functions of the gifts that the Corinthians most prized, prophecy and tongues, which leads into his severe regulation of their use in the assembly, in the form of fifteen imperatives, followed by his statement that anyone claiming to be spiritual will recognize that what he tells them "is a command of the Lord" (14:37).

At several points in this long discussion, Paul seems to be doing more, however, than simply correcting false impressions concerning the nature of spiritual gifts or regulating their use in Christian worship. Rather, his language suggests that he would like his audience to see and feel the absurdity of their behavior. His analogy comparing the church to the human body contains hints of caricature in its portrayal of the foot who laments the fact that it is not a hand (12:15), or the head that proclaims to the feet, "I have no need of you" (12:21). The rhetorical questions that end chap. 12 seem likewise intended to hold the Corinthians' behavior up to ridicule. In 14:7-9, he judges as completely useless the very spiritual gift that the Corinthians most valued, speaking in tongues, by comparing it to a bugle that blurts out incomprehensible noises, and then, in 14:20, he upbraids his hearers for thinking like children. All of this indicates that part of what Paul sees as the antidote to their immaturity is not simply more information, but rather the flash of self-awareness that comes from having one's behaviors exposed as ridiculous and immature. In short, for them to truly change, they need to feel shame and embarrassment over their present attitudes and actions. Paul's challenge is thus not only to overcome the resistance to his instructions that might be expected, but to circumvent the defensive reaction that would naturally be felt to any direct assault on their dignity, especially to the dignity of people who fancy themselves to be πνευματικοί ("spiritual").

Instead of attacking their pride and immaturity directly, Paul's answer is to interrupt the flow of his argument and instruction in order to give his hearers a poetic experience of the sublimity of love. To be sure, 1 Cor. 13 does offer a convincing "argument" for the superiority of love over all other gifts and religious qualities, surpassing even faith and hope. But so many features of the text indicate that his goal is not just to convince his audience of that fact, but also to bring love's grandeur "before their eyes," taking them into an experience of that reality, as it were, from the inside. First, Paul shifts his voice from a direct, second-person form of address to the first-person pronoun, the dramatic or fictive "I." Second, he employs such formal structures as those in vv. 1-3 that symbolically reduce religious displays such as tongues, prophecy, and even self-immolation, without love, to "nothing." Finally, as Kennedy detected, Paul moves from an initial tone of agitation toward a resolution in which the "emotional energy is dissipated."[10] Through all this, Paul seeks to shift the audience's engagement with the content from one of being outsiders to explicit claims and arguments about the importance of love, to being insiders to a visceral experience through which they are emotionally transported by love's beauty. In this sense, 1 Cor. 13 represents the discursive equivalent to the experience of Peter in the story of Jesus' washing of the disciples' feet, recorded in John 13, where Jesus' act of love and service provokes in Peter a reaction first of awkward defensiveness, and then of humility and gratitude. Likewise, it parallels the "Christ hymn" in Phil. 2:5-11, which similarly employs poetic form in order to bring an audience into a mimetic experience of Christ's self-renunciation, moving from equality with God to taking on the form of a slave, and finally to undergoing death on a cross, as a representation of the kind of self-renunciation that he hopes the Philippian church, also embroiled in rivalry and division, will embrace. So also in 1 Cor. 13, Paul's hope is that his hearers will undergo an experience against which their own attitudes and behaviors will be clearly exposed as petty and immature. His strategy is to use poetic form to take them into the experience so that they will come to that conclusion on their own, so that he will not have to convince them of it himself. In this way, when he does tell them to stop thinking like children (14:20), he will only be giving voice to what they have already realized in their guts.

As with the other texts examined in this study, finally, the epistle to the Ephesians addresses a topic toward which Paul would likely have expected resistance, the unity of Jews and Gentiles in the Christian church. But even if he were able to win their consent to his position, he needs to do more than merely bring about an intellectual conviction about the importance or appropriateness of this unity. He needs to reshape his hearers' fundamental attitudes and emotional reactions toward people against whom they have harbored longstanding ethnic hostility. The epistle as a whole addresses the problem in a number of different ways, all aimed at reaching the audience's cognitive understanding of Christian unity. He twice retells their conversion stories, first emphasizing the common experience of all people (2:1-10), and then highlighting the inclusion of the Gentiles into the commonwealth of Israel (2:11-22). He recounts his own commission to apostleship (3:1-13) as

---

10. George A. Kennedy, *New Testament Interpretation through Rhetorical Criticism* (Chapel Hill: University of North Carolina Press, 1984), 156.

ultimately a calling to proclaim the mystery of God, long hidden but now revealed, that the "Gentiles have become fellow heirs" with the Jews (3:6). He tells them of his prayer for them, that they be "rooted and grounded in love," and he exhorts them to "maintain the unity of the Spirit" (4:3). In each case, his mode is one of direct address, explaining how unity lies at the heart of God's plan and urging them to pursue that unity. Even his prayer, which does shift that mode of address somewhat, still comes to them as the writer's explicit disclosure of how fervently he is praying that they will operate out of deep love.

In a way that goes even beyond that of the other poetic texts examined in this study, however, the blessing with which the epistle opens offers the audience a dramatically different position from that of the rest of the letter. By virtue of its generic form, a liturgy, it invites the audience to engage the content at a deeper, more personal level than merely weighing the merits of a claim or even taking in the information conveyed in an explanation. Now they are positioned as participants in the expression of praise, as insiders to an experience of the content expressed in the text. Further, by means of its complex structure, the blessing creates a sort of momentum that moves the audience from praising God for those things that they agree with toward a climax in which they praise God for the very thing that they are most reluctant to accept — that Jews and Gentiles have already been brought into unity in Christ, as the first concrete instantiation of the grand, cosmic unity to which God is taking the cosmos. As Ladrière pointed out, that expression of praise presupposes the attitude and agreement that it is intended to bring about, potentially, at least, disposing the participants to "welcome that which it suggests."[11] Paul thus addresses both the problem of audience resistance and the need for a deeply rooted change in his hearers' view of ethnic difference by crafting a text that offers them a mimetic performance through which the audience can enact the unity that they will later be challenged to pursue. As noted in the conclusion to chapter 5, it is telling that in his exhortation to unity in 4:3, Paul does not tell the Ephesians to seek unity but, rather, to "maintain the unity" that the Holy Spirit has already brought about. The reason he can issue that challenge is because, at some level, they have already known that unity through their common expression of praise to God.

11. Jean Ladrière, "The Performativity of Liturgical Language," in *Liturgical Experience of Faith*, ed. Herman Schmidt and David Power, trans. John Griffiths (New York: Herder and Herder, 1973), 50-62, here 58.

Conclusion

In their writings, the New Testament authors often sought to advance beliefs and behaviors against which they expected resistance, even in cases where the beliefs and behaviors they promoted were deeply valued and embraced, intellectually at least, by their hearers. The positions they advanced, moreover, reflected convictions that went to the very core of Christian theology — the resurrection of the dead and the second coming of Christ, salvation by grace, and the unity of all believers in one church. Even more importantly, what they sought to bring about in their hearers was not simply mental agreement with a particular tenet of the faith but, instead, a modified worldview. This new "social imaginary" would alter fundamentally the way that believers would experience God, themselves, each other, and the world, giving rise to such sustained emotional states as hope, gratitude, humility, and love, and issuing forth in behaviors that reflected the Christian moral ethos.

In short, they faced an immense persuasive challenge, one that went far beyond the kind of obstacles envisioned in the classical rhetorical tradition. They certainly faced the predictable kinds of challenges related to persuasion addressed by Aristotle and other writers in that tradition, for example, those related to the speaker's credibility or the audience's emotional state. But they also sought to bring their hearers into a worldview that was fundamentally at odds with the dominant philosophical and ethical value systems of their culture and that was often contradicted by their own experiences — in short, to believe that God was in control in a world where they were a persecuted minority, where their identification with Christianity put them at odds with their culture, and where, in some cases, they faced physical and economic hardship and even death as a result of their faith.

Perhaps more acutely than even the classical tradition of rhetoric could have imagined, then, the early Christian writers faced the challenge of how discourse situated the hearers in relation to the content. Rhetoric in the classical tradition positioned the hearer as a judge, critically analyzing the merits of argument "from the outside." Paul responded to that challenge by using many of the same argumentative strategies that Aristotle and other writers in the tradition recommended for reducing that distance. But as I have argued in this chapter, he also employed the power of mimesis to create communicative experiences that transported their hearers into a present consciousness of the ideas, dispositions, and events they spoke of. In those moments, their hearers were not simply being asked to believe *that* something was the case. Rather, in that moment the hearers experienced those realities as if they were present reality. In that imaginative moment, faith was caught up in sight.

CHAPTER SEVEN

Reconfiguring the Rhetorical Encounter, Part Two: Removing the Rhetor, Constituting the Community

When Paul, in 1 Thess. 4:16, abruptly turns from explaining the end time to actually bringing that cataclysmic event "before the eyes" of his hearers in a vivid, multisensory depiction, he radically changes his audience's relationship to the content of his discourse. No longer are they contemplating the parousia and the resurrection of the dead as propositions they might accept or as information that they might now understand. Instead, the end time becomes an actual event that, in some sense, they have now felt and witnessed. Paul's shift from argument to mimesis locates them "in" the content so that, for a moment, sight replaces faith.

That reconfiguration of the audience's relationship to the content, which accompanies the shift from argument to mimesis, in turn, has significant implications for two other core relationships in the persuasive encounter. First, it transforms the relationship of the rhetor to the audience, symbolically moving the rhetor out of a stance of explicitly attempting to change the audience's beliefs and behaviors. Second, it potentially changes the relationship of the audience members to each other, positioning them not as isolated judges of argument but as co-sharers in a powerful emotional experience. This chapter focuses on these implications of the turn to poetic form, exploring the potential that mimetic discourse has for removing the "empirical" rhetor from the position he or she was assumed to have by most writers in the classical tradition, and for constituting the separate members of the audience into a community. In this way, I argue, poetic form offered Paul a way to meet what the classical tradition recognized as one of the persistent obstacles to persuasion, the reputation of the rhetor, even as it also enabled them to reinforce what they recognized as one of the core values of Christianity, that of unity in the church.

The Problem of the Rhetor

Among the factors that make for successful persuasion, writers in the classical tradition recognized that perhaps none was more important than the identity and reputation of the rhetor. For all his desire to privilege logical argument over all other forms of proof, even Aristotle has to admit that the speaker's ethos, or character, "may be the most effective means of persuasion he possesses," since "we believe good men more fully and more readily than others: this is true generally whatever the question is, and absolutely true where exact certainty is impossible and opinions divided" (*Rhet.*, 1.2). Isocrates similarly observes that "words carry greater conviction when spoken by men of good repute" (*Antid.*, 278). Later, when the writer of the *Rhetorica ad Herennium* offers copious instructions for how to craft the speech's introduction, much of what he has to say concerns one simple task, that of securing the goodwill of the audience not only to one's cause, but also toward one's own person (1.3.5–1.7.11). Of course, Cicero includes among the three tasks of the orator not only "the proof of our allegations" but also "the winning of our hearers' favor" (*De or.*, 2.115; cf. 2.128, 310; 3.104; *Or. Brut.*, 68; *Brut.*, 185, 276), calling the character and reputation of the speaker "a potent factor in success" resulting, in the case of a jury, from "goodwill toward the advocate and the advocate's client as well" (*De or.*, 2.182).[1]

When one considers the relationship of speaker to audience in a typical persuasive exchange, it is not difficult to understand this pervasive concern with the speaker's character.[2] In any instance of human communication, the message is attached to the person of the speaker and so is inevitably filtered

1. As May pointed out, Cicero's conception of ethos was broader than Aristotle's, embracing not only factors in the speech itself but also the speaker's prior reputation; see James M. May, *Trials of Character: The Eloquence of Ciceronian Ethos* (Chapel Hill: University of North Carolina Press, 1988), 4-6.

2. The tendency of persuasive communication to provoke defensiveness has been the subject of a great deal of research among contemporary social scientists, an interest given great impetus by the research of Jack Gibb; see Jack R. Gibb, "Defensive Communication," *Journal of Communication* 11 (1961): 141-48. More recent examples of this research include Glen H. Stamp, Anita L. Vangelisti, and John A. Daly, "The Creation of Defensiveness in Social Interaction," *Communication Quarterly* 40 (1992): 177-90; Jennifer A. H. Becker, Barbara Ellevold, and Glen H. Stamp, "The Creation of Defensiveness in Social Interaction II: A Model of Defensive Communication among Romantic Couples," *Communication Monographs* 75 (2008): 86-110; and Matthew J. Hornsey, Erin Robson, Joanne Smith, Sarah Esposo, and Robbie M. Sutton, "Sugaring the Pill: Assessing Rhetorical Strategies Designed to Minimize Defensive Reactions to Group Criticism," *Human Communication Research* 34 (2008): 70-98.

through the audience's perception of that speaker. But even more importantly, any explicit attempt to change an audience's beliefs and behaviors
implies, at some level, a criticism of what they currently believe and do.
That communicative exchange places the speaker outside and even above
the audience, in the position of an identified subject who is self-consciously
addressing the audience from a position of assumed superiority. Rhetoric is
thus inherently agonistic, presupposing an adversarial relationship in which
the rhetor attempts to overcome the audience's defenses using the strategies
of persuasion.[3] Aristotle hints at the agonistic nature of rhetoric when he
describes the persuasive encounter using war language, where maximizing
the "power of speech" (*Rhet.*, 1.1) entails having "command" of the means of
persuasion (1.2), and where ineffective persuasion means suffering "defeat"
(1.1). He explicitly captures the adversarial nature of the speaker–audience
relationship in a rhetorical exchange when he describes the audience not
simply as a judge of the argument, but a judge of the speaker:

> We may say, without qualification, that anyone is your judge whom you
> have to persuade. Nor does it matter whether we are arguing against an
> actual opponent or against a mere proposition; in the latter case we still
> have to use speech and overthrow the opposing arguments, and we attack
> these as we should attack an actual opponent. Our principle holds good
> of ceremonial speeches also; the "onlookers" for whom such a speech is
> put together are treated as the judges of it (*Rhet.*, 2.18).

As Aristotle suggests, the problem of counterargument described in the
previous chapter derives to a large degree simply from the fact that an audience is being confronted with another person telling them how they should
think, feel, or act, an encounter that almost inevitably invites this reaction:
"Who are *you* to tell me this?" Thus, Aristotle says, it is crucial that persuasive speakers demonstrate good sense, good moral character, and especially,
good will, showing themselves to be "well disposed to their hearers" (2.1).
Doing so would at least mitigate that barrier between the audience and the

---

3. For an examination of the agonistic nature of rhetoric as it was rooted in the sophistic
tradition, see John Poulakos, *Sophistical Rhetoric in Classical Greece* (Columbia: University of
South Carolina Press, 1995); for a slightly different view, see Debra Hawhee, "Agonism and
Aretê," *Philosophy and Rhetoric* 35 (2002): 185-207. Of course, the proponents of "invitational
rhetoric" highlighted this dimension of persuasion in traditional rhetoric. See Sonja K. Foss and
Cindy L. Griffin, "Beyond Persuasion: A Proposal for an Invitational Rhetoric," *Communication
Monographs* 16 (1995): 2-18.

speaker by demonstrating the speaker to be a person of knowledge and good morals, one for whom the assumption of the audacious position of attempting to persuade the audience has at least arisen out of the motivation of seeking their best interest.

Consequently, much of what writers in the classical tradition say about how to persuade an audience to one's position, even those elements of the process that had to do with the arguments themselves, reflects their concern for how the audience perceives the speaker. For all of his emphasis on *logos*, Aristotle especially understands the importance of the speaker's reputation and devotes a great deal of his instruction to how to enhance the proof that comes from that reputation. Because it is not enough to make the argument of one's speech demonstrative and worthy of belief, he asserts, the orator "must make his own character look right" (*Rhet.*, 2.1). He shows, for example, how to heighten the nobility ascribed to one's actions by emphasizing that they were done intentionally and unselfishly (1.9). He offers guidance for how to clothe negative qualities in positive language, so that an "arrogant man" becomes "impressive," "rashness will be called courage," and the "stupid man" is now an "honest fellow" (1.9). He gives detailed instructions for how to overcome hostility toward oneself by denying the cause of the hostility, admitting but alleviating its effects by pointing to mitigating circumstances or claiming good motives, or if all else fails, accusing one's accusers (3.15). All of this reflects Aristotle's recognition that the audience's perception of the speaker himself or herself is a crucial part, perhaps even the threshold, of persuasion.

Remarkably, the poetic tradition addresses this crucial issue not by seeking to bolster the rhetor's credibility, but rather by removing the empirical rhetor from a direct encounter with the audience altogether. One of the principle characteristics of mimesis, Aristotle points out, is the poet's avoidance of speaking directly to the audience. As Bywater's translation put it, Aristotle counsels the poet to "say very little *in propria persona,* as he is no imitator when he is doing that."[4] For this Aristotle praises Homer:

> Whereas the other poets are perpetually coming forward in person, and say but little, and that only here and there, as imitators, Homer after a brief preface brings forth a man, a woman, or some other Character — no one of them characterless, but each with distinctive characteristics" (*Poet.*, 24).

4. Aristotle, *Poetics*, trans. Ingram Bywater (Oxford: Clarendon, 1920), 77 §3.24.

Whereas rhetoric calls attention to the character of the rhetor, in poetic discourse it is important that the poet's identity not stand out.[5]

Although he does not deal with the issue nearly so explicitly as Aristotle, Longinus also seems to recognize this transformation of the relationship of rhetor to audience that accompanies the turn to mimesis. He explains the power of several lines in Euripides in this way: "The poet himself saw the Furies and compelled the audience almost to see what he had visualized" (*Subl.*, 15.3). The symbolic implication is that the audience, caught up in that vision, no longer sees the poet himself, but rather they stand side by side in awe of the spectacle before them. Similarly, when he describes the power of *hyperbata* in a speech by Dionysius the Phocaean, recorded in Herodotus, he says that Dionysius

> suspends the sense which he has begun to express, and in the interval manages to bring forward one extraneous idea after another in a strange and unlikely order, making the audience terrified of a total collapse of the sentence, and *compelling them from sheer excitement to share the speaker's risk* (*Subl.*, 22.3, emphasis added).

Again, the rhetor's turn from prose explanation to mimetic imitation brings the audience alongside the rhetor in a shared experience of the emotion. No longer is the rhetor speaking "to" the audience but, instead, they are together caught up in the turmoil of the drama. Longinus similarly praises a courtroom speech by Demosthenes in which he suddenly turns from addressing the jury to addressing the villain. Longinus describes how the speaker, "appearing to abandon the jury . . . has yet by means of the emotion made his appeal to them much more intense" (*Subl.*, 21.3). Significantly, his suggestion that Demosthenes has given the appearance of having "abandoned the jury" once more accentuates the speaker's altered relationship to his audience as together their attention now focuses on the defendant. In each case, by means of poetic form, the rhetor is able to alter the relationship to the audience from the way it was envisioned in the classical tradition. In mimetic discourse, the rhetor as a subject self-consciously

5. C. S. Lewis's pithy description of the poet captures the distinction: "The poet is not a man who asks me to look at him; he is a man who says 'look at that' and points; the more I follow the pointing of his finger, the less I can possibly see of him. . . . I must make of him not a spectacle but a pair of spectacles" (C. S. Lewis and E. M. W. Tillyard, *The Personal Heresy in Criticism*, cited in Walter Hooper, *C. S. Lewis: The Companion and Guide* [London: Harper-Collins, 2005], 599).

seeking to persuade an audience recedes into the background, so that the boundary between "speaker" and "audience" becomes permeable or disappears altogether. As I shall argue, that shift is a significant feature in Paul's use of poetic form.

"Removing" the Rhetor

The NT writers, and Paul particularly, clearly understand the problem of the audience's perception of the rhetor and are often at great pains to enhance their reputations or to mitigate the influence of the audience's negative attitude toward them.[6] As Betz argued, Paul's entire epistle to the Galatians could be viewed as an *apologia* aimed at defending his credibility and authority as an apostle.[7] In 1 Cor. 2:3, Paul's characterization of his ministry among the Corinthians as being marked by "weakness and . . . fear and . . . much trembling" reflects his attempt to assume the persona of an apocalyptic seer as a way of bolstering his image among his audience — an aim which clearly dominates the first four chapters of 1 Corinthians.[8] In 1 Thess., Paul seeks to restore his reputation with the Thessalonian believers by reminding them that he had preached to them "in spite of great opposition" and insisting that his appeals to them did not "spring from deceit or impure motives or trickery" (1 Thess. 2:2-3). The same concern for ethos pervades much of the instruction from the Pastoral Epistles, which call Christians to live in a way that exhibits decorum and propriety, so as to "make the teaching about God our Savior attractive" (Titus 2:10). All of this reflects what the classical tradition said about the need, as Arisotle put it, "to make your hearer receptive . . . giving him [or her] a good impression of your character, which always helps to secure his [or her] attention" (*Rhet.*, 3.14).

It is instructive to observe, however, what happens to the position of the

6. For an extensive treatment of ethos and religious communication, including the rhetoric of Paul, see André Resner, Jr., *Preacher and Cross: Person and Message in Theology and Rhetoric* (Grand Rapids: Eerdmans, 1999).

7. Hans Dieter Betz, *Galatians: A Commentary on Paul's Letter to the Churches in Galatia* (Philadelphia: Fortress, 1979). For a response, see D. E. Aune, review of *Galatians: A Commentary on Paul's Letter to the Churches in Galatia*, by Hans Dieter Betz. *Religious Studies Review* 7 (1981): 323-25.

8. Gary S. Selby, "Paul, the Seer: The Rhetorical Persona in 1 Corinthians 2.1-16," in *The Rhetorical Analysis of Scripture: Essays from the 1995 London Conference*, ed. Stanley E. Porter and Thomas H. Olbricht (Sheffield: Sheffield Academic Press, 1997), 351-73.

rhetor in the NT's poetic texts when the audience is invited into a mimetic experience of some element of Christian theology. When Paul discusses the fate of the righteous dead in 1 Thess. 4:13-18, for example, he at first speaks to them directly: "But we do not want you to be uninformed, brothers and sisters, about those who have died" (v. 13). His mode of address becomes particularly self-conscious when he claims that his message to them has come by special prophetic authority: "For this we declare to you by the word of the Lord" (v. 15). Paul returns to that direct mode of address in the beginning of chap. 5, where he explains the implications of what he has just told them about the parousia, emphasizing in particular the importance of remaining faithful as they await that event: "Now concerning the times and seasons, brothers and sisters, you do not need to have anything written to you. For you yourselves know very well that the day of the Lord will come like a thief in the night" (vv. 1-2). In all of this, Paul is, as it were, standing at the podium explaining and arguing based on his authority as an apostle and their church's founder.

When he launches into the vision, however, his stance before the audience changes. Activating their capacity for *phantasia*, Paul's vivid, poetically structured and emotionally charged narrative shifts the audience's attention away from him and toward the vision itself as, in their imaginations, they see the heavens part, they hear the trumpet call and the shout of the archangel, and they feel themselves caught up in that glorious event. At that point, Paul goes from a stance of talking *to* them directly to one of coming *among* them, no longer calling attention to himself but pointing away from himself to the coming Christ.

Similarly, in much of Rom. 7, Paul addresses his audience explicitly and self-consciously, a stance he signals in the chapter's opening verse: "Do you not know, brothers and sisters — for I am speaking to those who know the law — that the law is binding on a person only during that person's lifetime?" (v. 1). In other words, he is in no sense speaking from the position of an imaginative persona to a hypothetical audience (as he does, for example, in 2:1 and 2:17). Rather, he sets up the discourse as if it were a dialogue between the "empirical Paul" and the "empirical audience." He continues that dialogic mode of address through most of the chapter, asking rhetorical questions and then answering them, even adding his personal experience in support of his claims about the role of the Mosaic Law in provoking human sinfulness.

But when we come to vv. 15-25, it is clearly no longer the "empirical Paul" speaking *to* the Romans, despite the fact that he continues to speak in the first person.[9] He shifts exclusively to the present tense and ceases using the second person ("you"), signaling that he is no longer addressing them directly but, instead, has now moved into a monologic mode of address. In Theissen's words, he enacts "the I . . . alone with itself."[10] Using a frenetic style and the vehement language of self-condemnation, Paul allows his audience now to overhear his anguished soliloquy, placing the hearers in a markedly different relationship to their speaker from that assumed by the earlier sections of the chapter. No longer the direct target of argument, they are free to lower their guard and draw closer to witness the performance. Indeed, Kenneth Burke would suggest that Paul here represents the universal experience of humans who are, as Burke put it, "goaded by the spirit of hierarchy and rotten with perfection," and who thus constantly replay in their personal and social lives a cycle of guilt, purification, and redemption.[11] By mimetically representing with such pathos the tragic despair of anyone who has tried to keep the law perfectly, Paul invites his hearers to engage the performance sympathetically, drawing them into the experience alongside the speaker. To use Longinus's language, Paul compels the Romans to share his emotion, in this case, the emotion of despair (*Subl.*, 22.3). Paul's performance reflects Gorgias's prediction that, "through the agency of words," the soul would feel as "the suffering of its own" another's "fearful shuddering and tearful pity and grievous longing" (*Hel.*, 9).

Paul thus "performs" the content of his argument in a way that minimizes the barrier that would have been posed by the typical persuasive encounter, where a speaker attempts to convince an audience of some claim. Before, he had confronted them with facts and deductions in a way that might be expected to arouse defensiveness in his hearers, voicing in his rhetorical ques-

---

9. Because Paul continues to use the first person here, it is not clear whether Aristotle would have included his soliloquy within his strict definition of mimesis. But as Hayden suggested, Aristotle may simply have been naïve "in assuming that first-person narrative or lyrical forms must represent the author himself and are therefore 'real' in some sense, like a memoir or a diary; that is, mimicry would not be involved. The question might even resolve itself into the absence of the concept of a persona (the use, by the author, of a fictitious first-person narrator who would always be the actual author himself, and, as such, he would always be too particular, not sufficiently universalized" (John O. Hayden, *Polestar of the Ancients: The Aristotelian Tradition in Classical and English Literary Criticism* [Newark, DE: University of Delaware Press, 1979], 47).

10. Gerd Theissen, *Psychological Aspects of Pauline Theology*, trans. John P. Galvin (Philadelphia: Fortress, 1987), 261.

11. Kenneth Burke, *Language as Symbolic Action* (Berkeley: University of California Press, 1966), 16.

tions issues that likely arose in the minds of his audience, only to shoot them down with a strident μὴ γένοιτο ("May it never be!"). But now, it is as if Paul ignores the audience altogether — much in the way Demosthenes appeared to abandon the jury — as he turns inward and begins to wrestle alone with his thoughts. Indeed, the personal nature of that performance may also have served to bring his audience alongside him by virtue not only of its emotion, but also through the way that it externalizes an intensely private experience. In his magisterial work, *The Rhetoric of Fiction,* Booth noted how authors "win over" the readers to a sympathetic stance toward certain characters in the novel by giving readers a glimpse into the character's inner processes of thought and emotion. As he put it, "The sustained inside view leads the reader to hope for good fortune for the character with whom he travels, quite independently of the qualities revealed."[12] The result is that readers are drawn into sympathy even toward characters they might not otherwise care for.[13] What Booth noted about the process of good writing, Paul enacts in his soliloquy. He gives voice to an inner anguish that, even as a dramatic performance, manages to represent extreme self-disclosure and vulnerability. In the presence of such naked self-condemnation, his hearers, potentially at least, would have felt deep sympathy toward what is depicted as Paul's own suffering, even as they vicariously joined with him in the experience of guilt and despair.

Turning to 1 Cor. 13, we find Paul creating a similar kind of shift from a direct, confrontational mode of address to one that is similarly monologic and interior, as he begins to rhapsodize on the majesty of love. As noted above, throughout chap. 12, Paul addresses his audience directly and explicitly (e.g, "Now concerning spiritual gifts, brothers and sisters, I do not want you to be uninformed . . . , 12:1), culminating in the staccato series of strident rhetorical questions in 12:29-30. All of this leads to the imperative in 12:31, where Paul issues this command to the Corinthians: "Strive [ζηλοῦτε] for the greater gifts," an order that will be repeated in 14:1 in a way that continues his argument focused on tongues and prophecy — only now, he hopes, shaped by the experience of the soaring poetry of chap. 13. In the second half of v. 31,

---

12. Wayne C. Booth, *The Rhetoric of Fiction* (Chicago: University of Chicago Press, 1983), 246.

13. To this insight can be added the axiom from interpersonal communication which says that using "I" language to express one's emotions and experiences tends to elicit a far less defensive reaction than one which addresses an audience directly. See, for example, Edward S. Kubany, David C. Richard, Gordon B. Bauer, and Miles Y. Muraoka, "Impact of Assertive and Accusatory Communication of Distress and Anger: A Verbal Component Analysis," *Aggressive Behavior* 18 (1992): 337-47.

however, Paul signals a shift in both tone and theme, as he tells his audience, "And I will show you a still more excellent way" (v. 31). His turn from second to first person signals that movement, as does his use of the term, δείκνυμι ("show" or "demonstrate") to characterize what he is about to do — not to argue but to depict.

As the opening verses of chap. 13 make clear, Paul drops the direct form of address ("you") as well as the imperatival verb forms that pervade chaps. 12 and 14, and he employs instead a series of leading verbs in vv. 1-3 in the first-person subjunctive mode, all indicating an unmistakable shift to the voice of what Smit calls the "rhetorical 'I,'"[14] who speaks in a hypothetical style. Together, these features give the eulogy on love its character as soliloquy, a mode of address that symbolically allows Paul to look away from his audience and turn inward. In an even more dramatic manner than the example of Rom. 7, Paul turns from being the prosecutor vehemently arguing with his audience to a solitary figure revealing his innermost thoughts. No longer the object of direct attempts to persuade them, the audience is free to move closer and "overhear" his lyrical performance.

Perhaps nowhere does the relationship of rhetor to audience shift more dramatically from what would be expected in the typical rhetorical encounter than in the liturgy of Eph. 1. Certainly, Paul will address the Ephesians directly and explicitly, explaining to them the central place of unity between Jews and Gentiles within God's salvation history and giving them arguments in support of his exhortation that they commit themselves to living in harmony with one another. But in the opening text, as noted in chap. 5 of this study, Paul begins not by addressing them directly, but instead by inviting them to join him in a traditional *berakah*, a ceremonial expression of worship to God. That form symbolically situates the audience in the position of being the "speaker" who gives voice to the text's content. Instead of hearing *about* God, they are together talking *to* God, ultimately expressing their gratitude and praise for the unity that they will later be urged to maintain. Of course, that symbolic reconfiguration has profound implications for the author's relationship to his audience. Instead of being in the position of the rhetor seeking to overcome their defenses with his persuasive strategies, his discourse now symbolically locates his own person as a fellow worshipper who comes alongside the Ephesians and joins them in their communal expression of praise. In essence, Paul has moved away from the podium and slipped into the pew beside them.

14. For discussion of this point, see above pp. 95, 100.

In each of the poetic texts examined in this study, then, when Paul takes up theological content and clothes it in mimesis, not only does he remove the barrier between the audience and the content, he also removes the barrier between rhetor and audience that the classical handbooks sought to overcome. But rather than offering reasons to trust the rhetor, these mimetic texts symbolically remove the empirical rhetor from the persuasive encounter. Caught up together in an emotional, imaginative experience of theology, it is almost as if the identity of the rhetor has ceased to matter. That shift has one further implication for the hearers themselves. In addition to reconfiguring the hearers' relationship to the speaker, the mimetic experience potentially transforms their relationship to each other.

The Problem of the Audience

Of course, no dimension of the rhetorical encounter was more central to Aristotle's understanding of persuasion than the audience. Building on Plato's grudging acceptance of rhetoric as the art of adapting speech types to soul types (*Phaedr.*, 271-72), Aristotle argued that the theory of rhetoric is concerned with "what seems probable to men of a given type," since the mark of a successful argument was not ultimately its logical consistency but simply the fact that "there is somebody whom it persuades" (*Rhet.*, 1.2). Similarly, in his tripartite categorization of rhetorical genres, Aristotle distinguished between each by the position of the audience, since "of the three elements in speech-making — speaker, subject, and person addressed — it is the last one, the hearer, that determines the speech's end and object" (1.3). In his discussion of the actual forms of proof that constitute the art of rhetoric, Aristotle's advice was consistently to ground the speech's arguments, evidence of speaker credibility, and arousal of emotion in what one knows of the audience's beliefs, hopes, and experiences, as, for example, in his counsel to "take into account the nature of our particular audience when making a speech of praise," so that "if the audience esteems a given quality, we must say that our hero has that quality" (1.9). In all of this, the audience was the central element in the *kairos* for which the rhetor sought to discover the available means of persuasion. But beyond that, Aristotle and the writers who followed him in the classical tradition generally assumed that the audience was the empirical group of auditors addressed by the speaker. It assumed the audience to be a relatively homogenous entity that brought a fixed identity to the rhetorical moment, so that the challenge of the rhetor was to "adapt" one's speech to that *a priori* identity, a challenge the rhetor sought to meet with a system of persuasive strategies that remains useful advice for any public speaker.

Contemporary scholars, by contrast, have challenged the assumption that the audience has a coherent identity prior to the speech, emphasizing instead that the audience is constituted to a large degree by the discourse itself. These scholars focus on the ways that language can "create" an audience in two ways: first, through the evocation of shared emotional states among the hearers, a psychological process known as "emotional contagion," and second, through the use of particular terms that encode an "ideal" audience role that the hearers are invited to play.

Although he certainly did not develop the concept to any degree, Longinus did hint at the possibility that the shared experience of mimesis in a poetic text could actually serve to constitute the separate hearers as a community by virtue of the common emotions that it can evoke in them. Toward the end of *On the Sublime*, where he compared the experience of hearing artistically arranged words in a poetic text to being put under a "marvelous spell" by the rhythm and tones of great music, he described the power of composition, a "kind of melody in words," to bring

> into the hearts of the bystanders the speaker's actual emotion so that *all who hear him share in it*, and by piling phrase on phrase builds up one majestic whole — must we not think, I say, that by these very means it casts a spell on *us* and always turns *our* thoughts toward what is majestic and sublime and all else that it embraces, winning a complete mastery over *our* minds? (*Subl.*, 39.3, emphasis added).

Again, although his main point was about the power of the language itself, Longinus's account recognized the transformation between the individual "bystanders" ("all who hear") into something like a collective identity by means of their shared emotional experience. What Longinus hinted at, of course, has been confirmed by an abundance of contemporary research into two important constructs of human social behavior, "emotional contagion" and "vicarious affect," which have to do with the way that humans tend to share particular moods and emotions, and particularly to "share emotions by vicariously experiencing others' emotions." Kelly and Barsade noted, "There is mounting evidence that we do automatically mimic and synchronize with the manifestations of emotional behavior in others."[15] As these researchers also emphasized, this sharing of strong emotions within a group plays a central role in the formation of group cohesion, serving "to bind group members to one another, to operate in a more group-centered manner, to better coordinate efforts, and to better enforce group norms and procedures."[16] Humans are hardwired to share in the emotional experiences of those around them, and that shared emotional experience is, to a large extent, what constitutes us as a group. This understanding helps to explain the role that the NT's poetic texts might have played in helping to build cohesion and unity in the early Christian church. On the one hand, part of their impact may have come from the fact that by shifting from direct argument to mimesis, they invited their hearers to lower their guard and shift away from the kind of critical stance that a more direct argumentative "assault" would have evoked in them, a critical stance that presumably would have carried over into their stance toward one another. But a key factor in these texts' potential for creating group solidarity was the shared experience of intense emotion that Longinus said was the result of the artistic creation of sublimity.

A number of contemporary rhetorical scholars, moreover, have viewed the audience not only as being brought together by the common experience of shared emotion created by the text, but also as a discursively constructed identity encoded within the content of the text itself. Although this conception has come to inform the work of much critical scholarship, its early articulation is typically traced back to the work of Edwin Black. For Black, the "audience" was not simply a specific group of auditors addressed by a speech, but was also a "persona" encoded within the speech which the rhetor would have the "real auditor become."[17] This shared identity was characterized by adherence to a particular ideology that could be discovered through careful attention not only to the rhetor's claims, but also to "stylistic tokens"

15. Janice R. Kelly and Sigal G. Barsade, "Mood and Emotions in Small Groups and Work Teams," *Organizational Behavior and Human Decision Processes* 86 (2001): 99-130, here 108, 107.

16. Jennifer R. Spoor and Janice R. Kelly, "The Evolutionary Significance of Affect in Groups: Communication and Group Bonding," *Group Processes & Intergroup Relations* 7 (2004): 398-412, here 405.

17. Edwin Black, "The Second Persona," *Quarterly Journal of Speech* 56 (1970): 109-19, here 113. The other figure often associated with this conception is Michael Calvin McGee, who likewise highlighted the rhetorical nature of the audience when he described the public identity often addressed in political discourse, "the people," as "a fiction dreamed by an advocate and infused with an artificial, rhetorical reality by the agreement of an audience to participate in a collective fantasy"; see Michael Calvin McGee, "In Search of 'The People': A Rhetorical Alternative," *Quarterly Journal of Speech* 61 (1975): 235-49, here 240.

contained in the discourse — for example, the particular terms used to characterize (or caricature) the rhetor's opponents. To use Black's own example, when encountering the phrase "bleeding hearts" to refer to proponents of welfare legislation, "one would be justified in suspecting that a general attitude — more, a whole set of general attitudes, were being summoned." Such terminology functions as a "vector of influence," with the power to activate powerful cognitive and affective associations and structure the audience's experience of the world, inviting them not simply to adopt a policy but to share a common identity. Building on that understanding, Charland's study of the "peuple Québécois" explored the way that discourse "constructs" or "constitutes" the hearer as subject, highlighting the way that discourse advocating the sovereignty of Quebec paradoxically constituted for its audience an identity as the "Québécois," even as it simultaneously assumed that identity "to be pregiven and natural, existing outside of rhetoric and forming the basis for a rhetorical address." Based on his analysis of this discourse, Charland concluded that "audiences are constituted as subjects through a process of identification with a textual position."[18]

While somewhat different in their focus and method, these scholars and those who have followed them all view the audience as more than simply a coherent, unified entity to which one adapts one's argument in style. Rather, they insist that the audience is in some sense a product of the discourse itself. That is, the "audience" is a role that discourse prompts its empirical auditors to "play," or a consciousness of shared identity that a discourse influences them to experience together. We see both processes at work in the NT's poetic texts examined in this study.

Constituting a Community of Believers

Although it would be impossible to determine the degree to which Paul was operating out of a conceptualized sense of poetic discourse's potential for constituting a unified community out of a collection of disparate hearers, his poetic compositions nevertheless do show evidence that one of his aims was to create that kind of shared experience. Certainly Paul was concerned, in one way or another, with fostering unity in the church.

Paul's treatment of the end time in 1 Thess. 4:13-18 contains several

18. Maurice Charland, "Constitutive Rhetoric: The Case of the *Peuple Québécois*," *Quarterly Journal of Speech* 73 (1987): 133-50, here 137, 147.

features that seem explicitly intended to foster unity. Of course, the vision itself, by virtue of inviting the audience into a common, emotional, imaginative experience, might have been expected to create a sense of unity between them. But more specifically, Paul alters his use of pronouns in a way that moves him and his hearers toward a communal identity. The passage opens in v. 13 by referring to three different persons or groups: Paul, his audience ("*We* do not want *you* to be uninformed"), and the fellow Christians whose deaths they now grieve ("those who have died"). When he gives them the logical argument confirming the resurrection ("For since we believe that Jesus died and rose again, even so, through Jesus, God will bring with him those who have died," v. 14), the argument situates Paul and his audience as a single collective, distinct from the righteous dead. That distinction continues through the vision itself, which seems to depict the living as witnesses to the resurrection of the dead who rise to meet the returning Christ first, after which the living are "caught up in the clouds together with them to meet the Lord in the air." His vision culminates in this reunion, reflected in the vision's conclusion, which now depicts only one identity, that of all the believers, living and dead: "And so we will be with the Lord forever" (v. 17). As his hearers move through the vision, they also move symbolically from being three separate entities to one community of believers who now enjoy a happy reunion with Christ. On this basis Paul can exhort them in v. 18 to foster the unity they have just experienced: "Therefore encourage one another with these words."

Because of its intensely private nature, Paul's expression of personal anguish in Rom. 7:15-25 seems less likely to have been intended to create a sense of community in Paul's audience, certainly when compared to texts like the blessing of Eph. 1. But when it is viewed in light of the epistle as a whole, there is strong evidence that even here Paul envisioned the experience created by this text to bring his hearers together. In the chapters leading up to this passage, Paul takes his readers through a conversion narrative that captures the movement from being hopelessly condemned in sin to receiving forgiveness as a gift from God, as a way of highlighting his hearers' common experience of grace. In 1:18–3:20, using strong language and a vehement style, he charges that Gentiles and Jews alike are in sin and under God's wrath, his harangue culminating in his assertion that this indictment leaves "every mouth . . . silenced, and the whole world . . . held accountable to God" (3:19). In the face of their condemnation, no defense can be offered. But then, having confronted them with the desperation of their condition, Paul can announce his gospel: "But now . . . the righteousness of God has been disclosed . . . the righteousness of God through faith in Jesus Christ for all who believe. For there is no distinction [e.g., between Jews and Gentiles], since all have sinned and fall short of the glory of God" (3:21-23). Reflecting his emphasis on the stark silence of all sinners who stand speechless before God's judgment, Paul emphasizes at several points that because salvation is a gift, no one is able to boast in relation to anyone else (3:27; 4:2). Then, in Rom. 7:5-6, he retells that basic "before and after" story in miniature, moving from the death of sin to liberation from the law's condemnation. Paul seems to believe that the key to unity in the church is a common experience of that conversion story.

His hearers' unwillingness to embrace that understanding of salvation is, in Paul's view, what leads them to "boast" in relationship to each other, that is, to view each other from a position of supposed superiority. Viewed in this light, Paul's dramatic enactment of the sinner's despair, though intensely personal, is crucial to his aim of building a sense of community in the Roman church. On the one hand, along the lines that both Longinus suggested and contemporary scholars have emphasized, simply by virtue of vicariously sharing in that strong emotional process of moving from despair to joy, the audience might have been expected to feel an enhanced sense of solidarity. But even more, his dramatic portrayal encodes a particular identity that he wishes his hearers to embrace by traveling that journey with him — one of the humble supplicant who knows full well that his or her salvation is entirely an undeserved gift. Experiencing that identity, of course, places them in an entirely new position relative to each other, as fellow beneficiaries of God's unmerited favor. In order to bring them into this new self-awareness, Paul performs a role that is diametrically opposed to that of boasting in one's superiority. His use of intensely personal language may thus be the very feature of the text that allows the audience to lower their defenses and enter fully into the common experience that it captures — as Longinus put it, "bringing into the hearts of the bystanders the speaker's actual emotion so that all who hear him share in it" (*Subl.*, 39.3).

At first glance, Paul's encomium on love in 1 Cor. 13, like the "performance of despair" in Rom. 7, seems more focused on the personal motivation of love rather than corporate unity, since Paul speaks most often in the first person ("Though I speak in the tongues . . ."). Of all the texts considered in this study, however, the larger context in which the passage occurs, 1 Cor. 12–14, is the one most explicitly focused on unity. Indeed, underlying the entire passage is the theme that all things should be done for the common good. This suggests that Paul's use of mimesis has constituting the Corinthian church as "one body" as at least one of its aims.

As with the other passages examined in this study, one way that 1 Cor. 13 would have reinforced unity would have been through the hearers' common experience of the sublime, and especially their common "journey" through the mimetic process that Kennedy outlined, which begins with a "nervous" and "emotional" tone at the beginning, as Paul's syntax and form mimic the effusive frenzy of the ecstatic religious experience, resolving in a quieter tone "as the emotional energy is dissipated" when he depicts the cessation of tongues and prophecy.[19] As contemporary communication scholars have argued, that common movement from chaos to quiet order might have created among the Corinthians a shared emotional disposition that would have undermined the kind of intense rivalry that had characterized their relationships.

But beyond creating a kind of "emotional contagion," 1 Cor. 13 also encodes an ideal audience that Paul viewed as the prerequisite for unity in the church. Ultimately, that ideal audience is a community that values love above all manifestations of religious enthusiasm, in marked contrast to the way his actual audience in depicted in 1 Cor. 12. There, Paul highlights their jealousy and rivalry over the possession and exercise of particular spiritual gifts, which has caused division in their ranks. But then, in the opening verses of chap. 13, Paul mimetically captures the ostentation of religious display using hyperbole and crescendo, leading to a climax that goes from human to angelic tongues, from prophecy to omniscience, and from giving one's possessions away to undergoing self-immolation. In each case, he contrasts the ostentatious display of religiosity with a terse, two-word declaration of its utter uselessness apart from love, in a way that three times abruptly deflates the pretentious conceit of superiority that one might feel by virtue of one's religious performance. In short, Paul uses mimesis to drive a dramatic contrast between a genuine spirituality, marked above all else by love and humility, and the Corinthians' childish grasping for the limelight. His aim seems to have been to lure his audience, by means of the rhapsody of love that interrupts his often confrontational argumentation, into a poetic experience that would bring about a flash of self-awareness as they felt the distance between their own attitudes and those enacted in Paul's soliloquy. Chastened by the realization of their own immaturity, they would now be prepared to act out of the highest value, love. In this case, Paul's ostensible focus on himself actually encourages his hearers to lower their guard and en-

19. George A. Kennedy, *New Testament Interpretation through Rhetorical Criticism* (Chapel Hill: University of North Carolina Press, 1984), 156.

ter fully into a poetic encounter, where they would be indirectly compelled to let go of all of their pretenses to superiority.

Finally, the liturgy of Eph. 1:3-14 represents the clearest example of how a poetic text has the potential for constituting a unified audience out of separate auditors and, in fact, this appears to be the author's intent. As noted above, on account of its generic form as a communal expression of worship, the liturgy assumes the existence of a congregation of worshippers, a "we" who praise God for what God has done for "us," and through that assumption, actually constitutes them as such. Thus, the blessing itself positions the individual members of the audience as a united community, regardless of the actual content of the blessing. But as I argued in chap. 5, the content of the blessing is also organized in a way that underscores their unity. Paul takes the audience from praising God first for those elements of their Christian experience for which they are truly grateful — the fact that "we" have received grace and forgiveness through Christ — and moves them to praising God for that which they are reluctant to accept, the idea that their unity represents the first, concrete representation of the end to which God is taking the entire cosmos. The text, moreover, is cast as an expression of praise for what the audience has, together, received from God, a theme reflected in the copious use of the first-person plural pronoun (e.g., "who blessed us," v. 3, "chose us," v. 4, "destined us," v. 5, etc.). That emphasis is especially strong in vv. 11-13, where Paul distinguishes between the two groups who are now at odds with each other, "we who were the first to believe" and "you also, who heard the word of truth," who are joined as one community by their common reception of the Holy Spirit who is "the guarantee of *our* inheritance. . . ." By uniting form and content, the blessing functions to create phenomenologically the unity that it proclaims. Having enacted that unity, the Ephesians' challenge will not so much be to seek unity, but rather to "maintain the unity" that they have already glimpsed in their common performance of the epistle's opening blessing.

Conclusion

In the previous chapter, I examined one crucial implication of the author's shift from argument to poetic in the passages examined in this study, which has to do with the reconfiguration of the audience's relationship to the content of the discourse. In a typical rhetorical mode, the audience is "outside" the discourse, considering ideas as abstractions and critically evaluating the merits of the arguments, whereas in mimetic texts, the hearers are transported into an imaginative experience of the content. This chapter has explored two additional implications of that shift from argument to mimesis, which grow out of audience-content reconfiguration. The first of these has to do with the way that poetic discourse deals with the problem of the rhetor's identity and credibility. Whereas rhetoric offers strategies for enhancing the reputation of the speaker, poetic symbolically removes the rhetor from the process altogether by offering the audience some kind of visionary, liturgical, or dramatic experience with the power to draw their attention away from the literal speaker. Caught up in the imaginative experience, the identity of the rhetor ceases to matter. The second has to do with the way that poetic discourse has the potential to constitute the hearers as a united community of believers. Although it is unclear to what degree Paul, or even writers like Gorgias and Longinus, possessed an explicit conception of this element of persuasion, there are certainly hints that they might have had at least a basic grasp of what contemporary scholars have come to understand about that potential. Using mimesis, Paul was able to take his audiences through an emotionally charged experience that fostered group cohesion. At the same time, we find encoded in his poetic representations a depiction of an ideal audience — one that is united by faith and personal affection toward each other. Again, caught up in the common experience of transport, they were prepared to respond to each other in a new way.

Poetic form thus did more than provide Paul with a discursive resource for creating an ecstatic, transcendent experience that could serve as the basis for sustained faith. It also provided a way to handle two other pressing issues, the problem of the rhetor's identity and the problem of unity in the church. In this way, poetic passages, embedded within contexts that were largely argumentative and hortatory and reflecting the "rhetorico-poetic" tradition embodied in writers such as Gorgias and Longinus, represented a form of discourse uniquely suited to sustaining the Christian life.

A Discourse for the Church

In his essay "Rhetorical Depiction," Michael Osborn highlighted the unique power of visual images to "telescope remote and abstract antecedents and consequences into the present." Whereas enthymemes operate out of "diachronic or linear demonstrations," visual images have a unique power to compress "multiple, simultaneous meanings" in a compelling "perceptual encounter." He also noted their potential for fostering communion between larger and disparate groups, who are "sustained by simple but mythic pictures that embody common values and goals." Although depiction could be "a cynical hoax, a manipulative vision that poses as disclosure for the sake of exploitation," it could also "provide a benign moment of sharing, as rhetors overcome abstraction to disclose the world as it is revealed to them."[1]

In this book I have argued that Paul used the poetic strategy of mimesis, or representation, in order to create such numinous, extrarational experiences for his audiences, as a crucial element in his efforts to nurture and sustain Christian faith. These texts provided hearers with a momentary, phenomenological apprehension of the ideas and dispositions that they were promoting, creating for them an imaginative vision that, in Sullivan's words, "fills the consciousness."[2] In what follows, after a brief overview of the book's overall argument, I draw on Osborn's treatment of "depiction" in order to summarize the key persuasive functions of the poetic texts examined in this study. I end by returning to the question with which the study opened, which

1. Michael Osborn, "Rhetorical Depiction," in *Form, Genre, and the Study of Political Discourse,* ed. Herbert W. Simons and Aram A. Aghazarian (Columbia: University of South Carolina Press, 1986), 79-107, here 79-81.

2. Dale L. Sullivan, "*Kairos* and the Rhetoric of Belief," *Quarterly Journal of Speech* 78 (1992): 317-32, here 327.

has to do with the way that this form of discourse was uniquely fitted to the needs of religious faith. I note especially how the shift from argument to depiction, with its reconfiguration of the rhetorical encounter, aligns with key conceptions at the heart of early Christian theology. In this way, I conclude, rhetorico-poetic discourse uniquely represented a discourse for the church.

Rhetorico-Poetic Discourse in the New Testament Epistles

Osborn's account of the differences between persuasion by depiction and persuasion by enthymeme recalls the divide between rhetoric and poetic made by authors in the classical tradition. Beyond this, his incorporation of depiction as a welcome counterpart to abstract, logical argumentation echoes what this book has argued formed the natural, conceptual "home" of early Christian discourse — what Halliwell called the "rhetorico-poetic" tradition of persuasion.[3] This tradition, represented particularly by Gorgias and Longinus, drew on the poetic tradition of mimesis, through which ideas, events, and dispositions were imitated or represented by language as a complement to logical argumentation. Such forms of discourse activated the audience's capacity for *phantasia*, the ability to experience sensations as a result of their exposure to imaginary rather than literal occurrences. Although it is most often identified with the audience's ability to visualize events, people, and places not literally before them, Aristotle was careful to include other forms of artfully induced sensation besides just the visual.[4]

Reflecting this understanding, Gorgias highlighted the almost magical power of language to transport hearers into the past or the future, as well as to cause them to feel as their own the intense emotions attendant to the "good and ill fortunes of other people's actions and lives" (*Hel.*, 9). Similarly, Longinus used the term *ekstasis*, transport, to describe the vivid, imaginative experience that poetic language could give to an audience, noting its potential to inspire "wonder, with its power of amazing us," which always "prevails over what is merely convincing and pleasing" (*Subl.*, 1.4). Beyond merely persuading the audience, the "effect of genius is . . . rather to transport them out of themselves" (1.4). Whereas rhetoric offered claims and evidence as

---

3. Stephen Halliwell, *Between Ecstasy and Truth: Interpretations of Greek Poetics from Homer to Longinus* (Oxford: Oxford University Press, 2011), 277.

4. Ned O'Gorman, "Aristotle's *Phantasia* in the *Rhetoric*: *Lexis*, Appearance, and the Epideictic Function of Discourse," *Philosophy and Rhetoric* 38 (2005): 16-40, here 20.

abstract ideas to be considered, poetic form offered hearers an imaginative transport in which auditors felt the emotions and physical sensations as if they were literally happening, as "a vivid actuality" (25.1). Combined with logical argument, Longinus said, mimetic discourse "not only convinces the audience, it positively masters them" (15.9).

In precisely this way, I have argued, the texts examined in this study offered their hearers a vivid, imaginative consciousness of the theological realities that they proclaimed. Paul's apocalyptic vision in 1 Thess. 4 calls on the resources of mimesis in order to bring the parousia of Christ before the eyes of his audience. Rather than simply arguing for a particular understanding of that event, his vision uses poetic form and vivid, provocative language in order to dissolve the boundary between their world and the world to come, transporting the audience out of their present circumstances and into an imaginative glimpse of Christ's return and the resurrection of the dead. In Rom. 7, Paul shifts from explaining and arguing about the role of the law in salvation history to performing the role of the anguished sinner overcome by guilt and self-condemnation, then miraculously freed from the law's curse by the free gift of grace. The result is a mimetic experience of the helplessness and despair of the person who longs to keep the law but is utterly powerless to do so, which Paul sees as a prelude to the consciousness of conversion that he believes is the prerequisite to any future unity in the church. Paul's rhapsody of love in 1 Cor. 13 likewise interrupts the flow of rational argument in order to transport his hearers into a state of consciousness in which they feel the sublimity of love. His encomium mimics the ostentation of the Corinthians' most valued religious displays, and then the abrupt debasement of each "spiritual gift" when performed without love. He also enacts the broader movement from emotional fury to peace and order marked by the cessation of tongues and prophecy, which he will explicitly argue for in the chapter that follows. Having imaginatively and emotionally encountered love's grandeur, Paul hopes, his hearers will see themselves and their petty squabbles in a new light and will aspire to a higher plane of living. Finally, the liturgy of Eph. 1 symbolically enacts the kind of unity that the writer will later explicitly urge the hearers to seek. As a communal expression of praise, the text has the potential to unite worshippers and to make present and actual the kinds of ideals that it expresses. Further, its structure moves the audience from praising God for those blessings that they truly embrace to praising God for those which they might resist, blessings all centered on the bringing together of Jews and Gentiles into one church. Having provided a mimetically created consciousness of unity, the author then exhorts them to maintain the unity that they have just glimpsed. In each case, the author creates an imaginative experience of the ideas and behaviors they seek to advance, transporting their hearers, in Longinus's words, "out of themselves," and exploiting poetry's "irresistible power and mastery" to create experiences and memories that would be "stubborn and indelible" (*Subl.*, 1.4; 7.3-4). When taken alongside the arguments and logical explanations that formed their broader discursive contexts, such uses of language offered their audiences, in Stark's words, a "rhetorical-logical-ethical-mystical apprehension" of the beliefs and values they sought to instill in the early Christians' minds and hearts.

I have argued, further, that this shift from argument to mimesis has the effect of reconfiguring the three most significant relationships in the rhetorical exchange: the relationship of rhetor to audience, of audience members to each other, and most importantly, of audience to the content of the discourse itself. The NT's poetic texts transform the relationship of rhetor to audience, symbolically decentering the literal rhetor from a position external to the audience. In some cases, the rhetor slips into a fictive persona in which he performs some aspect of Christian theology. In others, he moves into the position of a co-witness to a dramatic vision or, in the case of the liturgy, a fellow worshipper. Whereas rhetoric traditionally seeks to offer reasons why the audience should trust the rhetor, mimetic texts simply remove the rhetor from the persuasive encounter. The NT's mimetic texts also reposition the audience members relative to each other, moving them from being isolated critics of argument to co-sharers in a powerful emotional experience with the potential to foster a deep sense of group cohesion. Finally and most importantly, this study has argued that the NT's poetic texts reconfigure the audience's relationship to the content itself. Whereas in rhetoric the audience is viewed as being "outside" of the discourse, considering ideas as abstractions and weighing the merits of exhortations to act, these mimetic texts transport hearers *into* an imaginative experience of the content. In those moments, the audience is not being asked to believe that something is true. Instead, these poetic texts place hearers "in" the content, encountering ideas, events, and dispositions as present reality.

Functions of the Poetic Form

The thesis of this book is that although they employed a different suasory process from that of traditional rhetoric, the texts examined in this study were nevertheless intended to be persuasive. Osborn's analysis of depiction explored a variety of ways such imaginative experiences can alter an audience's perspectives and behaviors, providing a useful lens through which to view the persuasive functions of the NT's poetic texts. I focus on three such functions, noting the crucial role of each in the development of religious faith.

Creating Theological Reality

In his discussion of the functions of depiction, Osborn first discussed depiction as "presentation," underscoring the potential for visual images to make ideas and dispositions "present" by appealing to the human perceptual capacities most closely related to our sense perceptions — sight, hearing, touch, etc. As he put it, "We experience the world either directly or through depiction, and even direct experience can be mediated and predisposed by previous depictions that prepare us for the experience."[5] Paul's encomium of love, for example, appears structured not simply to convey ideas but to offer something that approximates a sensory experience of love's grandeur, which will provide a perceptual lens through which the Corinthians can see themselves and each other, and hear Paul's further instructions for their behavior in the Christian assembly. Even more, his vision of the end in 1 Thess. provides a depiction that can mediate their perceptions of the harsh realities of persecution and death that are part of their ongoing lives as believers.

Osborn especially noted the power of "innovative presentations," through which depictions overthrow existing, often deeply held views by bringing together jarring incongruities in a single imaginative experience.[6] Thus, in Rom. 7 we encounter Paul the Pharisee, the one who would elsewhere describe himself as "a Hebrew born of Hebrews; as to the law, a Pharisee . . . as to righteousness under the law, blameless" (Phil. 3:5-6; cf. Rom. 11:1), now vividly presented as the anguished sinner who despairs over his utter helplessness before the law's demands. Similarly, in the blessing of Eph. 1, part of what draws the audience into collaboration with the liturgy's flow of thought is the fact that they are praising God for timeworn convic-

---

5. Osborn, "Rhetorical Depiction," 81.
6. On "perspective by incongruity," see Kenneth Burke, *Permanence and Change: An Anatomy of Purpose* (Berkeley: University of California Press, 1984), 90, 119.

tions related to God's providence, only to find themselves celebrating the jarring culmination of that providence in God's act of bringing together Jews and Gentiles in one body.

Closely related to Osborn's discussion of presentation is that of depiction as intensification, which has to do with the way that depictions strengthen feeling — how they "color what we see and make our reactions smolder." What is at issue here is the human tendency to rationalize as a way of maintaining an intellectual distance from claims and arguments. Depiction "thus corrects a certain ironically self-enervating tendency of human reason, which, Francis Bacon observed, deals typically in abstraction." Osborn stressed the synecdochal function of depiction, that is, its potential for collapsing and integrating complex, formless ideas into a single, vivid instance "for which it is possible to develop human recognition."[7] Again, Paul's "performance of despair" might be viewed as paradigmatic for the way that it unites Paul's identity as a Pharisee and devotee of the law with his anguish over his inability to keep the law, all condensed in one emotionally charged vision.

By fulfilling the functions of presence and intensification, then, the NT's poetic texts create theological reality for their audiences. In those moments of mimesis, hearers pass from thinking about to actually experiencing a consciousness that closely approximates that of their own senses. Osborn wrote, "By engaging our perceptions, intensification counters a certain tendency of our rationality to establish distance between ourselves and the object of perception. Thus through its intensifying function, rhetorical depiction invites action and discourages us from becoming detached onlookers of life."[8] In the moment of mimetic transcendence, the world of Christian theology is real.

Forming Community

Osborn also accentuated the role depiction can play in creating identification, which fosters a sense of connection between members of an audience and their co-auditors. He wrote, "If humans are imprinted as cooperative, sharing beings, then the sharing of symbols must be a profoundly satisfying experience, a terminal as well as instrumental function of depiction. Just to

---

7. Osborn, "Rhetorical Depiction," 86.
8. Osborn, "Rhetorical Depiction," 88.

merge in the use of certain symbols is deeply reassuring." Beyond simply sharing in the form of depiction itself, moreover, the content being conveyed visually becomes a source of group cohesion, as "certain presentations become authorized as legitimate group perspectives" and as "intensified feeling . . . [is] converted into group emotion: we discover together that we share feelings . . . [and] in that discovery we affirm our identification in a community." He notes especially the role of archetypal images and motifs around which communities build a common identity, the crucifixion motif for example, or the themes of "heroism, martyrdom, and villainy."[9]

As emphasized in the previous chapter, writers in the rhetorico-poetic tradition, at some level, recognize the power of sharing in vivid, imaginative experiences to bring hearers together in a common sense of identity. Indeed, this seems to have been an explicit aim behind the NT's poetic texts, as the writers employ particular forms of discourse that create shared emotions, and as they encode an ideal group identity for their hearers in those forms, as the undivided "body of Christ." All of this reflects what Osborn said about the power of depiction to foster identification. But as he suggested, the source of identification may also lie in the way that the authors embed archetypal themes within those depictions. Thus, Paul, in his performance of despair in Rom. 7, adopts the familiar guise of the helpless supplicant who cries out to God, just as the Hebrews in Egypt did when their cries "came to God" and prompted God to bring about miraculous deliverance through the exodus (Exod. 7:7-12). Even more basically, he enacts the motif of death and resurrection as he follows the path of surrender to dereliction and then to deliverance and exaltation, the path followed by Christ and depicted in another of the NT's poetic texts, the Christ hymn of Phil. 2:5-11. Similarly, his vision of the end in 1 Thess. 4 and his encomium of love in 1 Cor. 13 draw on familiar motifs from Greco-Roman political culture and philosophy, as well as from Jewish apocalyptic traditions. Finally, the liturgy of Eph. 1 calls to mind the deeply held theme of providence, as God graciously but inexorably unfolds an eternal plan across human and even cosmic history. The poetic texts examined in this study thus served to create collective emotional experiences, to symbolically cast hearers in a mutual persona as a unified community, and to engage hearers with familiar, shared archetypal patterns and motifs. As Osborn noted, "Such appeals presume and reinforce identification in the social order."[10]

9. Osborn, "Rhetorical Depiction," 89-90.
10. Osborn, "Rhetorical Depiction," 90.

Motivating to Act

Throughout this study, I have drawn a sharp distinction between these poetic texts, which were intended to create visceral experiences of theological content, and forms of discourse that were self-consciously hortatory,
texts more traditionally "rhetorical" in their explicit calls to action. But this
is not meant to minimize the fact that these mimetic discourses were also
ultimately aimed at changing Christians' beliefs and actions, a role Osborn
highlighted when he described "depiction as implementation." At its most
basic level, depiction can offer "graphic lessons that can influence and lend
urgency to present decisions." But beyond serving simply as "premises" for
calls to action, this function can also provide the kind of ongoing motivation that people need to sustain their commitment to a movement: "Often
the way is weary and perilous, and the faint of heart begin to falter. At that
moment the fate of a program may depend upon symbols of sustenance,
upon the depictive powers of communicators to show what is at stake, to
renew hope, and to remind audiences of the dedication required of them."[11]

The poetic texts examined in this study serve this implicitly hortatory
function. Paul's apocalyptic vision gives his hearers a glimpse of the end time
that can provide hope in the midst of grief over recent losses and ongoing,
severe challenges. But it will also serve as the basis for his challenge that they
live soberly and vigilantly, as they await this welcome event that will come
"like a thief in the night" (1 Thess. 5:2). The dramatic soliloquys of Rom. 7
and 1 Cor. 13 both appear intended to promote the kind of self-awareness
and humility that lie at the heart of Christian spirituality, offering a powerful
motivation for Christian behavior. In the case of the Corinthians, this will
mean using their gifts "for the common good" (1 Cor. 12:7), while for his
Roman listeners, it will mean no longer thinking "of yourself more highly
than you ought to think, but . . . think[ing of yourself] with sober judgment"
(Rom. 12:3). Finally, the liturgy of Eph. 1 gives the audience an experience
of the kind of unity that they will later be urged to maintain.

In each case, these and the NT's other poetic texts transport their hearers into an imaginative experience of the larger Christian narrative that establishes ontological and teleological reality for the adherents of the movement. It tells them who they are, it situates them at a particular moment in
salvation history, it explains why things are the way they are, and it envisions
the blessed consummation toward which God is taking all things. But to the

---

11. Osborn, "Rhetorical Depiction," 93.

degree that believers "enter" the world created by the discourse, they will face inevitable moral and ethical demands. If they truly possess the consciousness of the alternative world into which they have been transported, they can no longer live in conformity "to the pattern of this world" (Rom. 12:2, NIV), or face their circumstances "as others do who have no hope" (1 Thess. 4:13). Without directly exhorting them to behave like Christians, then, the imaginative experiences that these texts create serve as powerful, implicit motivations for embracing what is elsewhere described explicitly as the appropriate Christian lifestyle.

The Discourse of Faith

Osborn's analysis emphasized the role that depiction can play in political and civic discourse, serving as the basis for structural and legal changes in society as well as for altered attitudes among the populace. But when we consider the nature of religious faith, the vital role of imaginative experience becomes even more evident. As I emphasized in the introduction to this book, Christian faith was never conceived of as being a matter of mere "belief," that is, holding to certain ideas, possessing knowledge, or simply giving consent to certain claims. Rather, it was an entire reorientation of one's fundamental way of being in the world, involving, as Tillich emphasized, one's "total personality."[12] It entailed the creation of a new social imaginary, in a way that altered believers' "gut reactions" to themselves, others, and their world.

They were challenged to live, moreover, out of a social imaginary that flew in the face of much of their own empirical experience of the world. They were urged to embrace values that were fundamentally at odds with the values of the world, as when Paul confronted the Corinthians with an orientation toward the worth of various manifestations of religiosity that was the reverse of all they had experienced in paganism. The early Christians found themselves ushered into a reality that overturned centuries of racial hostility between Jews and Gentiles, as when the liturgy of Eph. 1 engaged them in praise for the way that their unity reflected the concrete instantiation of God's eternal plan for the cosmos, or when Paul enacted the despair of the sinner who is utterly powerless before the law, as a way of setting Jews and Gentiles on the same moral footing. As 1 Thess. made clear, believers found themselves called to hold to this worldview even when it was contradicted by

---

12. Paul Tillich, *Dynamics of Faith* (New York: Harper and Row, 1957), 4.

the data of their own perceptions, as they grieved the deaths of their fellow Christians and tried to hold up under the crush of persecution.

In short, they were asked to embrace a radically different worldview from that which they had hitherto known, but not only to hold to it intellectually, as an abstract claim to which they gave their assent, but to live fully in it, so that it truly became their "second nature" perception of the world. Even more, Kirkwood pointed out, the goal of Christian spirituality was not only new thinking, but also a sustained state of affect and awareness. As he put it, in Christianity, as in most religious traditions, such persistent "moods and states of mind (e.g., equanimity, quietude, awe, devotion) are not just the means, but the ends of spiritual discipline."[13]

Finally, as the opening chapter made clear, the generation of faith, as the early Christians saw it, was a conversion experience that, while always including conceptual explanations of the gospel, was equally centered in what psychologists call "ultimacy experiences." As the NT depicts it, converts witnessed the power of God and were filled with wonder at what they saw and heard. In other words, rather than being a rational judgment made in response to logical arguments, it was more nearly a vivid, extrarational, life-altering encounter with God, accompanied by amazement, literally, ecstasy (ἔκστασις).

Paul found in poetic mimesis a persuasive resource uniquely suited to sustaining that kind of faith. Along the lines Longinus suggested, it offered him the possibility of using language to create or recreate the kinds of ecstatic experiences that had been a central element of early Christianity's conception of the conversion process. By creating powerful emotional experiences, these texts could give the audience a momentary consciousness of the kind of affective state which, it was hoped, would eventually become a stable disposition, while at the same time overcoming the barriers to new ways of seeing the world posed by the persistent human tendency to intellectualize and counterargue. Most of all, it "transported" hearers into an alternative state of awareness, in which the radically alternative Christian worldview was accessible to their sense perceptions, providing the kind of "ultimacy experience" that contemporary psychologists see as being foundational to religious faith.

At a much broader level, finally, Paul's use of poetic form accorded with early Christianity's deepest theological convictions. Obviously, a core

13. William G. Kirkwood, "Storytelling and Self-confrontation: Parables as Communication Strategies," *Quarterly Journal of Speech* 69 (1983): 58-74, here 66.

principle in early Christianity was the unity of all believers in the church, a conviction that is enacted in the way that these poetic texts reconfigure the position of individual audience members as sharers in a communal imaginative experience. Further, the NT persistently downplayed the role of individual leaders within the church. Jesus repeatedly warned his disciples against self-aggrandizement and rivalry, as when he rebuked their attempts to grasp power and position with these words: "You know that the rulers of the Gentiles lord it over them, and their great ones are tyrants over them. It will not be so among you; but whoever wishes to be great among you must be your servant" (Matt. 20:25-26). Paul similarly minimized his own role and that of Apollos in the Corinthians' conversion when he asked, "What then is Apollos? What is Paul? Servants through whom you came to believe, as the Lord assigned to each" (1 Cor. 3:5). Remarkably, the mimetic texts analyzed in this study likewise minimized the symbolic role of the rhetor by repositioning him in relationship to the audience. Rather than the rhetor being an agent who explicitly sought to persuade the audience to believe or act, these poetic discourses decentered the rhetor, placing the rhetor behind the mask of a fictive persona or positioning the rhetor as merely a co-participant in some kind of liturgical or visionary experience. In each case, within the experience created by these ecstatic texts, the identity of the rhetor ceased to matter. As Kennedy put it, "The orator himself is nothing; his words are not plausible; all lies with God."[14] Most importantly, as Kennedy's examination of the theological assumptions undergirding early Christian persuasion emphasized, God's power and authority were at the center, rather than the skill of the orator. God provided the word. Persuasion was God's work. "The reaction of the speaker to the *kerygma* is like his reaction to a miracle, the direct evidence of authority."[15] While it is true that Christians were being invited to inhabit a social imaginary that was contradicted by their culture, history, and often, their own experience — to believe what was unseen — mimesis offered a way of using language to create the imaginative display of that miraculous reality. Caught up in the visionary experience, what they were asked to believe became real to their senses.

All of this helps to clarify the character of early Christian persuasion, a persuasion that embraced both rhetorical and poetic discourse in a way that prefigured what would eventually be codified in Francis Bacon's famous

---

14. George A. Kennedy, *Classical Rhetoric and Its Christian and Secular Tradition from Ancient to Modern Times* (Chapel Hill: University of North Carolina Press, 1980), 131.

15. Kennedy, *Classical Rhetoric*, 127.

statement, that the purpose of rhetoric was "to apply Reason to Imagination for the better moving of the will."[16] They understood that the inculcation of hope, the development of character, and the promotion of a Christian world-view were not achieved exclusively, or even primarily, through doctrinal explanation or argument. These came about through religious experiences that were both cognitive and visceral. Accounts of early Christianity attest to such extrarational apprehensions of theological meaning coming ecstatically, through what were viewed as outpourings of the Holy Spirit. But Paul also pointed to the creation of such experiences symbolically, through strategic and intentional uses of language. In their mimetic performances, these texts allowed the early Christians to witness imaginatively in the present what was not yet, creating, as poetic theory suggested, momentary and fleeting dispositions that would hopefully become stable virtues and perceptions of the world. In this way, mimesis offered early Christian rhetors a persuasive discourse uniquely suited not for the legislative assembly or the courtroom, but for the church.

---

16. Frances Bacon, *The Advancement of Learning*, in idem, *Major Works*, ed. Brian Vickers (Oxford: Oxford University Press, 1996), 120-299, here 238.

Modern Authors Index

Subject Index

apocalyptic, 46n13, 163
  discourse, 5-6, 13, 46n13, 47-48
  Jewish tradition, 54-55
argument, rhetorical, 36, 133-34
  classical rhetoric, 129-31, 140
  counterargument, 128-30, 132-33
  poetic and, 162-63
  resistance / reception of, 28, 121, 130-33, 134-38, 143-45, 149-50
Aristotle, 14, 19-21, 22-23, 101, 140
  enthymeme, 124, 129-30, 134
  on epideictic rhetoric, 119n34
  on ethos, 143, 145, 147
  on persuasion, 144-45, 152
  on poetic / mimesis, 24-25, 26-29, 31-34, 39, 149n9, 162
artistic form, 20, 121-22. *See also* mimesis.
audience / hearers, viii-ix, 107
  appeal to emotions, 71-74, 149-51
  character of, 26-27, 90-91, 116-17, 152-55
  Christian, 1-3, 16-17, 39, 46-50, 54
  in classical rhetoric, 13-15, 20-25, 84n12, 140
  ethos / author and, 130, 164, 171
  Gentile, 55-56, 67
  ideal, 158, 160
  identity, 107, 153-56, 167

imaginative experience, 27-28, 30-32, 34-36, 77-79, 140-41, 160
  as judges, 129-30, 133-34, 140, 144
  participation, 119-20, 122-24
  Paul's relationship to, 50-52, 56-57, 63-64, 66, 93-96, 151-52
  relationship to discourse, 154-55, 159-60, 164
  relationship with each other, 16, 120, 125, 142, 157, 160, 164
  resistance / reception of argument, 28, 121, 130-33, 134-38, 143-45, 149-50
  shared ideology, 154-55, 166-67
Augustine, 8

Bacon, Francis, 166, 171-72
baptism, 68n22, 69
behavior, changing, 16, 168, 142, 144, 164-65
belief, 9
  changing, 19, 37-38, 124-25, 127-28, 137-39, 157, 165-66
berakah, 112, 114, 124, 151

catharsis, 25-26, 29, 39
child imagery, 99-100, 138, 158
Christ hymn, 138, 167
Christian
  audience, 1-3, 16-17, 39, 46-50, 54

Scripture and Ancient Sources Index